BEAR WITNESS

BEAR
WITNESS

*The Pursuit of Justice
in a Violent Land*

ROSS HALPERIN

Liveright Publishing Corporation
A Division of W. W. Norton & Company
Independent Publishers Since 1923

For Mark A.R. Kleiman, 1951–2019

For information about permission to reproduce selections from this book, write to
Permissions, Liveright Publishing Corporation, a division of W. W. Norton & Company, Inc.,
500 Fifth Avenue, New York, NY 10110

For information about special discounts for bulk purchases, please contact
W. W. Norton Special Sales at specialsales@wwnorton.com or 800-233-4830

Manufacturing by Lakeside Book Company
Book design by Daniel Lagin
Production manager: Louise Mattarelliano

ISBN 978-1-324-09078-6

Liveright Publishing Corporation, 500 Fifth Avenue, New York, NY 10110
www.wwnorton.com

W. W. Norton & Company Ltd., 15 Carlisle Street, London W1D 3BS

10 9 8 7 6 5 4 3 2 1

CONTENTS

BOOK ONE

Locuras

~ 1 ~

TEGUCIGALPA SITS IN A CRATERLIKE VALLEY HIGH UP IN THE Sierra Madres. The ridges that surround the city make a head-on landing impossible, so pilots approaching from the north must perform a circle-to-land approach: dip a plane into the basin, bank it aggressively to the left, and then trace an elliptical and descending path that avoids promontories, hills, and buildings. This is tricky in bluebird skies, and variables like wind, clouds, and rain can make it harder. When, in 1989, a Boeing 727 carrying 146 souls crashed into a slope, one of the few survivors was the pilot.

And the actual landing was precarious, too. Toncontín International's runway was one of the shortest airstrips that jets were allowed to land on, and right at the end of it, the precipice of a sixty-five-foot cliff awaited. To stop short of that deadly nosedive, pilots had to stick a small landing zone and then hit the brakes hard. For all these reasons, touching down in Tegucigalpa felt miraculous, and once firmly stabilized, the first thing sensible travelers did was clap.

As of the new millennium, this million-person capital city was divided in two. The base of the valley was where rattletrap buses, trucks, cars, and motorcycles huffed and puffed in gridlock on two-lane boulevards, and it was where a veritable army of private security guards watched over fast-food restaurants, banks, pharmacies, malls, condos, hotels, colleges, and federal buildings in various states of disrepair.

The other half of the city consisted of the mountainside barrios that encircled this core. The twin-peaked Montañita was to the southeast—its upper reaches were a forest of oaks and pines, and its bottom half, on the Tegucigalpa-facing side, was a barrio called Nueva Suyapa.

Toward the top of that neighborhood was a three-story schoolhouse, and across the alley of reddish dirt that ran along its backside was a concrete wall with two black metal doors, one of which was car sized, and one of which was human sized. On the morning of March 19, 2005, Kurt Ver Beek was behind that wall, loading luggage into his station wagon, which was parked on an open-air slab of rubble-stone masonry. Being a six-foot-one, ocean-eyed American made him an oddity here; Nueva Suyapa was a community that taxi drivers, garbage collectors, and pizza-delivery men—let alone other gringos!— were generally too afraid to even set foot in.

It was the Saturday before Holy Week, the festive stretch between Palm Sunday and Easter Sunday when pretty much everyone found some way to break loose of the normal austerities. Homemakers accustomed to working with little more than eggs, beans, and corn tortillas would splurge on some dried whitefish fillets, and since it was the start of the dry season—the temperature that week would top out at ninety-five—parents would buy or build miniature pools for their kids. This was a major indulgence in a barrio where water was scarce; it ran through the pipes to each household only about one day per month, and on all other days, people had to get by with whatever they had stored up in bottles, pitchers, buckets, barrels, and tanks. Some residents would spend the holiday in the rural towns where they were born, and the luckiest ones, Kurt and his family included, would head to Honduras's Caribbean coastline to let loose between lush tropical forests and one of the largest barrier reefs on earth.

The Ver Beeks were excited to snorkel and swim, but before they could get going, Kurt's cellphone rang—unexpectedly.

Kurt, a forty-one-year-old sociologist, had two professional pursuits: He taught American undergrads who were studying abroad, and he ran a small Christian charity called the Association for a More Just Society, or ASJ, which, up until now, had been doing a hodgepodge of heartwarming but unspectacular good works like helping poor families procure land titles and helping abused wives get divorced. An ASJ middle manager named Carlos del Cid was calling to relay some news. The police had just arrested four Puchos, including Chelito, the leader of that *mara* and an individual who, according to the next day's *La Tribuna*, "had corralled the approximately fifty-thousand residents of Nueva Suyapa with his constant acts of bloodshed."

Corralled. A word typically used to describe livestock.

The Puchos had commandeered the barrio by being tactical—for instance, they were known to confiscate firearms from residents to both beef up their arsenal and disarm potential threats—and also by being horrifying. "They held nothing sacred," one local recalled. "They terrorized the community. It was complete chaos." Their repertoire of criminal activity included muggings, burglaries, extortion, and hurting people every which way. Chelito's uncle and three other Puchos had recently abducted a pair of sisters who peddled candy and forcibly ushered them down to a secluded area by a brook. The older sister, who was twenty-one, begged them to keep their hands off her sibling, but the uncle proceeded to stick a gun in the fourteen-year-old's mouth and rape her, at which point his henchmen had their way with the elder one. Later on, after the sisters reported this crime, someone they identified as "Chele," who was almost certainly Chelito, threatened to murder them if they didn't retract their complaint.

Post-crime intimidation was one of the reasons why the Puchos almost never seemed to get punished. Sure, the cops had worked up the courage to capture Chelito and three of his cronies, and sure, *La Tribuna* would soon regurgitate the force's self-congratulatory contention that the "whole mara" was now "dismantled." But Kurt knew the drill, knew those detainees would soon boomerang back to the barrio. Because while people in Nueva Suyapa might have been willing to report a crime in the heat of the moment, they generally weren't willing to testify against the Puchos in court, partly because they feared retribution, and partly because they didn't trust the cops, prosecutors, and judges who jointly administered criminal proceedings. And when witness testimony wasn't available, cases almost always had to be dropped.

There was a broader issue, too. Though Lady Justice was rendered in black bronze in front of the judiciary's headquarters—her tunic elegant, her blindfold taut, her scales balanced, her sword at ease—in truth, the justice system here was an ungodly mess, a vast fiasco of contaminated crime scenes, uninterrogated suspects, unanalyzed blood samples, shelved prosecutions, nonsensical rulings, easy-to-escape prisons, and disappeared files. One reason for that was extreme poverty. In the facilities where cops, prosecutors, and judges tried to do their jobs, there were desks without computers, printers without ink, cars without fuel, and bathrooms without toilet paper. And those absurdly unequipped functionaries were also preposterously overstretched. For example, while the United Nations recommended one judge for every four thousand citizens, as of 2003, Honduras had one for every fifty-five thousand. Which was even worse than it sounded, because the country was also superlatively violent. For five years running, it had had either the highest, second-highest, or third-highest homicide rate in the world.

In other words, the country's justice system was chock-full of breaking points where a case could collapse, and consequently, the cops had been hunting the Puchos on what appeared to be a catch-

and-release basis. Chelito's rap sheet, which probably wasn't even comprehensive, showed him getting arrested in September 2002, in May 2003, in October 2003, in October 2004, in December 2004, on March 14, 2005, and now, yet again, just a few days after that.

What del Cid was calling about, the apprehension of four *mareros*, would not normally be of urgent interest to the director of an NGO, but Kurt, who had been doing charitable work in Honduras for about fifteen years, had come to conclude that what impoverished people like his neighbors needed—*really* needed, right now, more than anything else—wasn't additional aid, development, or evangelism, the standard instruments in the do-gooder's tool kit; what they so desperately needed, he believed, was protection from violence.

And as it happened, he was harboring a plan to subdue the Puchos. Del Cid had typed it up into a half-page, eight-point outline titled "Secret Group." Kurt's doodle in the margin summed it up— an abbreviation for the word "lawyer" was connected by four separate arrows to the words "victim," "police," "prosecutor," and "judge." Step one was going to be hiring that "lawyer," and that was precisely why del Cid was calling.

He asked his boss for the go-ahead.

Kurt, who was probably wearing his standard weekend outfit— baseball cap, tank top, running shorts, and flip flops—was a man who made life-and-death decisions with an attitude that can be described as either serenely decisive or recklessly nonchalant. He gave del Cid the green light, knowing full well that it was going to be difficult to recruit an attorney at the start of Holy Week. But the good news for del Cid was that there was basically only one ironclad employment requirement— the new hire had to be a churchgoing Christian—and in a country as pious as Honduras, that didn't seem to be a major constraint.

Kurt hung up. He felt like del Cid could use some help but wasn't about to cancel his family vacation, so he wanted to make one last arrangement before taking off.

There were three attached town houses in this compound behind the wall. The Ver Beeks lived in the one farthest from the alley, and right next to theirs was the freestanding, cinder-block structure where Carlos Hernández and his family lived. Kurt knocked on the door and was welcomed inside, where, beneath a drop ceiling typical of an office, there was a kitchen, a dining-room table, and some upholstered seating in front of a TV.

Carlos, a thirty-five-year-old who wore glasses and a mustache, grew up a little inland from where Kurt and his family were itching to head. The two of them had met in the early nineties when the charities they used to work for shared an office. Now, almost every night, as Carlos walked through the narrow space between their homes, he would knock on Kurt's window, and then they would chat. "One more thing" often led to an invitation inside, a cup of tea, maybe a pastry, and a long and stimulating conversation, usually about how to improve the barrio, which was something they could effectuate through either ASJ—Carlos sat on its board of directors—or the charity he ran out of that building across from their compound. It was called Genesis, and it operated a school, a health clinic, and a microlender.

During their nightly dialogues, Carlos was prone to fall into dreamy run-on rambles, his voice melodic and throaty, his body bouncy, never at ease. Kurt was calmer, almost pastorlike in demeanor. He liked to fold his lanky limbs into more comfortable architectures, and in a Spanish that was fluent but made bland by his Midwestern drawl, he would tweak his word choices as he talked and arrange his thoughts into finger-counted lists. Carlos could tell he was excited when he nodded in slow motion and twisted his mouth into a tight-lipped grin. The two of them strived to not let cynicism, fear, or conventional wisdom prick whatever ideas bubbled up within the effervescent space between them. This emboldening quality of their discourse would eventually get them into entanglements with a military-grade serial killer, a shady tycoon who had about a thousand armed men under his command, multiple attorney generals, the Honduran National Police's top brass, a sitting president, and someone who, according to the head of the DEA, was "a central figure in one of the largest and most violent cocaine trafficking conspiracies in the world." But for the time being, the Secret Group was, without a doubt, the wildest thing they had ever cooked up.

Bringing murderers, rapists, and thieves to justice didn't sound like something private citizens could possibly get involved in, but if you thought about how that happened, step by step, you quickly realized that a lot of the legwork didn't require credentials. For instance, you didn't need a badge to track down witnesses or to convince them to testify. And while, yes, an average Joe couldn't legally arrest anyone, in Nueva Suyapa, the kicking down of doors and the clicking on of handcuffs usually weren't the factors that inhibited apprehensions. The bigger issues were that the cops often didn't know what mareros looked like, what their legal names were, or where they lived, and also that the force had so few gassed-up vehicles. There was no reason why a private citizen couldn't gather all that biographical information and also transport officers. Finally, though prosecutors had to do the actual arguing in court, and though judges had to make the rulings, when dealing with a justice system as ramshackle as this one, there were likely all sorts of ways to both assist and cajole them.

The Secret Group was going to be a semiclandestine division of ASJ. Its two employees, a lawyer and a private eye, were going to try to bridge the crevasse between witnesses and law enforcement and to compel cops, prosecutors, and judges to incarcerate the Puchos. Kurt and del Cid planned to manage the program's duo day-to-day, while Kurt and Carlos planned to introduce them to potential witnesses and informants in the barrio.

When Kurt asked his best friend to help del Cid recruit an attorney, Carlos would have understood the rush. If they found someone immediately, and if he or she managed to escort cooperative witnesses to a judge before the jailed Puchos were released, then Chelito would remain in a cell—that is, he would be stuck in a place where he couldn't hurt any more of their neighbors.

That was what made the prospect of the Secret Group so exciting, but in truth, the outline describing it was more of a sketch than a blueprint, and taking a step back, there was no getting around the fact that Kurt and Carlos were middle-aged dads hatching a cloak-and-dagger plot to shackle homicidal mareros in what may have been one of the most dangerous neighborhoods on the planet, a neighborhood where *they themselves* lived with no more protection than a gate that was often left unlocked. This experimental program's staff was going to be interacting with a large number of bureaucrats and Nueva Suyapa residents, so there was a decent chance that, sooner or later, the Puchos would figure out what it was and who was behind it.

That risk was not a crippling deterrent, however, because Kurt liked to point out that the Bible doesn't say "Be Safe!" and that the living-breathing Jesus was a gutsy renegade who once cracked a whip as he defied authority. And then there were his earliest acolytes, who wouldn't stop proselytizing his message even though they knew that would get them executed in the most dreadful ways. Kurt didn't appear to have much in common with those ancient desert dwellers—save for the fact that they all wore sandals—but he still found inspiration in their acts of reverent courage.

Kurt and his wife, Jo Ann Van Engen, got into the front of their station wagon, while their daughter and son hopped in back. Anna was only twelve but had already figured out that her parents sometimes confronted choices that, in her kid-mind, broke down into a safe option and a selfless option. She was never privy to the details of those decisions but would always silently wish that they prioritized *her* security over what they perceived to be *their* moral duty.

Kurt turned left out of the compound and then made two quick rights to wrap around Genesis, the vehicle swaying and rumbling over the badly rutted lanes. The bus terminal was a half-moon-shaped swath of dirt in front of the schoolhouse where, not too long ago, a group of Puchos allegedly ripped a man out of a car, told him to stop snitching, and shot him in the abdomen. The barrio's main artery, which had three gooseneck turns separated by long straightaways, bottomed out at a bridge that spanned a polluted brook. After exiting the barrio, the Ver Beeks passed a small factory that manufactured coffins, curved right on a road cut into a cliffside, and passed by a stall that sold calla lilies, hydrangeas, bromeliads, and at this time of year only, skinny palm leaves, too.

Because tomorrow, on Palm Sunday, many Hondurans were going to loop those into bouquets to commemorate the long-ago Sunday when, according to the biblico-historical record, a carpenter rode into Jerusalem astride an ass, along a pathway that his adherents had carpeted with palm branches. On Wednesday, they were going to commemorate the long-ago Wednesday when one of that carpenter's disciples agreed to turn state's evidence. On Thursday, they were going to commemorate the long-ago Thursday when the carpenter, now a wanted man, ingested intoxicants at a gathering of his criminal syndicate. And on Friday, they were going to commemorate the long-ago Friday when this troublemaking outlaw was arrested, charged, tried, and punished in accordance with the law of the land.

Among the infinitude of lessons that have been drawn from this tale is a warning that justice can be miscarried, and that childish simplifications like "good and evil" and "hero and villain" do not always neatly correspond to the punisher and the punished. Meting out justice is ethically complex, always, but especially when it is meted out to the young. Jesus was crucified at thirty-three. According to *La Tribuna*, Chelito was a twelve-year-old boy.

———

AS THE VER BEEKS WENDED THEIR WAY NORTH, CARLOS HEADED TO ASJ's office, a green stucco house that was located in a wealthy residential neighborhood a mile west of Nueva Suyapa.

In the conference room on the second floor, he and del Cid pitched the Secret Group to two attorneys del Cid had invited. Unsurprisingly, they both passed.

Del Cid didn't have many options—it was a Saturday, and it was one of the deadest weeks of the year—so he reached out to a lawyer he knew through his personal involvement with a fringe political party dedicated to radical progressivism.

Macario Pavón and a second attorney soon arrived.

The professional world in Honduras tended to be decorous and formal, and generally speaking, counterculture was synonymous not with quirky bohemianism but criminal deviance. Macario had deep-set eyes and boxy cheeks; he had shown up in jeans; and his hair was pulled back into a ponytail. He wasn't overtly rude, but a harsh sarcasm and a mercurial edge were detectable in his voice, and it's safe to assume those qualities served him well when he used to do debt collecting for a bank. He did know the Bible inside and out, but the only reason he had studied it, it seemed, was so he would be able to ridicule it knowledgeably.

Carlos did not normally engage with metalhead atheists, but he was at a crossroads and understood that in starting the Secret Group, he was becoming something of a transgressive himself. He had spent the last decade doing everything he possibly could to help the barrio's youth, including Chelito and some of the other Puchos—he had educated them, mentored them, and showed them fatherly love. And now, all of a sudden, he was going to start locking them up? *In Honduran prisons!* Something about that felt inherently unholy, but the thing was, he had purchased too many coffins for too many neighbors—at one point, as a cost-saving measure, he had just paid a carpenter to build them inside Genesis. And blood, all over his clothes, the smell of it, had transformed him. He knew it was time to lay down the law but also that doing so would require venturing into a demimonde where macho cops combated—and sometimes partnered up with—ferocious mareros. He and Kurt clearly weren't well suited to navigate that dog-eat-dog jurisdiction, but perhaps this hard-edged attorney was just the man they needed.

After Carlos and del Cid described their scheme to take down the Puchos, as far as Carlos remembers, Macario replied, "We'll cut 'em to pieces."

– 2 –

THREE DECADES EARLIER, IN 1974, A BODY OF LOW-PRESSURE
air coalesced off the coast of Africa, traveled across the Atlantic, curled up above the Caribbean, and slammed into Central
America as Hurricane Fifi. The river that bisects Tegucigalpa inundated some of the shantytowns along its banks, and many of the dispossessed relocated to the Montañita, which, at the time, was the site
of the municipal garbage dump.

The settlers claimed plots of land on its slopes, ridges, and hollows and built with whatever they could—they cut down trees, turned
cliffsides into quarries, mixed dirt, water, and pine needles to create adobe, and supplemented that natural bounty with cloth, tarps,
cardboard, sheet metal, and cinder blocks. Their ersatz shacks were
connected by a network of paths and lanes that collectively resembled
a crooked cat's cradle. Though outsiders derogatorily called this newborn barrio Rag City, the residents of Nueva Suyapa preferred that it
be called its name.

Over the ensuing decade, thousands of destitute campesinos came
in from the countryside. The Montañita's spring water was salty and
not potable, but since there was no other source—the pipes hadn't

been installed yet—women lugged it home to drink and cook with anyway. Catching a ride to work in the morning required queuing up at the bus terminal much earlier than you needed to leave and then, if you were lucky enough to squeeze aboard, praying as the dangerously overfilled jalopy crossed the unbanistered bridge out of the barrio. Some people scavenged the dump for food and materials, and all that exposed rubbish spawned infestations barriowide. "It was intolerable," one resident recalled. "Sometimes we couldn't even eat. Flies got into our food. In our drinks. Clouds of flies. Everywhere."

Nueva Suyapa was a shelter of last resort, exactly the sort of place Carlos would have been expected to end up in when, in 1990, a destitute campesino himself, he boarded a bus bound for Tegucigalpa.

He was twenty and had never left the coastal lowlands before; he hadn't lined up a job or a place to sleep; and all he had on him was a round blue briefcase and a measly three hundred lempiras. And on top of all that, this journey of his was upsetting to his extended family, who, after his parents separated, had chipped in enough caregiving to see their pride and joy not only graduate from a vocational college but also get the best job they thought a country boy could possibly get— teaching. A few days after he had taken his post in the remote hamlet to which he was assigned, however, he quit. He felt bad about turning his back on those students, but he just knew he wanted more from life than an unelectrified village could provide.

By the time his bus passed over the lip of Tegucigalpa's highland valley, it was nighttime, and he therefore got to take in a truly breathtaking spectacle: a gigantic black basin speckled with a galaxy of lights.

Soon after he deboarded in a colonial-era district with cobblestone streets, however, reality struck. He learned that one night in a hotel would cost him fifty lempiras, or a sixth of his entire stash.

He managed to find a grungy room in what appeared to be a brothel for far less than that, but given that he also had to pay for food, local transportation, and, quite possibly, a humiliating bus ride back home, that didn't give him much time to find gainful employment.

Throughout his childhood, Carlos had lived with different relatives in order to always be within walking distance of a school that educated kids his age. His favorite stint had unequivocally been the three years he spent with his paternal grandmother in Sonaguera, a humid town surrounded by orange groves. Mami Calla, who used a wheelchair, hadn't received much of an education, but she knew how to read, and Carlos adored her even though she was strict. One of her unbreakable regulations was that he had to spend one hour each day teaching some of their adult neighbors how to read, and in an effort to do that well, he once ordered instructional materials from a radio station called La Voz Evangélica de Honduras. Now, years later, on his third day in the capital, he decided to go to that broadcaster's office.

A kind employee there gave him some food and, more importantly, showed him the classifieds. And there it was, right there, his lucky break, a job with his name written all over it. A Christian charity needed someone to lead adult literacy groups, to do precisely what Mami Calla had forced him to develop an expertise in. The salary was minuscule, but it was enough to scrape by on, and once he got hired, his hot streak continued.

He got a series of more lucrative jobs at several different Evangelical charities, and within a couple of years, he was leading a middle-class life in a country where most everyone else was poor. Seemingly, he should have felt happy, but instead, he felt like something was wrong.

———

AT THE TIME, THE VAST MAJORITY OF HONDURANS WERE CATHOLIC, but a number of Evangelical churches, including Carlos's, the Sala Evangélica, were beginning to make their rise.

Carlos fully subscribed to his religion's metaphysics, but he was starting to feel like his particular sect's dogma—save your soul by praying, attending church, and converting others so they will, too—was so obsessed with the fate of the dead that it fostered a complacency about the living. Why waste time teaching math or curing tuberculosis when what's really at stake for the uneducated and ill is whether they spend an eternity in a torturous hellfire or a luxurious bliss?

The church elders and foreign missionaries who promoted that mindset seemed to be implying that Honduras was doomed, even godforsaken, which rubbed Carlos the wrong way. For a young man who prayed all the time and directed one of his congregation's choirs, this sense that his church was off base amounted to nothing less than a severe emotional crisis.

"Not speaking up is part of Honduran culture," Carlos later said. "People feel things, but if an authority is involved, they don't share them. In this case, however, I did. I said that I didn't feel good about something. . . . I felt like there had to be more to being Christian."

Carlos had contrarian instincts and a penchant for dramatizing his own life, and in truth, his church wasn't quite as head-in-the-clouds as he sometimes suggested. It *was* doing some charitable work, through an affiliated ministry that ran a health clinic. But in his mind, his point still stood, because that wasn't nearly enough. And to his credit, he put his money where his mouth was. Initially working as a part-time volunteer, he pulled his church's ministry in a bold new direction, to a place that was widely thought of as a down-and-out snake pit bedeviled by thieves.

Carlos had, of course, never been to Nueva Suyapa before, but once he concluded that it was the most hardscrabble neighborhood in the entire city, circa 1993, he started going there and strolling around. Though he had grown up poor in one of the poorest regions of the poorest country in Latin America besides Haiti, the poverty he witnessed on the Montañita shocked, disturbed, and moved him.

He got started Mami Calla style, informally teaching children how to read in the shade of an oak tree by the bus stop. These alfresco classes were a touching sight but obviously weren't going to cut it long-term, so Carlos convinced a Canadian foundation he had dealt with at a prior job to donate to the ministry. Those funds were then used to purchase an adjacent cantina that was closed down after several people were murdered there. Around the end of 1994, Carlos joined the ministry full-time and began supervising the construction of a schoolhouse at the site of the accursed barroom.

One day, he withdrew cash for the builders, crossed the barrio's entry bridge with the windows of his pickup truck rolled down, and started ascending a steep lane—slowly, as was the custom on the neighborhood's moonlike streetscape. As he was passing by a bodega, two men jumped him from opposite sides. His panicking feet lurched his truck into a stall, at which point he became aware of the fact that there was a knife pressed against his neck.

He thought this was it, The End. And the worst part about it was that he had brought this upon himself, first by disregarding his family's wishes in coming to Tegucigalpa, then by defying his church's teachings in getting *this* mixed up with the problems of the earth, and finally by flouting the most basic common sense in galivanting around Nueva Suyapa.

He gave the thieves the cash, but for a while after they ran off, he remained paralyzed.

He eventually managed to turn the key, shift the gears, and push the pedals. He then told the work crew to go home—in his mind, not for the day, but forever, because he had just decided to pull the plug on this *locura*, on this dangerous and idiosyncratic "lunacy" of his.

Carlos went back to his apartment and waited for his wife, Bernarda, a small woman with straight black hair and a cool, self-assured demeanor that must have commanded the attention of the students she taught English to at one of the most prestigious private schools in the city.

As soon as Carlos saw her, his tale of woe poured out, and all he was wanting back from her was a little bit of sympathy. Once he finished, however, she tersely reminded him, "Nobody ever said this was going to be easy."

———

ON OCTOBER 12, 1995, NINE DAYS AFTER THE COUPLE'S FIRST CHILD WAS born, the ministry's schoolhouse in Nueva Suyapa opened. Its exterior was sky blue, and inside was a roofless courtyard surrounded by three floors of classrooms. Carlos and his colleagues christened it Genesis, as though it were going to be illuminating a primordial darkness.

Their first class of first graders was outfitted in green-and-yellow uniforms—guayabera shirts and slacks for the boys, sleeveless pleated jumpers over Peter Pan–collared blouses for the girls. The school technically charged tuition, but parents just paid whatever they could afford to. Carlos planned to add one new class behind this inaugural group each year until the school encompassed all ages, and his goal was to someday send these students off to college, an aspiration which, in a country where less than a tenth of the lowest-income pupils even graduated from high school, sounded like nothing more than a gee-whiz pipe dream.

And from the start, Genesis was more than just a school—it was, metaphorically speaking, a multinecked crane dedicated to lifting the six hundred poorest families in the barrio up above subsistence poverty. There was a clinic on the ground floor where a doctor, a nurse, and an orthodontist provided care that was free for students and subsidized for everyone else. And because the city's financial institutions had always redlined Nueva Suyapa, Genesis set up a microlender that bankrolled women who wanted to start businesses and families who wanted to add elemental amenities to their homes, like a concrete floor, a sheet-metal roof, a concrete water basin, and a latrine.

Carlos's role was technically managerial, but he was more of a dreamer than a taskmaster, and what he enjoyed most was spending time with his beneficiaries. "He knew how to make people feel happy," a former colleague explained. "He was like a politician." He often delivered construction materials to homeowners himself, and when he wasn't doing that or motivating children or encouraging borrowers or soliciting donations, he might have been leading women's workshops about domestic violence.

Each and every school day began with an hour of prayer and scripture, and within this educational cocoon, which was often enlivened by the echoes of kids dressed in avocado colors, Carlos experienced a religious awakening. His epiphany was sappy and simple but entirely heartfelt: Being Christian meant walking alongside those suffering the most, putting biblical principles into action in addition to all the praying, the preaching, and the singing of hymns. Said another way, he had finally discovered the correct balance between the earthly and the ethereal, and because of that, the psychic discord that had been tearing him apart had been replaced by internal harmony.

WORKING WITH DEVOUT PUPILS, FEMALE ENTREPRENEURS, AND striving homeowners was all well and good, but because Carlos wanted to assist the seamier side of the barrio, too, he came up with a way to safely approach it.

In 1997, he offered to host the annual dinner of Come to Serve, a buildingless congregation that focused on helping addicts and wrongdoers turn around their lives. According to one of that church's pastors, the guest lists for these events typically included "thieves, prostitutes, and alcoholics—all underworld people."

The night of the gala, tables with seating for 170 were set up in the Genesis courtyard. The plan was for Carlos, one of his colleagues, and the two Come to Serve pastors to be waiters in the faux-fancy restaurant, serving chicken, veggies, and soda to the rogues' gallery come to life. It was impossible to predict what was going to happen once all these supposedly dangerous individuals were crammed into an unfamiliar space, but at first, everything went smoothly.

At one point, however, Carlos looked out across the atrium and was startled to see a face he recognized—it was one of the men who had robbed him.

He didn't know what to do.

He wanted to avoid a confrontation, but the thief, who seemed to be in his twenties, walked right up to him and said, "Don't be afraid of me. I'm sorry for frightening you that day."

They shook hands, and from then on out, as strange as it may sound, Carlos felt safer in Nueva Suyapa than anywhere else on the face of the earth. He and Bernarda soon ditched their apartment and moved into a room on the third floor of Genesis.

– 3 –

I N 1982, KURT'S FRESHMAN YEAR AT CALVIN COLLEGE, A PROTES-
tant university located in Grand Rapids, Michigan, two courses
rocked his world, not because of the professors or syllabi, but
because another student was taking them, too. Jo Ann had blue eyes
and wavy brown hair, and her red corduroy bowling shoes stood out.
Their first date was a tandem-bike ride.

Both of their lives had thus far been contained within the Dutch
Midwest, a regional subculture of corn-fed Americans with names
like Vanden Bosch, Beerens, Hoksbergen, and De Roy. Jo Ann grew
up near campus, and Kurt grew up in South Holland, an unusual
Chicago suburb that had a rural feel and a God-fearing population.

While Kurt had always adhered to their subculture's principal denom-
ination, the Christian Reformed Church, Jo Ann had some doubts, so he
gave her a copy of C. S. Lewis's *Mere Christianity*. She reciprocated with a
subscription to the *Chicago Tribune*, which became their lens to the wider
world. On Valentine's Day of their senior year, Jo Ann proposed, and two
weeks after graduating, they got married in their own unique, no-frills
way—a ceremony on one of Calvin's lawns was followed by a sandwich
buffet and a swimming party inside the gymnasium.

The newspaper articles the two of them read about faraway places had caused them to hate President Reagan so much that they protested against him on their fairly conservative campus. His administration was arming and funding the rightward side of right-versus-left-wing civil wars in Guatemala, El Salvador, and Nicaragua, the three countries that bordered Honduras. Whether or not the United States should be doing that was a major foreign policy debate at the time, and what really enraged the country's progressive youth were the reports about America's allies committing atrocities as grotesque as smashing infants' skulls against boulders.

Kurt and Jo Ann didn't have a specific vision for their life, but they did feel abstractly obligated to alleviate suffering. Though neither spoke Spanish nor had ever left the United States before, just six weeks after their wedding, they flew down to Costa Rica, which was where the Christian Reformed World Relief Committee, a charity affiliated with their church, had offered them jobs. This abrupt move, to a country that was next to multiple war zones, made both of their mothers cry.

They shacked up with a Costa Rican family in a tiny, thin-walled house, which was the perfect environment for learning a new language, but a bad one, privacywise, for two religious newlyweds learning how to cohabit.

Two years later, in 1988, they relocated to Tegucigalpa on a new assignment for the same charity. They quickly fell in love with Honduras, though they could explain why only in the vaguest of terms—Hondurans were open, genuine, funny; they just liked them a lot.

Kurt's job was to distribute funds to local charities and to train their employees. With the passage of time, he came to realize that that made him something of an overseer, which he found discomfiting, because he knew all about the imperious carpetbaggers who had come before him—the conquistadors, the lost-city hunters, the bananamen, the canal diggers—and understood that, for the most part, they had believed, as he now did, that what they were doing was going to ben-efit the locals. He seemed to be way more sincerely altruistic than any of those old-timey characters, but there were also some do-gooder archetypes he wanted to avoid becoming—the adventurer getting his exotic thrills under the banner of philanthropy, the lost soul playing the part of the white savior, and the gentleman-abroad enjoying the maids, cooks, and chauffeurs he could never afford back home.

Kurt didn't think that attempting to improve one's adopted home-land was inherently inappropriate, but he did feel like he was currently unqualified to do so. That was why, in the fall of 1992, he began work-ing toward what he liked to call "a PhD in how to help the poor."

PROTESTING IN HONDURAS HAD LONG BEEN DANGEROUS, BECAUSE though the country avoided a major internal conflict during the Cold War, its US-backed military still repressed Marxist agitators as well as some of the peaceful activists it put in the same bucket. Neverthe-less, in July 1994, thousands of Indigenous people, most of whom were Lencas from western Honduras, descended on Tegucigalpa with a long list of demands, ranging from a ban on logging in their region to the construction of a road to connect their villages to the rest of the country. Salvador Zúñiga, the leader of the entity behind this show of force, the Committee of Popular Organizations of Intibucá, or COPIN, was betting that, with the Soviet Union no more, he was shepherding his flock toward getting what they wanted, not toward what they could have expected in the past: tear gas, jail cells, emer-gency rooms, and funerals.

And the incoming marchers were not entirely unthreatening themselves. Salvador and Berta Cáceres, his wife and work partner, admired the Zapatista Army of National Liberation, the Indigenous militants who were then waging a war against Mexico, and the couple had injected a dose of pugnaciousness into COPIN. Earlier that year, one of their antilogging protests outside of a sawmill had climaxed with a face-to-face standoff between hundreds of COPIN protesters holding sticks and rocks and dozens of soldiers armed with batons and M16s; this highly combustible situation had de-escalated only when the governor of that state, who was then surrounded by hundreds of additional demonstrators, agreed to shutter the mill.

Clearly, there was the potential for a lethal clash in the capital, but that wasn't what ended up happening. The COPIN pilgrims made an effort to not cause a ruckus, and for the most part, they were received warmly—a children's choir sang them songs; the government provided fresh water; beauty-school students gave away free haircuts; and provisions were donated by schools, businesses, and even some military officials. On the pilgrims' fifth day in the city, President Carlos Roberto Reina agreed to nearly all of their demands.

This magnanimous denouement probably had a lot to do with the global do-gooder zeitgeist. Two years earlier, as some celebrated the five hundredth anniversary of Columbus's landfall in the Americas, others called for a reevaluation of his legacy vis-à-vis the genocides his discoveries wrought. And those historical revisionists also lobbied for greater compassion toward the present-day Indigenous. The United Nations had actually just declared that the International Decade of the World's Indigenous People was about to begin, which meant that there was now diplomatic pressure on countries like Honduras to take better care of those populations.

At the time, Kurt was working toward a doctorate in development sociology, and having already completed the two years of coursework at Cornell in central New York, he decided that COPIN's pilgrimage was going to be the subject of his dissertation, because he wanted to study an initiative that was (a) successful and (b) locally led.

A few months after the pilgrimage, he, Jo Ann, and their one-and-a-half-year-old daughter traveled to La Esperanza, the mile-high town four hours west of Tegucigalpa where COPIN was based. After staying there with Berta's aunt for three months, the gringo family hiked seven hours on a mule trail to San Francisco de Opalaca, the mountainous hinterland where many of the pilgrims lived, primarily in hilltop dwellings surrounded by corn fields and coffee shrubs. Your average American parents would have never ever brought a toddler to such a remote, indigent, and undeveloped place; the grass that roofed most of the homes there was a habitat for an insect that was known to carry a life-threatening parasite.

"Participating in and observing daily village life was personally rewarding," Kurt would later write in his dissertation, "but often anxiety-provoking. . . . People piled up rocks to stare into our bedroom window, we felt self-conscious about our 'stuff,' and we had to deal with daily requests for loans and ever-present overnight guests. . . . I also made lifelong friends and learned that we can enjoy life without running water, electricity, or electronic gadgets."

Over the course of their six months there, Kurt interviewed many people in twenty-one different villages. In doing so, he discovered some fascinating inconsistencies.

Back in 1993, an agronomist working for a group of NGOs had announced that there was a famine in San Francisco de Opalaca; journalists subsequently reported that the villagers were subsisting on ants, and foreign aid money was soon donated to alleviate the crisis. Many Opalacans Kurt spoke to, however, denied that this famine occurred.

He wasn't sure what to conclude but had an inkling that this was an example of altruists embellishing the plight of the poor. Maybe advancing a philanthropic agenda in the competitive marketplace for deep-pocketed sympathy does require the use of melodrama, but in his dissertation, Kurt identified some downsides to that brand of sensationalism. For example, one villager told him about getting humiliatingly taunted in La Esperanza—"Here come the anteaters!"—and at least one local organization diverted its agenda away from getting a road built, which was what the villagers desperately wanted, to famine relief, which was what attracted international donations.

And then there was the fact that COPIN had presented the pilgrimage as, first and foremost, a long-overdue assertion of Indigenous pride, while up in the forest, Kurt learned that many Opalacans hadn't even thought of themselves as Lencas until quite recently, until COPIN and its precursors began pushing a revivalist campaign. "I had no idea what Lenca meant," one told him. ". . . No one knew we were Lencas. Sometimes we find it strange or think it's a joke."

To be clear, Kurt wasn't suggesting that this was a fraud. In fact, what had pulled the Opalacans' ancestors away from their traditional language, religion, and sense of identity, he argued, wasn't their apathy but the systematic persecution of church and state. His point was simply that, for the most part, the villagers' decision to ally with COPIN had less to do with them having patrimonial grievances or a soft spot for trees and more to do with them desiring the most prosaic infrastructural modernities, such as roads, schools, and clinics. And he was touching this third rail because he thought it mattered. By the time he finished his dissertation, 15 percent of the promised road had been built, but some of the other projects that grew out of the pilgrimage had already flamed out. The reason why, Kurt argued, was that the Opalacans found COPIN to be overbearing, and consequently, their relationship had soured.

All things considered, he was still a big fan of Salvador and Berta. They had won new resources for their people and were courageous enough to stand up for the rights of minorities in a country where doing so was a game of Russian roulette. That's no exaggeration—Berta would not make it to forty-five.

After Kurt shared his findings in La Esperanza, Salvador graciously told him that they "helped clarify many things," but in truth, his feelings weren't that anodyne.

First of all, he had no doubt that a famine occurred and felt Kurt did not understand the nuances of local communication, did not know that, out of shame, some people might not be willing to admit that they lived through a quote, unquote, famine. And Salvador believed that the gringo's oversights weren't just attributable to his naivete. He suspected that Kurt was a spy on an undercover mission to delegitimize COPIN, and that he had cherry-picked interview subjects in an effort to paint the organization in a bad light.

That allegation might sound cockamamie to someone who does not know that during the Cold War, the United States had used Honduras as its regional hub, which meant that, not too long ago, the nation was teeming with an untold number of gringo spooks, mercenaries, and commandos. That was the context through which Salvador, who once volunteered with the leftist guerrillas in El Salvador, saw Kurt, and if you were looking to concoct a conspiracy theory, there was certainly enough raw material there. For example, American soldiers stationed in Honduras had been airlifting food into San Francisco de Opalaca, and at one point, Kurt's daughter slipped, broke her collarbone, and was evacuated on a gringo chopper.

Suspicious, no?

Or is it?

There was a lesson in all this. Kurt was trying to distinguish himself from the various gringo archetypes, but to the ultraleft flank of Honduran society, if he did not toe their party line, he was always going to be just another Ugly American.

――――――

CALVIN, KURT'S ALMA MATER, HIRED HIM AS AN ASSISTANT PROFESsor of sociology, and in 1996, two weeks after his son was born, his first batch of study-abroad students arrived in Tegucigalpa.

He loved teaching and getting to work with Jo Ann, who graded papers, sometimes cotaught, and on a weekly basis, whipped up a feast of American classics for the class. "Kurt and Jo Ann know a lot," one of their former students said, "but they were more about asking questions than giving answers. . . . We got to hear different voices—

average Hondurans, microlending organizations, schools, educational initiatives, embassies, congress, community organizers, Indigenous people who had been shot. . . . It was all about why poverty exists and what humanity does to solve it."

Kurt and Jo Ann were critical of one of the more faddish solutions: the missionary and student groups who spent, say, $30,000 to travel to Honduras for a couple of weeks in order to build a house that an underemployed local contractor could have built for $2,000. And their disapproval wasn't purely economic—they taught their students that, in contrast to those sojourners, they should experience poverty firsthand before endeavoring to help the poor.

The couple had set an example for that by spending half a year in San Francisco de Opalaca, but given that their current residence was in a middle-class neighborhood, they were no longer living up to their own yardstick. This was something they managed to ignore until they heard that Carlos, who, at this point, was closer to an acquaintance than a friend, had moved to Nueva Suyapa. Kurt's initial reaction to this was to feel jealous, because though he and Jo Ann had previously considered doing that, too, they hadn't had the guts to actually follow through.

The gringos soon visited Carlos and Bernarda at their apartment inside Genesis. Carlos told them that he loved living in Nueva Suyapa but insisted that it wouldn't be safe for an American family. He knew Kurt and Jo Ann somewhat, but apparently not well enough to know that his earnest warning would hit them like a double-dog dare.

The Christian Reformed Church teaches its devotees that they will all go to heaven, that nothing they do, good or bad, could possibly change that, and that even so, they should try to make every square inch of the earth better. Nueva Suyapa contained plenty of inches that needed bettering, so Kurt and Jo Ann decided to violate the first rule of parenting. "Keeping your kids safe has become an unquestioned explanation for not doing really good things," Kurt later said. "We don't think that's right."

Around 2000, they moved into the cinder-block house that they had built for them in the compound owned by Genesis. The gringo family of four would walk to church on Sundays, and whenever they passed by the seedy cantina en route, the inebriated men who seemed permanently affixed to its facade would heckle them with faux-English words. The kids liked going to school across the street at Genesis and had no clue that the reason they went there, instead of to a top-tier institution like the one where Bernarda taught, was not because their parents felt it was in their best interests but because their parents didn't want them to be overly privileged. This was arguably a bit excessive. When it would come time for Carlos's two sons to enroll, Bernarda put her foot down—they would be going to her school, not his.

In the popular imagination, extreme do-gooders are thought to be highfalutin oddballs, but Kurt was a winsome guy who liked to make pantomimed dad jokes, like yanking his hand away from a teenager's handshake. He found deciding whether or not to eat out to be a serious moral dilemma, because he couldn't help but compare the cost of four professionally prepared meals with what that amount of money could buy someone in Nueva Suyapa. Jo Ann had similar qualms, though what embarrassed her most was the size of their house, which Kurt had been in charge of designing. It wouldn't have turned any heads in Grand Rapids, but in the barrio, it qualified as palatial, and Jo Ann hated how, when her local friends saw it for the first time, they would say, "Wow."

After about a year, they moved into one of the town houses next door, at which point the Hernándezes took over the Taj Mahal. Carlos needed the space, because people came to him for assistance, day and night. His family dinners usually included a number of interlopers, and he kept spare mattresses in the living room, in case any local kids were in need of shelter. "It felt like Carlos adopted a bunch of us," one of the boys who used to pass through later said. ". . . If a young person had a problem in his own house, he would go to Carlos's. The door was open. You just entered."

Kurt was making an impact on the barrio, too. A water infrastructure had been installed by then, but it was a shoddy patchwork of tanks, pumps, and PVC pipes, so ASJ, which was newly up and running, paid a hydraulic engineer to study it. Kurt then rallied the local water board around making some improvements, and for about two years thereafter, water arrived at each house every ten or so days, instead of every twenty-five.

He and Jo Ann also found a myriad of small ways to assist their neighbors. "They have helped people in our church with economic problems, house problems, and work problems," their pastor said. ". . . They have been the number one force in developing our community."

Nueva Suyapa was much maligned, but for all its faults, it did have a certain charm to it. There was an array of palm trees, orange-flowered acacias, pink-flowered jacarandas, white-flowered hizotes, and trees known as "butt plugs" because of what their fruits did to digestive tracts. Whenever the power fizzled out in the early evening, audible jeers would momentarily overwhelm the nightly dog-bark chorus; and as soon as the outage ended, a collective cheer would resound, which was also what happened when one of the city's soccer teams scored. It was a community where unsupervised kids roamed around, where vendors operating out of wheelbarrows and stalls sold just about anything you might ever want, and where a shirtless glue addict could knock on a door and expect to receive a sugary cup of coffee.

Kurt would commute to his classroom by rolling down the switchback on his bicycle and then pedaling halfway across the city, wearing a helmet, a button-down, a backpack, and khakis with a strap around his chain-side ankle. It was quite the image. His skin, education, job, and passport all put him at a major advantage to his neighbors, but he had reduced the gulf between him and them enough to combat poverty without feeling like a phony.

— 4 —

NEXT TO GENESIS WAS A LANE THAT PLUNGED INTO FLORES DE Oriente, the most sequestered sector of Nueva Suyapa, a hollow where thousands of people lived in rudimentary dwellings dispersed among a sea of fruit trees. Chelito lived there, in a one-room shack, near a salty brook. He wasn't yet *the* Chelito, just a "Chelito," a common nickname for fair-skinned boys.

His father, a shoeshine man, had moved out when he was eight, which was probably for the best, because as Chelito himself would later admit, he hated that drunk for abusing his mother. The boy had apparently been enrolled in first grade three times but was unlikely to have received any more schooling than that. One of his earliest odd jobs was at a fruit stand that paid him and his older brother Junior in kind; they would share one of the portions they received as wages and bring the other one home for their younger siblings. According to a social worker who would later meet with Chelito's mother, "I asked her directly, 'Did you force him to steal or deal drugs?' She replied, 'That's what everyone says about me.' I also interviewed Chelito. He said his mom sent him out to sell things like tortillas, but he was the one who decided, once he got out there, that stealing and dealing drugs was an easier way to make money."

Had Chelito come of age in a prior era, he may have never graduated beyond that sort of petty vice. But because of a force with roots that stretch across decades and countries, the nature of criminality in Nueva Suyapa had mutated.

This story begins, oddly enough, with the Salvadoran Civil War. Many of its refugees settled in the sunny flatlands of Los Angeles, which, in the eighties, wasn't exactly a refuge from violence; it was a gangland where Bloods, Crips, the Mexican Mafia, and a slew of other crews battled, an inharmoniously multicultural environment where a group of young Salvadorans decided to form a posse called MS-13. They and their local rival, Barrio 18, eventually opened up their ranks to Latinos of different national origins, and they also eventually attracted the attention of law enforcement. From 1994 to 1997 alone, 11,235 Salvadorans, Hondurans, and Guatemalans with rap sheets were deported from the United States. "Many were gang members," said a United Nations worker who greeted the castaways at Toncontín International. "They were easily recognizable because of their tattoos."

These exiles, who now found themselves in a weakly policed country where what had qualified as gang violence before were fair fistfights staged outside discotheques, achieved their manifest destiny with a pestilential ease. By the turn of the millennium, most barrios in Tegucigalpa were occupied by MS-13, Barrio 18, or both of them.

These local cells knew their Gangster 101. They posted graffiti, stationed lookouts, ran protection rackets, and loitered like outlaws in a frontier outpost—smoking, drinking, dancing, glancing, just generally putting the mood on edge. This peacocking was obviously a means to intimidate, but it was also a tactic to entice. Since the mareros rocked oversized Dickies pants, threw up devil-horn salutes, and tattooed themselves in occult iconography, they embodied American countercultural cool, which was something barrio kids knew all about from watching movies. Add to that the bacchanal of parties, drugs, sex, and brotherhood they got to enjoy in an otherwise poor and pious country, and then ask yourself, What wayward boy wouldn't want a taste of that?

As of 2003, Carlos had about four hundred students enrolled in his school, and during its annual December-to-February break, he bused hundreds of kids to Genesis's seven-day, open-enrollment camps in a nearby mountain town. Part of what he was trying to do with all this was convince youngsters that, even though they happened to be born in a besmirched community where most of their parents were either unemployed or working for poverty wages as janitors, bus drivers, and the like, they, the next generation, could become doctors, lawyers, engineers, or cops. This game of persuasion had always been challenging, but once Barrio 18 sank its claws into Nueva Suyapa, the difficulty and stakes of it increased, because now there was a tantalizing wrong turn to make, one that, unlike your typical teenage rebellions, had no coming back from.

Chelito, who once went to a Genesis camp and sometimes played in the school's gymnasium, was one of the many kids Carlos tried to steer away from street life. "A classmate of mine sometimes wouldn't show up," a former Genesis student recalled. ". . . When that happened, Carlos would say, 'I'm going to go grab him on my moto.' The kid wasn't coming in because his shirt was dirty or shoes were broken, that sort of thing. So Carlos and his team would just go get him shoes."

And Carlos's efforts to counter the draw of the mara often continued after the bell had rung. "At night, we'd be so tired, really fatigued," he later said, "but I'd still stay at Genesis. . . . As long as kids were there, they were safe. We'd play volleyball. I'd invent obstacle courses. . . . Sometimes I'd stay until eleven, midnight, one or two in the morning."

Yet some of the boys in Carlos's orbit did make that wrong turn. It was a Barrio 18 marero known as Siniestro, or the Sinister One, who took Chelito and Junior under his wing. One of the brothers' licit hustles had been keeping an eye on cars parked outside downtown restaurants in exchange for tips, and it was their new mentors who encouraged them to start stealing the in-dash stereos. Once, when the brothers didn't bring back enough plunder, Siniestro's crony pistol-whipped Junior's head.

RECRUITMENT WASN'T CARLOS'S ONLY PROBLEM WITH THE BARRIO 18.

Though there were no reliable georeferenced crime statistics back then, it was quite clear to the residents of Nueva Suyapa that with the mara entrenched, and several groups rising up to combat it, the barrio had become more violent than ever.

Javier Arasli, the father of two Genesis students, lived in the Diecisiete, a gridded sector built on top of the old garbage dump. He did well enough as a security guard to own a car and earned enough extra cash moonlighting as a driver to be able to take his sons to Tae Kwon Do classes. And he also somehow found time to scrub mara graffiti off walls on his block, which was a very daring hobby indeed.

His wife, Fidelia, worked at a supermarket, and on the last night of September 2003, she did inventory until three in the morning. Then, about an hour after she climbed into bed, Javier woke up, because a neighbor of theirs needed a ride. The couple's indefatigable work ethic was what facilitated their happy home life, but ever since the barrio had become this dangerous, Fidelia did not approve of her husband driving late at night.

"Go tomorrow," she insisted.

"I have to take advantage of this work," he replied.

"I'm scared. I'm scared."

"Why?"

"Don't go. Just leave later."

He departed, and the next thing Fidelia knew, she woke up to knocking.

It was her niece. A few blocks away, on the lane that gently slopes down from the Diecisiete to Genesis, Javier had been robbed and murdered. In other words, Fidelia, a petite woman with big brown eyes, had suddenly just become a widow.

Not long after that, while she was dropping off her sons at school, Carlos invited her into his office, a square room with a large bookshelf. She told him that she had asked her boss for a leave of absence but had been forced to resign instead, which was an absolute catastrophe, since it meant her family had zero streams of income left. This corporate ruthlessness wouldn't have surprised Carlos, but what did was Fidelia's reason for wanting a sabbatical.

To an American ear, the word "impunity" may sound old-fashioned and lawyerly, but in Nueva Suyapa, where *impunidad* reigned, it was ordinary parlance. It basically means getting away with murder, and there was so much of that in Honduras—maybe 10 percent of serious crimes were even investigated—that relatives of the slain were known to utter a cliché of surrender: "Leave it in God's hands."

But Fidelia, for one, wasn't ready to delegate justice to the afterlife. She wanted her husband's killers to be punished via the jurisprudential trinity of arrest, prosecution, and incarceration, and she had needed time off work to try making that happen.

Whodunits are typically dramatized as booby-trapped mazes only the cleverest detectives could possibly make their way through alive, but Fidelia, the amateur sleuth, had already cracked the case. It was simple. A few of her neighbors had directed her to the witnesses, and those witnesses had fingered the culprits.

That wasn't the hard part. The next part was.

The police told Fidelia that they couldn't make any arrests unless the witnesses gave official statements directly to them, but when she asked the witnesses to do that, they refused. This logjam was all too common. At the time, national polls indicated that about two-thirds of Hondurans were afraid to report the criminals who lived in their neighborhoods, and a similarly large fraction had little or no trust in the police. And those numbers were almost certainly higher in a community as marginalized and crime-ridden as Nueva Suyapa, where, according to one longtime resident, "There have been situations where someone denounced a marero or delinquent, and the police told the criminals who denounced them. . . . The cops used to show up in the small hours of the night and do deals with the delinquents."

Fidelia asked Carlos to help her break this impasse.

He was supposed to be the guy who resolved people's problems . . . but *this*? Hunting down murderers? He was out of his element here, so later on, he discussed it with Kurt, who, by now, was his best friend.

The two of them wanted to support Fidelia; having said that, they knew next to nothing about the criminal justice system and worried that the perpetrators would retaliate. Their understanding—which seems to have been based on conjecture, not facts—was that the suspects Fidelia identified were members of the Encapuchados, or the Masked Men, a vigilante group formed with an antimara mission that now purportedly assaulted completely innocent people like Javier. Kurt and Carlos didn't know how to handle this obviously dangerous situation, so as a next step, they decided to reach out to some friends for advice.

———

SINCE AMBULANCE DRIVERS USUALLY WOULDN'T ENTER NUEVA SUYAPA after dark, Carlos's front door was sometimes people's only pathway to urgent medical care. Soon after his heart-to-heart with Fidelia, in the early evening, a woman and her adult daughter knocked.

Carlos immediately drove them around the corner to a church, in front of which the woman's son, a scrawny seventeen-year-old known as Niño, was lying, with blood gushing from a bullet wound on the left side of his torso. Carlos wanted the teenager, who had recently attended one of his camps, to survive, but many others might have rooted for the opposite outcome.

Niño was basically a prototype for what Chelito was in the process of becoming. His childhood had been very difficult—his dad was an alcoholic, his mom was psychologically unstable, and he and his six siblings had all been crammed into a small shack. But his adolescence had been quite exciting, because he and some friends had had the moxie to invent their own mara. Their flag was planted in the steep sector where Kurt's church was located, and they were known to vandalize property and assault pedestrians. Nevertheless, Carlos had not given up on Niño. He felt, perhaps somewhat delusionally, that the teenager could still get back on the straight and narrow. Unfortunately for Niño, however, a Ouija board had recently informed him that he was never going to get to turn nineteen.

Carlos loaded him into the back seat, sped downhill, and hurtled three and a half miles west on a straightaway boulevard, alternating his gaze between the fading teenager behind him and the road, the taillights, and the neon pole-top signs up ahead.

Once they arrived at the hospital, Niño was pronounced dead. Carlos then purchased a coffin down the street before returning to the hospital to retrieve his camper's corpse.

Carlos believed that the Encapuchados were the ones who had shot him. This was speculation—and it was probably incorrect—but he wasn't yet in the business of solving murder mysteries, and the back-to-back killings of Javier and Niño were just two of the many crimes to wonder about at the time. For instance, in October 2003, a fifteen-year-old girl was shot in the eye for resisting a rape; later that month, a father of four was shot in the head for refusing to hand over his wedding ring; that same day, a body was found on the Montañita; in late November, a twenty-two-year-old man was murdered; in mid-December, a logger was taken out; and in late December, it was another twenty-two-year-old's turn. Carlos came into contact with some of this stretch's carnage—he recalls lifting and transporting three additional victims to the hospital. He once did so late at night, and though he wanted to immediately return home and shower, he worried that the barrio, at that hour, right after a murder, would be extra treacherous, so he just paced around the emergency room, waiting for the sun to rise, his attention lingering on the stench of the blood that was drying on his shirt.

After each of these gory transports, he would wash his upholstery and clothes, but he still couldn't rid himself of that ferrous odor; at a certain point, he wondered if he was hallucinating.

One byproduct of extreme impunity is confusion, because if detectives, prosecutors, and judges don't suss out and rubber-stamp the Truth, then people are forced to rely on gossip and inherent bias. Determining who was responsible for this spasm of violence was thus largely an unscientific exercise, and the same could be said of the spike in violence nationwide.

For much of the Honduran electorate, however, its cause was not at all uncertain—mareros were clearly to blame. That was why President Ricardo Maduro had ridden into office on an ardently antimara ticket, and that was why the police were now aggressively rounding up mareros as well as some people who just seemed to be. And dragnets weren't the force's only tactic; there were also covert detachments that summarily executed suspected gang members. Some of that clearly did go on, but just as the right-wing charlatans seemed overeager to pin every last unsolved murder on mareros, the left-wing bleeding hearts seemed overeager to pin every last one on the cops, and while there was certainly a measure of truth in both of those explanations, the only real truth in places like Nueva Suyapa was that the Truth did not exist.

Four months after Javier's murder, on January 19, 2004, a twenty-two-year-old cop with three kids told his girlfriend that he was afraid to start his new assignment at the Nueva Suyapa police post. A few days later, he responded to an armed robbery reported near the bus terminal and was killed in a shootout with the culprits. Within hours, 150 cops and soldiers swooped into the barrio with a helicopter supporting them from above. This atypically large incursion was memorable; nevertheless, what really happened that day is not entirely clear.

According to *La Tribuna*, the armed robbers were Barrio 18 mareros, and one of them died in the initial shootout with the twenty-two-year-old cop. That may have been accurate, but given that the press was hungry for salacious mara-related stories, and given that crime reporters seemed to be overly reliant on not-totally-reliable police sources, it wasn't necessarily. And Kurt and Carlos's understanding, which presumably came to them through the barrio's rumor mill, was different. They believed that the armed robbers were Encapuchados, and that during the megaraid, the police killed one of Javier's murderers and arrested another. This was the version that solidified in their minds and precipitated a come-to-Jesus moment in their own bildungsroman.

Because it forced them to face a humiliating fact. In the pursuit of justice, Fidelia had risked her life and lost her job, whereas all they had done was make a few phone calls—*to seek advice*. The thirteen people they believed the Encapuchados had killed since Fidelia approached Carlos bore down on their consciences, because theoretically, they could have gotten them arrested based on her intel.

Kurt had an ability to rapidly transform his negative emotions into focused reasoning, and a natural place for doing that was his classroom, where he could typically be found perched on the edge of his desk, a plastic tea mug in hand and a map of the world behind him. He liked to riff on the proverb that had become a platitude in the development world: Give a man a fish, and you feed him for a day; teach a man to fish, and you feed him for a lifetime.

Kurt now believed that neither "fish" nor "fishing"—neither aid nor development—helped the poor as much as advertised, because most of the impoverished people in the world lived in semilawless places where bullies could get away with stealing their "fish," snapping their "poles," and fencing off the "lakes" for themselves. In other words, giving a Honduran farmer seeds or a lesson about crop yields wasn't going to make a difference if a bunch of thugs subsequently extorted him, drove him off his land, or emptied a clip into his chest.

Where Kurt was going with all this was that justice, not in the vague sense of the word, but as in, the administration of the law, was the "unserved niche in the global-how-do-we-help-the-poor agenda."

In most English translations of the Bible, the word "justice" appears frequently in the Old Testament, which was originally written in Hebrew and Aramaic, but infrequently in the New Testament, which was originally written in Greek. This makes it seem as though Jesus prioritized sweet concepts like righteousness and love over justice and retribution. But a theologian Kurt studied with at Calvin, Nicholas Wolterstorff, felt that that interpretation was flawed.

The Greek words *dikaios* and *dikaiosune*, which appear hundreds of times in the New Testament, are typically translated to "righteous" and "righteousness." When the scripture was penned, however, those words could also mean "just" and "justice," and that's usually how they are translated in Aristotle's and Plato's works.

In the Sermon on the Mount, Jesus proclaims, "Blessed are those who are persecuted for the sake of dikaiosune." Wolterstorff argued that, in that case, "justice" was the superior translation, because people generally don't get persecuted for being righteous, or broadly moral. In his version, Jesus goes on to declare, "Blessed are those who hunger and thirst for justice."

The idea for the Secret Group began taking form.

CHELITO AND JUNIOR GOT THEIR FEET WET AS BARRIO 18 MINIONS, but at some point in 2004, they and Siniestro decided to start their own gang. How exactly the Puchos, or the Bunch, usurped the barrio's other criminal outfits is not well understood, but by the end of that year, Barrio 18, the Encapuchados, and Niño's mara no longer had a meaningful presence.

All said and done, there were about thirty-five Puchos, and though many were minors, they precociously understood that dominating was a lot more fun than playing around. Their coming-out party, if you will, happened on the evening of December 4, 2004, when Siniestro, Chelito, Junior, and another Pucho waltzed up to a buzzing nightclub near Genesis. The establishment's owner, Armando Jevawer, was a prominent local figure then running for a seat in the National Congress. Nevertheless, right by the disco's entrance, Siniestro fired three bullets into the candidate's head, apparently because he had dared to ask the youngsters to surrender their guns before entering.

Two days after that, *La Tribuna* reported that Siniestro was a suspect in a handful of cop killings, and that the police wanted him, dead or alive.

Weeks later, on Christmas Eve, lo and behold: Siniestro's mutilated corpse was dumped on the Montañita. *La Tribuna* characterized this as a Christmas gift, and that was, in fact, how a lot of people felt. But his elimination did not incapacitate his mara.

Once upon a time, it was impossible not to feel sorry for Chelito, and pretty soon, you would have to wonder if he truly was as freakishly wicked as portrayed. But now he was indisputably *the* Chelito, and part of his legend was the way he consistently yo-yoed from the barrio to police custody and back, as though he were the Honduran Houdini.

Another component of his notoriety was that, as one former Pucho put it, "He was one of the smallest kids but also one of the evilest. If killing someone served his purposes, then he would kill them. No problem. He wouldn't feel a thing. . . . He once shot one of our buddies in the foot . . . just to show he was in charge."

When the police arrested him on March 18, 2005, they took a

mug shot out in the field. In it, he is wearing a tucked-in white tank top; he has acne, a buzz cut, and a sort of elfin face; and he is pursing his lips and squinting one of his eyes, as though he were trying to look menacing. But he doesn't. In fact, he could momentarily be mistaken for a middle schooler at a science fair, because his body is only partway through puberty, and because there is a homemade poster to his rear. An inspection of its exhibits, however, reveals that his interests weren't, say, photosynthesis or seabed ecology. It has images of guns pasted onto it, as well as an illustration of a graveyard with ghosts floating above, and in one corner it reads, "Welcome to the Barrio."

Chelito must have felt like Nueva Suyapa was his.

- 5 -

MACARIO WAS NOT WHAT KURT HAD IN MIND WHEN HE asked Carlos and del Cid, the ASJ middle manager, to hire a churchgoing attorney, but by the end of the Ver Beek family vacation, the Secret Group had made an impressive amount of headway toward its immediate goal: keeping Chelito's yo-yo extended.

According to their detailed report, during Holy Week, Macario and that second attorney (a friend of his who would soon back out) had visited the juvenile courthouse, where a judge informed them that one of the arrested Puchos had already been released, but that Chelito and the other two were still in custody. Macario and his partner had then assured this judge that they were going to do what was necessary to keep them there, namely, bring in witnesses who could testify to their crimes.

And that was already in the works.

On Palm Sunday, the two lawyers, Carlos, and del Cid had met up with two influential community members to arrange another clandestine meeting. Then, two days later, at eleven in the morning, seven concerned citizens surreptitiously gathered in a private room at a pan-Asian restaurant in the city's urban core. Macario and his partner asked everyone there to become their confidential informants, which would entail providing intelligence about the Puchos as well as introductions to potential witnesses.

Kurt chose to keep Macario on board even though he didn't know much about him. He liked to mountain bike; he owned a motorcycle; his political views were very left-wing; he seemed to have an on-again, off-again relationship with the mother of his two kids; and he sometimes laced his speech—proudly, it seemed—with the telltale signs of a barrio childhood: the profane slang, the machine-gunned r's, the gangsterish melodies. He was clearly sharp, brave, and persistent, but according to his former colleagues at ASJ, these sorts of phrases could also be used to describe him: "pompous jerk attitude," "huge problems with authority," "not open to input," "verbally abused people."

So be it.

The fact that he was willing to give the Secret Group a shot made him indispensable. To prevent Chelito and the others from snapping back to the barrio, Kurt and Carlos needed witnesses to start singing—soon. And in case the seriousness of this ticking-time challenge was at all unclear, there had already been a reminder. That one released Pucho—who was possibly Junior, using an alias—had allegedly just helped murder a twenty-four-year-old man.

———

IN THE LATE NINETIES AND EARLY AUGHTS, THE UNITED STATES HAD pushed Honduras to replace its inquisitorial justice system with a replica of America's accusatorial one, which meant redefining the roles of cops, prosecutors, and judges and scrapping written trials in favor of oral ones. This was done with good intentions—oral trials are faster, and in theory, since every last thing is open to instantaneous challenge and counterchallenge, they are fairer, too. But this new legal system was essentially stillborn, because the country's functionaries were struggling to comply with the due-process standards that had been exported from a much richer place. And then there was the fact that oral trials forced witnesses into face-to-face confrontations with the defendants whose liberty largely depended on their testimonies. They're there together, in the same room, spitting distance, two sides locked in a duel. Perhaps people were willing to volunteer for that in Iowa and Maine, but in Honduras, who the hell was going to sign up?

That was the challenge Macario now faced.

One thing working in his favor was that Chelito and the others had been arrested for illicit association. This meant that, for the time being, the lawyer didn't need to track down witnesses who had seen one particular crime; instead, all he needed were witnesses who could attest to the fact that the detainees were members of a gang. Between Kurt's church community, Carlos's beneficiaries, and the Asian-restaurant-informants' Rolodexes, there were plenty of people who could do just that, and through those channels, Macario was able to quickly track down six witnesses.

While Fidelia's investigation had stalled out there, Macario managed to get one step further, to convince those witnesses to actually testify. Maybe it was his rock-and-roll bravado that reassured them, or maybe what made the difference was that he was effectively sponsored by Kurt and Carlos, two of the barrio's most respected residents, given that all his introductions had chained person-to-person from them.

The Public Ministry, the institution that employed the country's prosecutors, was headquartered in a three-story building on a road that curves up a hill in central Tegucigalpa. Macario went there with his witnesses and told a prosecutor that they would testify against the Puchos—but only if Article 237 were invoked.

The success of the Secret Group largely hinged on this provision in the Penal Procedure Code, which stated that witnesses' identities could be concealed if their testimonies were going to put them or their loved ones in danger. But that was basically it. The clause didn't provide a comprehensive road map for actually going about doing that or a stream of funding to pay for it, so, unsurprisingly, Article 237 was rarely ever utilized.

But this prosecutor agreed to request it, and a judge soon approved, which meant that at all hearings and in all publicly available records, Macario's witnesses were going to be referred to by aliases—Witness C, for example.

The judge also sent summonses to attend a hearing to the Public Ministry; normally, they would then be forwarded to Criminal Investigation, the police force's detective bureau, which would be responsible for delivering them to their ultimate recipients, the witnesses. But handling this basic clerical task like that would entail revealing the witnesses' identities to police officers who, theoretically, could have been in cahoots with the Puchos. After Macario insisted on cutting through this life-threatening red tape, the judge agreed to let the Secret Group handle the process serving itself.

One morning, not long after that, four people slipped out of the barrio, went to a prearranged rendezvous, and got into the car Macario was driving, most likely his Volvo sedan. He then drove them to the juvenile courthouse, which, consistent with the juvenile justice system's euphemistic style—a punishment was "a socio-educational measure," and a prison was "a pedagogical complex"—looked nothing like a courthouse. A squat stucco low-rise, it would later get converted into a tight-quartered motel, and in a serious affront to the tenets of NIMBYism, it was located in a fancy residential neighborhood. Macario cased the surroundings before leading his witnesses inside.

The front vestibule was connected to the back of the building by a low-ceilinged hallway with multiple doors; they led to a courtroom, a social work office, a holding cell for girls, and a holding cell for boys that presumably then contained Chelito and the two other Puchos. The prosecutor Macario previously met at the Public Ministry asked him and his wards to wait in the hallway until the hearing was called to order.

Macario was confused. That would put them in plain sight of whoever walked into the building, including, in all likelihood, the Puchos' attorney and relatives. Therefore, he asked the prosecutor to escort them to whichever room was typically used to shelter protected witnesses.

Now the prosecutor was confused. She had thought Macario was going to bring balaclavas. There had been a miscommunication.

They all rushed up a half flight of stairs to consult with the judge. He considered Chelito, a regular in this building, to be exceptionally dangerous, and he was accustomed to throwing out cases due to witnesses not showing up for hearings. But now here, before him, were four flesh-and-blood cooperators who were ready, willing, and able to testify against the boy who always slipped away.

The judge had dealt with this type of situation before but apparently not enough times to have bothered developing a procedure that wasn't farcically haphazard. He kicked the clerks out of their office down the hall and locked Macario and the witnesses inside of it. This was the first maneuver in what would turn out to be a game of cat-and-mouse.

Once courthouse security cleared out the second floor, the judge brought Macario and the witnesses back into his office, which had a balcony that was closed in with tinted windows—they weren't as opaque as the mirrored glass typically seen in American interrogation rooms, but they were dark enough to do the trick.

A bailiff brought the Puchos out onto the gated parking lot behind the courthouse as the witnesses, from their blackened higher ground, told the judge what they knew about them. Then, after security cleared out both the lot and the ground level of the building, Macario and his crew descended the stairs, exited into the lot, and were driven away in the courthouse's microbus.

Juvenile court records generally aren't accessible to the public, but according to Macario, the judge ruled that Chelito and the others were going to remain imprisoned until their trial. For the Secret Group, this was a huge early win.

But, no, of course it wasn't going to be that easy.

This provisional victory would amount to nothing.

Actually, worse than nothing.

On May 8, Chelito and some other Puchos broke out of Renaciendo, a juvenile detention center located about an hour northwest of Tegucigalpa. He had probably not enjoyed being exhibited like a zoo animal before a plate of black glass, and according to a document Kurt would soon write up, "the day they escaped, they killed a woman and cut up a bus fare collector's face. They thought they were witnesses (they weren't)."

Many years later, neither Kurt nor Carlos would be able to recall this murder in any detail. "I think it was an older woman who sold peanuts" was the best that Kurt could do.

One possible victim was Zoila del Carmen Avila, a twenty-four-year-old who, according to *La Tribuna*, was the third sibling in her family to be killed by "mareros who brag about bearing the blood of their now-extinct boss, Siniestro."

Whoever the victim was, the fact that Kurt and Carlos do not remember her is a bit startling given that, according to Kurt's own write-up, they may have unintentionally contributed to her death. Asked to address this, Kurt replied, "What we were focusing on was, we have to get these kids arrested, because they're just going to keep killing. . . . The fact that they had killed another person didn't require—well, maybe we should have thought more about, are we safe ourselves? But I don't think we went there. . . . It was just, once again, we have to get these guys off the street, because they're just going to keep killing."

That was his mantra. He repeated it over and over again as he tried to explain this, and it was clearly one of the moral alibis he leaned on back in the day as his program struck ethical land mine after ethical land mine. Around this time, he gave the Secret Group a new name: Peace and Justice. Those two beatific concepts were his endgame, and on the arduous journey there, he wasn't going to paralyze himself by tracing every last tragedy through the butterfly effects of his own actions—the barrio was way too bewildering for that. And furthermore, he was willing to accept that there might be some collateral damage on this quest, so whenever setbacks like this occurred, instead of wallowing in shame or closing up shop, he would double down on his mantra: *We have to get these guys off the street, because they're just going to keep killing.*

– 6 –

BERNARDO LAGOS LIKED TO HUNT RABBITS ON THE MONTAÑITA. He was a tall man with a blunt chin, arched eyebrows, and a full head of ebony hair; people called him Pan Blanco, or White Bread, because his skin tone was so light.

His lifestyle was peculiar—he traveled throughout the country to work on large-scale construction projects, and in addition to the nine children he had with his partner of over three decades, Martha Isidro, he had fathered thirteen more with five other women. It will come as no surprise that he and Martha had had their ups and downs, but for the most part, things were copacetic in their brick house on the slope above Flores de Oriente.

Like a lot of great blood feuds, Pan Blanco's beef with the Puchos had surprisingly modest origins. According to the family lore, the foundational incidents had been the Puchos demanding his shotgun, and the Puchos attempting to recruit his son. It was from there that things escalated.

Pan Blanco was close with his extended family—on Sundays, they all got together to play soccer and eat beef soup—and the two sisters that Chelito's uncle and his cronies raped down by the brook were his nieces. After that happened, Pan Blanco and a handful of like-minded men started watching over their sector and patrolling out beyond it. If they came upon a Pucho, they fired their guns. "It felt like a war out of the Wild West," one of them later said. ". . . We were just neighbors trying to protect ourselves. Calling the police would have been pointless."

Vigilantism was not terribly unusual in Honduras, a country where adults could legally own up to five small firearms, and where Cold War detritus like AK-47s could be purchased illegally for a pittance. Of course only a sliver of any imperiled population actually had the mettle and moral dexterity to fight fire with fire, but those who did had a certain amount of tacit backing, because "social cleansing," which is what Latin Americans call the lynching of criminals, was not unpopular. A survey conducted by Vanderbilt University's Latin American Public Opinion Project would soon indicate that only about 45 percent of Hondurans disapproved of people taking justice into their own hands in places where the state didn't punish lawbreakers. Kurt and Carlos were not among those who condoned the extrajudicial killing of mareros, and in their minds, incarcerating them through Peace and Justice was a counterintuitive act of compassion, because as the murders of both Niño and Siniestro demonstrated, the likely alternative was that they would be killed by either the police, a vigilante group, or a rival gang.

And what was going to happen to Pan Blanco once one of his slugs actually struck a Pucho? Would the taste of blood change him? Would he lose his sense of proportion and just go ahead and execute all those nihilistic little shits? After how much ammunition purchased, and how much danger endured, would he start "asking" merchants to compensate him for the security he was providing?

That right there was the fundamental problem with vigilantes—it was so easy for them to become almost indistinguishable from the mareros they supposedly despised. And Kurt also worried that if Pan Blanco crossed either of the two irreversible thresholds before him—

killing a Pucho, or a Pucho killing him—a tit-for-tat cycle of bloody vendetta would ensue.

That was why he asked Macario to speak to Pan Blanco, to try convincing him that he could protect his community in a different fashion, by helping Peace and Justice get the Puchos jailed. The fact that Pan Blanco quickly agreed to this indicated that he really would have rather not resorted to cowboyish vengeance. He and his posse, which was known as the Pan Blancos, immediately became some of the program's most active informants.

Now Peace and Justice had to live up to its end of the bargain.

Kurt had been operating under the assumption that there had to be some upstanding cops, but Macario didn't have time to sift through the force, searching for hidden gems, because who knew how long the Pan Blancos would eschew a shoot-out. Therefore, when the lawyer received tips about the Puchos' whereabouts from his growing network of informants, he simply passed them along to whoever would listen at Criminal Investigation and the Public Ministry.

But the police didn't immediately go and arrest them, which was a big problem, because it seemed like the barrio was inching closer and closer to a battle royale. According to a sworn statement given by one of Pan Blanco's sons, on May 16, four Puchos went to his brother's school and "said they were going to kill him if he didn't hand over his bicycle and gun."

The following day, Pan Blanco purchased a twelve-gauge.

Then, finally, two days later, just before daybreak, a fleet of patrol cars containing over fifty cops as well as Macario and five of his informants headed toward Nueva Suyapa. The informants, who were going to be acting as guides, were wearing balaclavas, but the ponytailed attorney elected to leave his face au naturel.

———

AT THAT VERY MOMENT, A YOUNG MAN NAMED JHONNY LOPEZ WAS fast asleep at his grandmother's house. He had already endured a seemingly backbreaking amount of adversity in his life—his father had drunk himself to death before his eleventh birthday; cancer had taken his mom before his twelfth; and he had spent his adolescence in a countryside orphanage, until he couldn't take it anymore and escaped back to Nueva Suyapa.

His uncle was the pastor of Kurt's church. The gringo sometimes gave him money and advice, and though Jhonny was twenty, he was matriculated at Genesis, which, given the limited number of spots, was a serious privilege. But Jhonny didn't like studying. What he liked was booze, drugs, and guns, so, predictably, he had fallen in with the Puchos.

At six a.m., the bells of a nearby basilica tolled, and the police fanned out across the barrio. According to the officers' report, Jhonny's grandmother gave them permission to enter her home, at which point they notified the young man of his right not to be subjected to "mistreatment, threats, physical or psychological violence, torture, or the application of mind-altering substances, hypnosis, or a lie detector." According to Jhonny, however, the public servants who wrenched him out of bed that morning tied him up, showed his face to a masked individual, transported him to an isolated spot up the Montañita, and gave him a beating. And this was no mild slapping around; he would not be able to eat solid food for an entire month.

The cops nabbed a total of twelve Puchos and also took statements from a number of witnesses, at least some of whom were Macario's— one claimed that after Chelito ordered two Puchos to attack his boss, they had cracked the man's teeth with a pistol.

This was quite an impressive haul, but the scariest Puchos, including Chelito and Junior, were still at large, and Macario had observed some disturbing behavior, such as cops barging into homes without warrants, cops striking already apprehended suspects in the head, feet, and genitals, and cops threatening to cripple a detainee with an aluminum baseball bat. And it must be emphasized that they had done all that *in front of* an attorney who worked for an NGO.

This brazen thuggery rattled Kurt and his team. The gringo immediately started wrestling with the issue in internal meetings and correspondence with a donor, but ultimately, when it came to deciding how to respond to it, he relied not on hard-and-fast principles but decision-tree logic. The charity could have submitted a complaint to internal affairs, but as everyone knew, internal affairs was an absolute sham. Then there was the idea of publicly denouncing the abuses; in Kurt's opinion, that would have merely added one more voice to an already ignored chorus of human rights activists. And if they did either of those things, Peace and Justice would likely cease to exist, because the cops would never work with them again.

Kurt felt like his hands were tied, so he more or less tabled the issue, even though implicit in that was stomaching some amount of police brutality as a cost of imposing law and order. Carlos was on the same page. "We felt bad about this," he later said. ". . . There is an ethical part of me that says the police should start behaving differently, that they shouldn't beat people up. But on the other hand, it would have been cynical if I didn't also consider that the entire community was suffering. . . . When you live outside the community, you can think about things like human rights in a more theoretical fashion. . . . But being a human rights defender inside the community is different. When you are inside, you justify certain things, up to a certain point. . . . Nobody wants to say that out loud, but that is how it is."

This was not a radical stance in Honduras, and there were those who took an even harder line. Adrienne Pine, an anthropologist who had done research in Honduras a few years prior, wrote about discovering that most of her acquaintances there supported state-sponsored extrajudicial killings—which, to be clear, Kurt and Carlos opposed. One of her friends was upset she even questioned it: "Who was I, he said, to come here from the first world and tell Hondurans that what they had done to protect themselves from such violence was wrong? What right did I have to say gang members should live, when I didn't even know what it was like to narrowly escape being murdered by these people who didn't give a damn about human life, to see family members killed and not be able to do anything about it? Who the hell did I think I was?"

———

SEVERAL DAYS AFTER THE RAID, MACARIO MARSHALED A FEW balaclava-clad witnesses to the courthouse, where they testified about some of the captured Puchos. Jhonny would ultimately get a thirteen-year sentence, and throughout that atrocious stretch in prison, Kurt would occasionally visit him.

Peace and Justice seemed to be finding its footing. Around May 24, Kurt and Macario met with a senior official at the Public Ministry to discuss formalizing their institutional collaboration. Then, on June 3, soon after Kurt and his family arrived at Jo Ann's parents' house in Grand Rapids for their annual six-week summer visit, del Cid sent him and Carlos an email that referred to Carlos Bruner, a private eye who briefly worked alongside Macario, and Flor del Campo, a barrio in Tegucigalpa: "Thanks to all the work Macario and Bruner have been doing with the patrol cops and Criminal Investigation, this morning, a group of mareros was captured in Flor del Campo. Chelito was among them. He tried to flee but was shot in the leg. He is currently at Hospital Escuela. Bruner and Macario are going there now to make sure he's being watched. . . . We have already spoken to the prosecutors' office and the judge in charge to ensure the case moves quickly."

"EXCELLENT news," Kurt replied. "A prayer has been answered."

– 7 –

K URT'S TRIPS NORTH WERE HIS CHANCE TO MEET DONORS AND catch up with family, and with Peace and Justice off to the races, it seemed like a fine time for a getaway. That being said, in his absence, his charity continued to play with fire.

Apart from Peace and Justice, ASJ operated three open-to-the-public clinics, one in Kurt's church, and two in churches in other barrios, that were staffed by a lawyer and a psychologist on a rotating basis. These were places where poor people could get whatever legal or psychological assistance they needed for next to nothing. Through the Nueva Suyapa clinic, a friend of Kurt and Jo Ann's named Rosa Reyes had recently submitted a complaint to the Public Ministry, alleging that one of her neighbors had knocked down her fence.

That may have sounded like a fairly innocuous dispute, but unfortunately for Rosa, the vandal, an ex-con known as Olanchano, lived by the sword, and demolishing fences wasn't his only transgression. In fact, the ASJ clinic had recently facilitated a second complaint against him, this one alleging that he abused his kids.

On the morning of June 3—coincidentally, the same day Chelito was recaptured—agents working for the Public Ministry went to his house and took his children into protective custody. The identity of who initiated the child-abuse complaint was not in the public domain, but it soon became clear who Olanchano blamed.

Later that day, Rosa saw him walk past her front door with a machete in hand and, in short order, would learn what he did. After locating her twenty-one-year-old daughter in front of a nearby bodega, he rendered his sicko spin on eye-for-an-eye revenge: *You take my children; I butcher yours.*

Embedded in this grotesque tragedy was a lesson. Since quasi-lawless environments like Nueva Suyapa are natural habitats for gangsters, vigilantes, and hotheads of every stripe, they are spring-loaded at every turn with the potential for violence. An awful paradox results—though the long arm of the law is the very thing that should ultimately make such a community safer, the process of introducing it gets people hurt, because it inevitably triggers some of that spring-loaded violence. Kurt and Carlos had already received enough of that lesson for a lifetime, but that very same day, they were going to get another reminder.

Night fell, and up in the Diecisiete, Gárgola, a sixteen-year-old who once participated in a Genesis program, went to buy a juice box at a bodega. While he was there, a group of people grabbed him. Then, after leading him around the corner, they punched him, kicked him, and pulverized his face with a stone the coroner would later estimate to be the size of a car battery.

The murderers' identities were not yet known, but because the attack happened so soon after Chelito's arrest, the timing suggested that they were Puchos retaliating against a presumptive snitch. This forced Carlos, who managed all of ASJ, including Peace and Justice, whenever Kurt went out of town, to wonder whether this was yet another side effect of their altruistic machinations. "I have to confess that this whole situation has made me afraid," he wrote to Kurt, three days later. "The murder of the girl was so cruel, and same with

Gárgola. . . . And now there are rumors that five Puchos are going to leave prison on Wednesday and take vengeance on the snitches. . . . I fear that people are going to lose confidence in the program, and I fear for del Cid, Macario, and everyone else involved. Please pray a lot."

"I don't think it would be that difficult or expensive for me to come back down for a few days," Kurt replied. "What do you think?"

"Let's wait. Things have been manageable up until now. . . . Thanks for worrying."

But were they ever going to be manageable again? Sure, Chelito and a number of other Puchos were in Renaciendo, but realistically, they might not remain there long, and what if Peace and Justice accidentally precipitated additional casualties? An American security expert Kurt consulted seemed to think it almost certainly would. "ASJ has taken several precautions to protect the identities of the witnesses, the attorney who has been contracted, and ASJ itself," he wrote. "These precautions are effective in the short-term, but the identity of all will eventually be revealed."

The charity's staff thought of Kurt as their boss, and Carlos as an occasionally involved board member, so while the gringo was away, he kept receiving messages. "The security measures we have in place for ASJ employees are very empirical," Macario wrote to Kurt, on June 17. ". . . I have already spoken to you about getting me some safety 'implements': a bulletproof vest, a second cellphone, and a balaclava. . . . I also took the liberty of getting a quote for a pistol (don't freak out). Honestly, I would feel safer if I carried a gun, and I want to know if ASJ will support me in this. If not, I am going to get one myself, with my own money. (Because I'm sorry to say that, unlike the rest of my colleagues, I don't have any spiritual beliefs to stand on). . . . Yesterday, there was a massive escape attempt by the Puchos (approximately fifteen members). The prison guards stopped them, presumably because they haven't been paid off yet."

Kurt replied, with Carlos copied, "Regarding the vest, I think it would be best to get a quote on the internet. I am almost certain you can find a cheaper and higher quality one in the US, and it wouldn't be that hard for me to bring it down. Regarding the pistol, I think we should discuss it, but my first thought is that I do not really agree. Since you're an employee of this institution, that could expose us to many possible problems."

"It is hard for me to follow some of this discussion," Carlos wrote, "because I am getting copied on Kurt's replies but not on emails sent to him."

"Call me if there's anything I can do to be helpful," Kurt wrote directly to Carlos, the next day. "I miss you."

Nine days later, on June 27, Carlos told Kurt about the latest gut punch. "I just confirmed the rumors I heard this weekend," he wrote. "Chelito has escaped. . . . We are going to have to come up with some sort of strategy for stopping this prisonbreak vice, because without that, we will get nowhere."

When Kurt left for Michigan, it had seemed like they were gaining traction, but now it felt like nothing was falling their way. Even previously reliable partners like the Public Ministry were starting to look shaky; according to a memo seemingly written by Macario, prosecutors were resigning from their cases because of "the constant threats they receive."

And as bad as things seemed, Kurt and Carlos didn't even know what was, by far, the most ominous aspect of this monthlong maelstrom. The Puchos hadn't killed Gárgola. His corpse was an omen. A new terror was gaining strength but had yet to rise into view.

———

We have to get these guys off the street. We have to get these guys off the street. We have to get these guys off the street.

Peace and Justice was going to have a better chance of incarcerating the Puchos for an extended period of time once it fully staffed up.

Bruner, the private investigator, hadn't worked out, so Kurt, who was back in Honduras, found a potential replacement through a friend of a friend of a friend of a friend.

Cholo was a short meaty boulder of a man who strutted around like a bodybuilder. Given what it was he did for a living, his self-reported biography might not be entirely true: shanghaied into the military at seventeen; trained in marksmanship, antiterrorism, psyops, and skydiving; served in military intelligence; and then, after his discharge in '98, worked as an investigator for the tax authority while simultaneously freelancing for the spooks. "Cholo was a person who acted like he had experienced everything and knew everything," an ASJ employee recalled. "If we were talking about planes, then he had jumped out of a plane. If we were talking about a car flipping over, then he would say, 'Well, my car flipped over twice.' Everything had happened to him. He was able to prove some things, but otherwise, you had to take his word."

On the one hand, Cholo was dutiful, enthusiastic, competent, learned, and totally obsessed with completing his mission; on the other, he was enigmatic, cocky, boastful, militant, and totally obsessed with completing his mission. He was more or less a walking-talking Faustian bargain, an asset you might be willing to deploy only when dealing with the most desperate of situations, like trying to rescue your daughter from a sadistic kidnapper. Some of his cop friends had nicknamed him "Cholo," which, in Honduras, basically means "gangbanger," because they thought he smacked of, in his devil-may-care audacity, the mareros they were after. This was a small man with a gargantuan personality—he ate at warp speed, smoked an occasional cigar, drove a tan station wagon, and in addition to listening to the completely predictable satanic metal, was also a big fan of Madonna.

Growing up in a violent barrio in Tegucigalpa had imbued in him a burning hatred for criminals as well as a deep compassion for their victims. Peace and Justice sounded like a floundering project he alone could remediate with his unique set of skills, and also, it would put him in a position to lay the smackdown on a bunch of pissant mareros. He obviously wanted in, but Carlos, who had been a student activist back when the military treated student activists like they were part of the global communist conspiracy, wasn't sure they should hire him, because in the operative he saw hallmarks of the institution he used to fear.

As always, Kurt took a pragmatic approach. He would have preferred hiring an investigator who didn't have a cutthroat aura, but he hadn't been able to find any other qualified candidates. So Cholo it was.

At first, the two prongs of Peace and Justice did not click. In fact, Cholo was so skeptical of Macario that he snooped on him. "I can report with absolute certainty," he wrote to Kurt, "that he has a number of shady friends. . . . I would suggest that someone speak to him in order to make him aware of his shortcomings, which include impunctuality and a number of personal issues."

Managing these two mavericks was clearly going to be a wild ride. But Kurt needed them to start working together immediately, because in addition to the tasks described in the original Secret Group outline, they were going to have to somehow harden a distant juvenile prison. "In a facility with about 140 people," Kurt wrote in an email, on July 8, "there were over forty escapes in the last six months (and that is probably underreported)."

And soon after he sent that message, another urgent matter arose. The program's closest allies, the Pan Blancos, found themselves trapped in a life-threatening bind.

———

ABOUT SEVENTY MINUTES BEFORE SUNSET ON JULY 11, 2005, FOUR detectives who were accompanied by a masked person surprise-searched Pan Blanco's house. They found two shotguns, a nine-millimeter handgun, four military fatigues, and three balaclavas. Pan Blanco, who happened to be out of town working at a construction site, didn't have to see what happened next: His nineteen- and twenty-four-year-old sons, Kerin and Lenin, were perp walked into patrol cars.

A prosecutor threw the book at the two brothers, charging them with illegal possession of firearms, robbery, and illicit association. At their arraignment the following Monday, a masked witness claimed that the two of them had jumped him and stolen papers, but not the cash, from his wallet; a second masked witness echoed the first, despite not having personally seen the alleged theft; and the detective who led the search party asserted that the Pan Blancos were a gang—an illicit association—based largely on his observation that people he had chatted with on the street were afraid to testify against them.

This was not a strong case. Nothing of value had been stolen; the second witness's testimony was hearsay; the two shotguns were legally registered; it wasn't clear who owned the unregistered pistol; and the detective came off as unprofessional on the stand. For example, he admitted that he had not written down the first witness's complaint, the complaint that had supposedly spurred him and four colleagues to rush to Nueva Suyapa. Furthermore, he committed a major faux pas: He burned confidential informants in public when he stated that Kerin and Lenin had been helping the police pursue the Puchos.

The judge dismissed the weapons and robbery charges but upheld the illicit association charge, mainly because the fatigues and balaclavas seemed fishy. Kerin and Lenin were thus shipped off to the national penitentiary, which was perhaps the most dangerous place on earth for two Hondurans who had just been outed as snitches.

One of Cholo's first assignments was to determine if the Pan Blancos had broken bad, if the against-the-ropes watchmen had morphed into villainous desperados. This hadn't been the only allegation levied against them. Back on July 6, the mother of a sixteen-year-old with the surname Ibran had told a human rights organization, "For the past two months, I have been hearing about the Pan Blancos, a group that assaults people and delivery trucks. There used to be Puchos, but now all of them are in prison, and the Pan Blancos are saying they have authorization from the police to patrol and kill teenagers in Flores de Oriente."

Cholo organized a get-together with Pan Blanco at the house of another informant. Pan Blanco's side of the story was that the masked person at the arrest and the two anonymous witnesses at the arraignment were either Puchos or their relatives, and that the detective orchestrating this whole charade was a lackey on the take. According to an official statement given by Martha, Pan Blanco's partner, on the day Kerin and Lenin supposedly robbed that anonymous witness, a group of Puchos had threatened Lenin's wife with machetes. In that same declaration, she described another incident, which, frankly, is a bit hard to believe. Allegedly, at three a.m. one day, Chelito, Ibran, and five other Puchos had gathered outside her house and audibly discussed killing one of her kids.

Martha could have been lying. Pan Blanco could have been lying. Ibran's mom could have been lying. The anonymous witnesses could have been lying. The detective could have been lying. Adjudicating he-said, she-said standoffs is a seat-of-the-pants exercise, but it is fundamental to administering justice, because oftentimes, there isn't any conclusive physical evidence of a crime. Therefore, more often than not, verdicts are derived from the magic of reading minds: fallible people—in Honduras, judges, and in the United States, juries—listening to strangers testify and deciding what and what not to believe. In other words, justice relies on the honesty of human beings, and that is why an injunction against perjury—"thou shalt not bear false witness against thy neighbor"—is one of the most ancient moral imperatives of all.

Cholo believed Pan Blanco's version; Macario, who had attended the arraignment, thought that the anonymous witnesses were, in fact, conniving Puchos; and neither Kurt nor Carlos, who had tons of contacts in the barrio, felt that the Pan Blancos had crossed the line between self-defense and predation. The vigilantes probably had been threatening the Puchos and some of their relatives with guns, but it didn't sound like they had actually hurt anyone yet, so Peace and Justice decided not to cut ties.

Taking a step back, it seemed like the Puchos were retaliating against the Pan Blancos with a disingenuous version of what Peace and Justice and the Pan Blancos had been weaponizing against them— victims make complaints; masked informants guide cops; masked witnesses testify; defendants get locked up.

Kurt had an intern research the sleight of hand at the heart of this procedure. The intern's report explained that some consider shrouding witnesses to be unethical, because innocent people are exposed to guilty verdicts when they don't know who is accusing them. Case in point: If Kerin and Lenin's attorney had been able to confirm that the anonymous witnesses truly were Puchos, then she would have likely been able to impeach their testimonies. That is why many judicial systems guarantee the right to face-to-face confrontations in court— see the Sixth Amendment to the United States Constitution—and that is why the United Nations has issued stern warnings about faceless justice, even when utilized in egregiously dangerous settings like Colombia in the eighties.

But Honduras happened to be one of the many countries that did permit the cloaking of witnesses in certain circumstances, and the other type of witness protection, the type where undisguised witnesses are given new identities and homes, was prohibitively expensive. Therefore, all things considered, Kurt thought that his program's facial camouflaging was justifiable.

Eight days after Kerin and Lenin's arraignment, an appeal hearing was held, and it seemed to go as well as it possibly could have for the brothers. Their attorney explained that the fatigues and balaclavas, the only evidence the prior judge clung onto, were disguises they used to serve as protected witnesses, and the prosecutor, who previously demanded the utmost harshness, said that she had since spoken to Macario and now more or less agreed with the defense. This case clearly should have been dismissed right there, but as the judge explained, that wasn't possible, because the illicit association law prohibited that from happening at this stage in the process.

Pan Blanco soon visited his sons in the penitentiary that, years ago, he had helped to construct. His family was in a precarious spot. Until his sons' preliminary audience, God-knows-when, they were going to be locked in a cage with an army of mareros, some of whom were Puchos. And since his guns were impounded as evidence in their case, the rest of his family was defenseless. He and Martha had lived in Nueva Suyapa since they were children, since before the Puchos were even born. But now they had no choice but to flee it. They had clearly lost this war.

– 8 –

ONE WAY TO KEEP THE PUCHOS BEHIND BARS WAS TO PLUG up Renaciendo; another was to make sure they belonged there in the first place. Officialdom thought Chelito was a thirteen-year-old named Herlan Colindres, but when he was stripped naked after his most recent arrest, a respectable amount of pubic hair was observed.

And then there was his older brother Junior, who seemed to be the operational leader of the Puchos. His rap sheet stretched back over four years, to the time he allegedly assaulted a bishop, and with his double chin and bleached hair, he wouldn't have looked out of place on a college campus. Nevertheless, just recently, on May 8, he had escaped from Renaciendo, a facility exclusively for minors.

Honduran criminals coveted youth. In the mid-nineties, the country had set up a separate juvenile justice system with materially shorter sentences—if an eighteen-and-a-half-year-old adult was convicted of murdering three people, he would spend decades in prison; if a seventeen-and-a-half-year-old minor was convicted of that same crime, the max he could get was eight years, with eligibility for parole after four. Furthermore, as one former Pucho explained, "It was easier to escape Renaciendo than the national penitentiary, so we'd carry birth certificates of other people, people who were minors. It was just a piece of paper. All we had to do was memorize the identity number and names of the mom and dad. . . . It didn't have a photo."

Sometime around mid-July, Cholo began trying to figure out who the Puchos really were. Clearing that up would not only ensure that they were sent to the correct penitentiary but also prevent any biographical mix-ups from messing up their prosecutions.

According to the operative, he used a badge borrowed from a cop friend to impersonate a police officer. This allowed him to review the visitor logs at Renaciendo and then, at the National Registry of Persons, to see that the forty-four-year-old woman who visited Chelito in prison had one daughter and five sons: a twenty-two-year-old, a nineteen-year-old, a fifteen-year-old who was about to turn sixteen, and two thirteen-year-old twins, one of whom was Herlan. Junior Colindres was the nineteen-year-old, which meant he had no business being in Renaciendo back in May or, for that matter, ever again.

The fifteen-year-old was Elvin Colindres. Carlos, who had known the family for years, was confident that that was Chelito—the judiciary would later confirm this, and Chelito himself would fess up. Though Elvin was still a minor, there were several reasons why he would have wanted to act younger. For one thing, Herlan, the twin he impersonated, had been under thirteen for most of Chelito's criminal career, and in Honduras, preteens could not be convicted of crimes. And despite the fact that Herlan had recently aged out of that immunity, pretending to be him still made sense, because it would buy Chelito three extra years of shorter sentences and three extra years of Renaciendo.

There were other elements to Cholo's groundwork. If he was going to help the police replace their meathead dragnets with high-precision strikes, he had to get to know Nueva Suyapa like the palm of his hand. There were no good maps of it, and home addresses didn't really exist, so after getting oriented by Kurt and Carlos, he reconnoitered.

According to him, he diagrammed sectors, memorized faces, scribbled down license plates, knocked on doors, recruited assets, culled intelligence, assembled dossiers, and hid in vegetation while photographing homes.

Macario had approached the cops as a lawyer with a hippieish hairdo and all sorts of scruples about roughing up suspects. Cholo, on the other hand, had a certain hawkish charm—he was one of them, and now he also had a portfolio of stellar policework to share. He met up with one of the brass at a pork-chops-off-the-grill type of joint, and unsurprisingly, they hit it off.

Soon thereafter, a joint operation ensued.

Cholo and a crew of undercover cops put on health department uniforms and drove to Flores de Oriente in cars emblazoned with the department's logo. Mosquito-borne illnesses like dengue and chikungunya were not uncommon, so residents were generally happy to let health officials fumigate their houses. Cholo and the officers went door-to-door with clipboards, wrote down people's information, and sprayed their residences. What they were really doing, of course, was verifying where their targets lived.

The Colindreses lived on a cockeyed lane, in a ramshackle dwelling with an unpainted wooden door. The mother of Chelito and Junior let Cholo enter.

Before initiating his extermination, he peeked around. "There were dirty shoes and dirty clothes," he recalled. "This was extreme misery. I don't get how people can live in such filth."

One photograph caught his eye, so he asked the woman, innocently enough, "Who is that?"

"Those are my twins," she replied, "and *that* is my Chelito."

———

THAT, AT LEAST, IS HOW CHOLO TELLS IT.

Kurt and del Cid recall authorizing the fumigation mission, and two other people remember seeing Cholo sashay around the barrio in a health department getup. That doesn't mean he didn't sprinkle some fictional tidbits into his caper, but there is no doubt that he had actually accomplished the most important thing: He had wedged himself between Nueva Suyapa and Criminal Investigation. According to the chief of the city's Homicide Unit, who only ever knew Cholo as "Roberto," which was not his real name, "Roberto would say, 'I need this type of support or that type of support,' and then I'd say, 'Tell me what you have.' He'd explain that he had witnesses lined up and could get even more, and then as a team, we'd go into Nueva Suyapa and do an operation. But Roberto was always our pincer."

On July 27, 2005, the day before the Pan Blancos' appeal was denied, Cholo emailed Kurt, who he typically addressed with the formal prefix Don, "TAKE NOTE. There was an operation last night. . . . I have identified the vehicle Chelito moves around in. I don't think we will have to wait long until he is captured."

This message encapsulated some of the quintessential elements of the Cholo Experience. There was the opacity around whatever the "operation" was; there was the use of the first-person pronoun—"*I* have identified"—to refer to what may have been a team effort or someone else's doing; and there was the tantalizing prediction about the mission's near-term completion.

Most of the informants, witnesses, cops, prosecutors, and bureaucrats Cholo interacted with had no idea he worked for Peace and Justice or its parent, ASJ. Some thought he was a concerned citizen. Some thought he was a policeman. Some thought he was military intelligence. Some thought he was linked to the American embassy. He was Cholo; he was Roberto; he was whatever he needed to be. Kurt understood that doing espionage and investigative fieldwork in a place as perilous as the barrio required duplicity, subterfuge, and shape-shifting, and he accepted that anyone who could pull that off would probably deceive his boss as well. But the Cholo Experience was still irresistible, because despite the shroud over his clandestine activities, and despite his seeming propensity to self-aggrandize and embellish, the main thrust of his claims usually checked out, and most importantly, he almost always delivered.

———

THE PATRON SAINTS OF A NUMBER OF LATIN AMERICAN COUNTRIES are specific renderings of the Virgin Mary. It is said that in 1747, a campesino named Alejandro Colindres and an eight-year-old boy he worked with in the cornfields northeast of what was then called Real de Minas de San Miguel de Tegucigalpa came across a two-and-a-half-inch cedar-wood statuette of the mother of Jesus. The Colindres family kept her on an altar in their home in the village of Suyapa for a few decades, until a military captain became convinced that she miraculously cured his gallstones. That was when a chapel was built to house her at the base of the Montañita, and much later, in 1954, an enormous basilica was erected next door to accommodate the thousands upon thousands of pilgrims who came to visit her on her annual feast day. Three years after Pope John Paul II went to pay his respects in 1983, Our Lady of Suyapa was stolen, stripped of the gold, silver, and jewels that festooned her, and left to be found in the tank of a toilet at a restaurant called La Terraza de Don Pepe.

The smaller chapel had an off-white stucco frontispiece with tan moldings, an arched entryway framed by four fluted columns, and two cupolaed bell towers with a clock tower in between. When the hands of the turret clock read half past eleven, on the morning of July 29, 2005, Timothy Markey, a balding, six-foot-two gringo a day shy of his forty-fourth birthday, got out of a taxi on the plaza in front of the chapel. He was near a bodega painted the colors of a Coca-Cola can when he heard somebody scream, "You son of a bitch! Give me your money!"

Chelito and Pico de Pato, a five-foot-three Pucho with a buzz cut, tried snatching Markey's backpack, and in the ensuing scuffle, Pico de Pato fired his nine-millimeter twice.

As the Puchos fled, Markey hobbled back to his taxicab. A bullet had lacerated an artery in his left leg, and by the time he reached the hospital, he was in grade four hypovolemic shock.

Murder was commonplace in Honduras, but on the rare occasion a gringo was killed, it was a newsworthy scandal. And this was way bigger than that—this was a full-fledged historic event—because Markey happened to be a sixteen-year vet of the Drug Enforcement Administration, and his killing therefore harkened back to a canonical tale.

In 1985, a DEA agent stationed in Mexico was kidnapped, tortured, and murdered. The US Department of Justice accused a Honduran narcotrafficker named Juan Matta Ballesteros of helping to plan this, but down south, Matta was thought to be untouchable, partly because Honduras didn't have an extradition treaty with the United States, partly because he had managed to evade justice for ages, and partly because he was the country's rags-to-riches antihero, a Pablo Escobar–like figure who employed thousands across his legitimate businesses and financed a number of schools.

But no way were the gringos going to let this slide. In 1988, a strike team of Honduran soldiers who were accompanied by a handful of US Marshals illegally abducted Matta, and before loading him onto an outbound plane, they gratuitously jabbed a stun gun into his testicles. In response to this breach of national sovereignty, approximately one thousand protesters stormed the American embassy's campus in Tegucigalpa and set a seven-story building ablaze.

An American jury handed Matta multiple life sentences, and he would end up spending much of his life in a federal supermax in rural Colorado. The moral of this story is that you do not harm an American lawman, because if you are loco enough to cross that line, then no matter who you are or what the law says, you will be hunted down, and you will spend the rest of your days on earth in a freezing pit.

There was no reason to think that Chelito and Pico de Pato knew Markey was DEA; they seemingly had not intended to kill him; and Chelito had not even been the triggerman. Nevertheless, the noontime killing of the towering fed elevated Chelito to a level of infamy that bordered on the supernatural, as though he had slain one of the X-Men. He and Pico de Pato were now Honduras's most wanted, and since at least one person incorrectly placed Junior at the scene, so was he.

The Honduran National Police had been spun out of the military, so its culture was more Rambo than Sherlock Holmes. In a situation like this, the brass couldn't afford to wait around while some cerebral detective with a notepad did his behind-the-scenes work responsibly. That would be political suicide. What mattered was feeding the news cycle telegenic action, so hours after the Markey murder, a swarm of cops conducted what *La Tribuna* would call "A Hunt Without Limits in Barrios of Terror." A close reading of that article, however, reveals that the group of young men the police rounded up and showcased that day had absolutely nothing to do with the Puchos.

According to Cholo, the night of the murder, he got Kurt's blessing to attend a meeting at Criminal Investigation with the homicide chief, two of his detectives, a DEA agent, and an FBI agent. At this point, the police didn't know much about the Puchos. Their case file misidentified Chelito as the thirteen-year-old twin and Pico de Pato as a seventeen-year-old when, in reality, he was nineteen; as had been the case with Junior, this fountain-of-youth gimmickry had put him in a position to escape Renaciendo a few months prior.

In Cholo's telling, he was the one who disabused the police of their misunderstandings, the one who yanked a collection of documents out of his backpack that proved, once and for all, who Chelito and Junior were. Also, he was the one who demonstrated, on the screen of his digital camera, how the cops should go about finding and cornering them inside Nueva Suyapa.

As hard as it might be to believe that Cholo finagled his way into such a momentous meeting, let alone played a heroic role at it, his story checks out. The homicide chief has confirmed that Cholo was in attendance and was the best source they had, and his boss recalls popping in that night and meeting a mysterious fellow who wouldn't reveal who he worked for but who had enough intel to justify his involvement in one of the biggest cases of the century.

The next day, around two in the afternoon, a fleet of squad cars barricaded Flores de Oriente, while a helicopter buzzed overhead. Officers in navy blue tops poured into Chelito's mom's house, dug up the dirt floor of a tin-roofed structure out back, and found the murder weapon wrapped in newspaper.

Chelito and Pico de Pato were apprehended fifty meters away in an unplastered adobe house. The cops must not have brought along any handcuffs, because they instead used shoelaces to bind their detainees' ankles and wrists. Then, in clear view of the bystanders, they put out cigarettes on Chelito's earlobe. "It wasn't me! It wasn't me!" the teenager apparently screamed.

His past arrests hadn't been that big of a deal, because they had always been negated by yo-yoing, but things were different now. The government couldn't afford to let such an iconic criminal abscond, and him being sixteen, as opposed to thirteen, meant Renaciendo had to hang on to him for just two years. In an effort to accomplish that, the prison would soon construct a special cell with steel-reinforced walls, above which, according to a Nicaraguan newspaper called *La Prensa*, "a guard in a tower monitored his movements, as though he were Hannibal Lecter."

Maybe Chelito's days were finally numbered, but the real driving force behind the Puchos, Junior, had eluded the raid, and one week after it, he murdered someone, someone near and dear to Peace and Justice.

– 9 –

ACCORDING TO A STATEMENT GIVEN BY ONE OF PAN BLANCO'S sons, "On Saturday, I drove to Nueva Suyapa with my father to check on our house. Around seven p.m., we started driving slowly out of the barrio. When we passed the entrance to Flores de Oriente, three armed individuals—Junior, Cris, and Ibran—suddenly came at us rapidly. They were all members of the Puchos. My dad got angry and jumped out of the truck. They attacked him. They shot at him. The first bullet missed but the second one didn't."

Not only was Pan Blanco unarmed, but he had also just left a cantina where he put down one too many and then a few more. Going anywhere near the Puchos' sector in that state was an uncharacteristic act of extraordinary foolishness. Maybe what had happened, at a psychological level, was that he had buckled under the pressure of his responsibilities—he had been working nomadically while his family was imperiled and dispossessed, and he had also been serving as one of Peace and Justice's most active informants.

Collaborating with the program might not sound terribly demoralizing, but it is important to appreciate that witnesses and informants are more or less strapped into a judicial roller coaster that threatens their lives and consumes their time. A witness, especially, must somehow maintain his resolve and sanity over a period of time when a dangerous criminal's Achilles' heel is his mouth, and while he is forced to keep revisiting whatever dreadful thing he happens to know. He doesn't get to move on from that painful memory because it is now a civic asset. And when it's his turn to take the stand, he will have to perform in front of illustrious judges, persnickety lawyers, an affronted marero, and the ghost of the victim he is trying to avenge. And if the ravages of time have distorted his recollections, or terror catches his tongue, then the case will collapse, and a guilty bastard will walk free. All because of him!

In other words, meting out justice isn't just an investigative and legal challenge; it's an emotional and psychological one, too. Macario and Cholo were clearly equipped to handle those first two components, but Kurt and Carlos were beginning to realize that their program was missing a piece.

A few months after Pan Blanco's murder, his mother passed away, and Martha was convinced that the cause was grief. Around that same time, the toothless case against Kerin and Lenin— neither of whom had been granted leave from prison to attend their father's burial—was dropped. Kerin, who had been doing homework at the time of his arrest, soon developed a bad drinking habit, and that seems to be why he would die a young man. According to his brother, the one who witnessed their father's demise, in the middle of that fatal altercation, one of the Puchos had uttered what may have been a hard truth: "You were always going to die, you dog."

Junior . . . Cris . . . Ibran. Junior . . . Cris . . . Ibran. Junior . . . Cris . . . Ibran.

Kurt's managerial style was corporate—establish weekly objectives and then hold employees accountable to them—even when it came to something like hunting down three killers. "I used to get super pissed off," he later said. "Everything always took longer than I thought it should. . . . I would be like, '*Come on* Cholo.'"

The operative had no excuses, because when the gringo last went to the United States, he had convinced a donor to give the program $50,000, which, in Honduras, could go a very long way. Cholo used some of that cash to garner goodwill with the absurdly underfunded police units he wanted to work with. For instance, according to one of his reports, he "had seven chairs repaired for the antigang unit in light of the fact that their office has no chairs."

He also found that he was able to compel cops to prioritize Peace and Justice's cases by covering the costs of their fieldwork and operations, by paying for things like fuel, car rentals, phone cards, pens, pads, and coffee. Right now, what he wanted them to do was bust the three Puchos who just killed one of his informants.

Cris was the first to drop; he was arrested on August 19, 2005. It isn't clear if that was Cholo's doing, but for what it's worth, there was a folder labeled "photos of cris" on his computer, and inside of it was a picture of a house taken just four days before the capture.

Less than a week later, Macario informed Kurt that he had caught the Public Ministry making a mistake, that a prosecutor had been about to charge Cris with illicit association instead of murder. These were the types of errors that had presumably facilitated some of Cris's past yo-yoing—he had been arrested in June 2003, August 2003, February 2004, August 2004, and May 2005. Unfortunately for him, however, his salad days were over. According to Macario's email, he got the ministry to correct the oversight.

On August 23, Cholo wrote to Kurt, "Ibran lives with his parents who sell fruit and gum from a booth on the street in front of a Tegucigalpa supermarket called Colonia that is located next to Hospital Escuela."

Nine days later, Cholo, Macario, and a masked person whose identity only they knew rode along on a police operation. After the cops arrested a teenager in front of that Colonia supermarket, the disguised witness confirmed that the detainee was, in fact, Ibran.

Two down, one to go.

September passed and still no Junior.

No dice in October either, even though Cholo, according to his reports, had scoured a number of barrios with the homicide detectives and a number of villages with the antigang cops.

On November 2, Carlos emailed Kurt, "Junior is supposedly in Nueva Capital"—another barrio—"which is where the fugitives are taking refuge. Also, someone apparently saw him yesterday around here in a little green bus."

Nothing came of that tip, or any of the other ones either, so on November 14, Cholo told Kurt that it was time to change strategy: "My number one priority is staking out the markets. . . . It's certain that he will go there for monetary reasons because Christmas season is approaching and for financial reasons he'll have to step into the light. . . . We might capture him this week when he goes to collect 'taxes.'"

TWO DAYS LATER, JUNIOR CRUISED AROUND IN A BEIGE TOYOTA Corolla packed with the trappings of business and pleasure: two nine-millimeters, a henchman, a wad of cash, a CD binder, a bottle of rum, a twelve-pack of beer, and three seventeen-year-old girls.

Sometimes, being him must have been fun—for example, who could forget the time he and Siniestro divided the Puchos into two soccer teams and wagered a gold chain on the game.

But being the skipper was hard work, too. Earlier that day, he had run an extremely ballsy mission after catching wind of the fact that Chelito was getting examined at the hospital. When his younger brother was on his way back to Renaciendo, sitting in the bed of a pickup truck beside a guard, Junior and some other Puchos intercepted them. With the two cars in motion, the Puchos took aim at the guard, and Junior hollered, "We're taking our homie. We're going to kill you, you bitch." This emancipation effort had failed only because the guard used Chelito as a human shield, and because after a five-kilometer, fender-to-bumper pursuit, they ran into a police cruiser, which forced Junior and his people to retreat.

But a good leader doesn't get discouraged, and he had more work to do before any festivities could begin.

About an hour after dusk, the Corolla started tailgating a bus that was on its cross-city route between Nueva Suyapa and the markets. After the two vehicles pulled over, Junior's henchman, a tall teenager in a jean jacket, boarded the bus.

This wasn't a stickup. Everything had been prearranged. When Junior called and told you to kick him some cash, you did it, period. These types of handoffs happened all the time, but what was unusual about this one was that there was a passenger in the back row of the bus who wasn't really a passenger, and who now signaled the nearby detectives.

They arrested Junior and his companions without a fight.

Cholo photographed various phases of this operation. In his telling, he was, of course, the one who figured out Junior would show, which is probably true, the one who planned the entire operation, which is probably false, the one who paid for it, which is probably true, and the one who was the undercover spotter in the back of the bus, which seems unrealistic, but which someone with reason to know believes to be true.

Election Day was less than two weeks away. Junior was old enough to vote, which meant he was too old to do time in Renaciendo. He was sent to the national penitentiary instead.

– 10 –

THE NATIONAL PENITENTIARY AND RENACIENDO WERE BOTH located in a shallow valley an hour northwest of the capital. The juvenile facility, which was separated from a dirt road by a corrugated fence topped with barbed wire, was composed of several walled-off modules, each of which had dormitories and outdoor space. Back in August 2003, one of the psychologists on staff was murdered, and according to a former warden, the reason why was that "he was in charge of verifying the inmates' ages." That incident and another made it feel like Renaciendo was out of control. In an effort to reign it in, the Maduro administration turned to an unconventional savior.

The Reverend Jimmy Hughes was a thick-bodied, charismatic preacher who claimed to have killed many people, first as a United States Army Ranger, and then as a self-described "mafia hitman." Clarifying this enigma's biography would be a tall task, and a contingent of conspiracy theorists who believe he is linked to an Illuminati-like cabal known as the Octopus have been trying to do so for a while. In Hughes's own resurrection story, however, none of that mattered— the past was the past. He had moved to Honduras in the nineties to deliver three concise messages to its populace: God loves you; your land is fertile; God will bless you. The new man in a new land founded an Evangelical rehab center for troubled teens, and on the back of its supposed success, he became, in the eyes of some influential people, an expert in that field.

Aguas Ocaña, a Spaniard who would be married to President Maduro for a total of just four years, took on Renaciendo as a pet project. Though the precise mechanism that allowed for this is a bit murky, by all accounts, she gave Hughes de facto control over the facility from late 2003 to late 2004. The first warden the reverend appointed was a thirty-year-old employee of his rehab center whose most relevant credential was that he himself had been a frequently jailed cocaine dealer until he found Christ at the age of twenty-five. Hughes subsequently replaced him with Erick García, a Nicaraguan who had recently been a sales supervisor at a car battery shop in Tegucigalpa.

One lasting legacy of the Hughes era was the segregation of Renaciendo—MS-13 was put into one module, Barrio 18 into another, and everyone else into a third, called Nuevos Horizontes. The goal of this practice—which was becoming standard throughout Honduras—was to prevent both forced recruitment and gang warfare. But in Renaciendo at least, it wasn't foolproof. In September 2004, a fragmentation grenade exploded in the MS-13 module, and five months later, a fourteen-year-old was beaten to death and hung on display, apparently by MS-13.

The sequestering of the big-league maras also had an unexpected side effect: It freed up a module for the Puchos to take over. As a matter of fact, Nuevos Horizontes proved vital to Chelito and Junior's rise, in part because being held there largely shielded them from Barrio 18's vengeance, and in part because it gave them a place to intimidate other teens. According to the judge who oversaw the facility, "One morning, at like five, the warden called me and said Chelito and some others were blocking an entrance, so I went out there with some cops and a human rights prosecutor. Chelito said he would kill us if we entered. . . . We said we're coming in and threw a tear gas grenade. This made Chelito angry. He said you can't do that; that's prohibited. Well, that's true, but what he was doing was even more prohibited. He had taken all the mattresses from the other teenagers and was sitting on them like a king."

This carceral fiefdom was clearly of strategic value to the Puchos, but even so, Chelito could not have enjoyed his time there, because Renaciendo was, simply put, a thoroughgoing hellhole. When Macario went there on a fact-finding mission in June 2005, the facts he found were alarming: The walls were easy to break through; the faucets barely ran; the bathrooms were nauseating; some inmates had to sleep on the floor; the floors were often wet due to roof leaks or subterranean seepage; teens sexually abused other teens; the guards beat up the juveniles; and when the juveniles denounced the guards, they retaliated by withholding food. In other words, Renaciendo wasn't just Peace and Justice's infuriating point of failure, it was also one of its ethical conundrums, because sending teenagers there was arguably inhumane.

The charity responded by trying to reform the facility, and one thing that necessitated was visiting it a lot. In September 2005, which was after Pan Blanco's murder but before Junior's arrest, Carlos drove out there with two ASJ employees and four teenagers affiliated with Genesis. They were shown into a meeting room with whitewashed walls, a red-and-gray tile floor, and benches that were bolted down and arranged in a square.

Chelito was soon brought in, wearing flip-flops, jean shorts, and a T-shirt with the phrase "Pool Party" on it. This was the teenager who had been labeled "a killing machine" by the security minister, the teenager who, according to *El Heraldo*, had sworn "to take the lives of judges, prosecutors, journalists, and the warden." When he saw all the familiar faces from Nueva Suyapa, however, he smiled, and in the photos taken of him that day, he looks, sitting there next to Carlos, not monstrous but, if anything, slightly embarrassed—he is rubbing his eye; he is scratching his leg; and he is planting his toes beneath his seat.

Carlos, who was wearing a magenta polo with sunglasses hanging off the placket, tried some conversation starters, and according to the notes taken by one of the ASJ employees in attendance, Chelito eventually opened up.

He said the Puchos were unfairly blamed for every last crime and claimed he had escaped Renaciendo in the past because Barrio 18 had threatened to bomb his cell. He wanted to improve his reading ability, but according to him, the teachers at the facility were scared of him— apparently, one had bugged out when he went to sharpen his pencil. But his real beef was with the guards. He said they had recently tried to smother him with a shirt saturated in feces, and when he resisted, they whacked him with a stick.

Who knows how much of what he was saying was true, but he was able to show his visitors some evidence of that last anecdote: a foot-long welt that angled across his spine.

Carlos felt that Chelito had to be incarcerated, but in this particular moment, he saw him as a victim. He assured the teenager that they were working to improve the facility, and he offered some encouragement: You are still young; you can still repent; you are a natural leader; and you can still do good things with your life.

Hearing that, in front of everyone, the killing machine cried.

ASJ WAS ATTACKING RENACIENDO ALONG SEVERAL DIFFERENT VECTORS.
What Macario and Cholo had been doing in Nueva Suyapa— investigate, capture, prosecute—they were now trying to pull off inside Renaciendo, except their targets were not mareros but the guards who abused inmates and the guards who sold them escapes.

On October 19, 2005, Macario went to the Public Ministry, whose archives, he had already discovered, contained several complaints from when Erick García was warden—one teenager claimed that the guards struck his head with a pipe; another that they handcuffed him for days; and another that "the warden saw them beating us and didn't say a thing." A medical examiner had verified some of those complainants' injuries, but even so, the ministry hadn't filed charges. This incriminating information had been dormant for about a year.

According to Macario, he and a prosecutor reviewed the documentation, and then, about five weeks later, he accompanied the prosecutors who went to interview the personnel at Renaciendo. Finally, on December 8, the ministry charged three guards with torture and Erick García with harassment.

Meanwhile, Cholo did Cholo stuff. According to one of his reports, that month, he and thirty-five cops raided the facility and confiscated the following contraband from the inmates: two marijuana plants, forty handmade machetes, and thirty-five ice picks. This disarmament must have made the other ASJ employees who had been visiting the penitentiary feel a little bit safer. One was a thirty-year-old reporter named Claudia Mendoza.

Kurt believed in the power of investigative journalism, so back in December 2001, ASJ had launched *Revistazo*, an online magazine that now had about six journalists on staff. Claudia, who had gotten her start as an on-air television correspondent, and who still freelanced for Univision, the American Spanish-language network, had joined the charity's periodical because she wanted to cover gritty topics to a depth that wasn't possible on TV.

Various sources told her that the prison's administrator had been stealing food from the cafeteria and selling it at a bodega he owned. This sounded too sleazy to be true, but Claudia was able to confirm it. On December 26, 2005, *Revistazo* cited a government document that actually acknowledged this misconduct. By then, the administrator had been dismissed, but he hadn't been charged with a crime, because according to a government spokesman that *Revistazo* quoted, "this was a private matter between a particular person and the administrator."

It sounded like the powers that be were hoping to sweep this under the rug, but partly because of Claudia's reporting, that was not possible. *Revistazo* ultimately published dozens of articles about Renaciendo's deficiencies, and eventually, the administrator was indicted.

The final vector of ASJ's attempt to reform the facility focused on the juveniles themselves. The Social Vagabond, as he was occasionally referred to by some of his colleagues at ASJ, was technically not a social worker yet—he was still studying to become one—but he was willing to work directly with mareros, so Kurt decided to give him a shot. By November 2005, he was hosting a weekly meeting inside Renaciendo with about a dozen teenagers, most of whom were Puchos. They would do activities like painting, and at the boys' request, he once led a three-hour workshop on sexuality. In one of their group discussions, Chelito admitted that, as a child, he had desperately wanted to know what pizza tasted like.

When the Vagabond wasn't at Renaciendo, he moseyed around Nueva Suyapa—hence the nickname—in an effort to get to know the juveniles' families. He also organized events for local teenagers, like movie screenings and soccer tournaments. Meanwhile, another ASJ employee, Melanie Holwerda-Hommes, a gringa who actually had earned a master's in social work, counseled female relatives of mareros and female victims of violence, both individually and in small groups.

The Vagabond and Melanie were jointly supposed to be the yin to Peace and Justice's yang—while Macario and Cholo pursued a punitive approach to crime control, the other two would try to prevent youngsters from erring in the first place and to rehabilitate those who had. Furthermore, Kurt and Carlos tasked Melanie with providing psychological and emotional support to the program's witnesses. She did end up doing some of that, but it was clear, almost from the outset, that the two camps could not coexist.

On the second floor of the charity's building, where nearly all its employees worked, the Peace and Justice guys kept photos of the perps they were after on the wall of their shared cubicle. Melanie once noticed the son of someone she counseled in their gallery. She knew exactly where he lived but, because of her commitment to confidentiality, felt she could not disclose that.

Cholo was no fool. Of course he realized that she and the Vagabond were privy to all sorts of intel he wanted to know. And do you think he gave a rat's ass about the ethical guidelines adhered to by shrinks? No, of course not, so he pressured the social workers to share information and, in doing so, made them uncomfortable.

Yet he wasn't the only source of friction on this two-way street. The Vagabond, who was green and gung ho, once unwittingly put the Peace and Justice duo in danger when, without warning, he brought a friend of Chelito's mom to the office, where she easily could have seen their makeshift wanted posters.

What was going on here was part of a broader culture clash that pitted Macario and Cholo against the rest of the charity's staff. The prototypical ASJ employee was a female professional with a strong religious conviction and an unwavering dedication to human rights. Macario and Cholo, on the other hand, looked and acted like lads you'd be wise to bring to a barroom brawl. Claudia felt they talked down to women, and by all accounts, they could be immature and disruptive. They sometimes skipped the charity's mandatory Monday morning devotional, where everyone else prayed and sang Christian songs, and on occasion, as the jazzed-up believers streamed out of the conference room, Macario would belt out sarcastic verses like "I want to fly! Up into the sky! I want to go there!"

And that wasn't his only musical number. In the open-floor-plan office, he and Cholo—who had clearly gotten past their initial differences—would sometimes blast Iron Maiden and sing together in broken English: "His eyes are ablaze. See the madman in his gaze!"

In Cholo's estimation, this whole interoffice conflict could be traced back to a simple root cause: "I'm a rocker. Macario is a rocker. We are rockers. The rest of ASJ is a bunch of hypocrites."

Kurt moved the two headbangers up to the third floor, an otherwise empty space, and in recognition of the fact that some grown men are in need of babysitters, he relocated his own desk beside theirs. He was willing to put up with their antics because, as he later explained, "They were catching the people who were killing my neighbors. They were good at that."

And he didn't just put up with them; he arguably took their side in the charity's ideological civil war. He and Carlos never abandoned preventive crime control—Carlos still ran Genesis, and ASJ would continue to operate a mentoring center for at-risk youth right next to it—but over the course of 2006, the Vagabond would be let go, and Melanie would quit.

"Sadly," the Vagabond later reflected, "we were sacrificed because, supposedly, we had made less of an impact on the community. . . . But you're not going to see therapeutic effects in a year. We needed more time."

———

KURT HAD HOPED THAT CAGING CHELITO AND JUNIOR WOULD CAUSE their mara to disintegrate, but that wasn't what happened. "The second-tier members of the gang have been given the assignment to get $1,500 (a lot for here) to pay for a lawyer to get their leaders out," he wrote in an email, on December 5, 2005. "So now there are about fifteen kids (most between twelve and sixteen years old) who are terrorizing about 30,000 people." A pack of them had recently kicked in the door of his pastor's house and forced him to lie prone as they stole cash, an iron, a telephone, a pair of sneakers, and a chicken from the fridge.

Peace and Justice responded forcefully to this plundering horde, and as it did, it came to function, in Cholo's mind, as beautifully as "a Swiss watch." According to his monthly report, detectives he accompanied captured seven suspects on December 12, two on December 22, two on December 27, and two more on December 29. And the next big thing the operative did was play a key role in Chelito's trial—he managed at least one of the anonymous witnesses who testified and likely took the stand anonymously himself. On January 19, 2006, the defendant was sentenced to four years for being an accomplice to the DEA agent's murder.

On February 5, *La Tribuna* reported that a group of Puchos had attacked two people and then engaged in "a fearsome firefight" with the police. Four days after that, according to one of Cholo's reports, he and a team of detectives arrested seven people, and the following morning, they got three more.

It was starting to feel like the Puchos were metastasizing, so at a meeting at ASJ's office the following week, Kurt asked Cholo and Macario, "Are we doing something wrong? Do we need to change our strategy?"

Macario argued that catching the big fish had already caused the homicide rate to drop, and that they should keep reeling more mareros in.

On February 23, someone reported that a group of Puchos, one of whom used the alias Coco, had threatened to kill some bus drivers. Cholo responded to this by staking out the bus terminal from inside Genesis between March 6 and 9, and then, on the 10th, his target, Coco, was apprehended along with five other suspects. Six days later, Macario put on a sport coat, grabbed his brown leather briefcase, and brought three anonymous witnesses to Coco's initial audience. The witnesses were essentially invisible to the outside world, because they were all wearing black head-to-toe robes that Cholo's mom had sewed; the garments looked just like burqas.

That month, Cholo, who, it should be noted, is a dog lover, pretended to be a government veterinarian in order to case houses in Nueva Suyapa, and one can only wonder whether or not he actually vaccinated any strays.

Indeed, one could only wonder what he was really doing on *all* his operations. Kurt prohibited him from bearing arms and expected him to hang back from the action, to just orient cops and marshal witnesses. But according to an ASJ employee, "We always had questions about what Cholo was doing with the police." And another one of his colleagues added, "People were concerned that if he was sure someone was guilty, he would lean on a witness."

In a series of interviews many years later, Cholo would speak with astonishing frankness. That being said, his words should not be taken at face value, in part because he seems to like to play the part of the provocateur, and in part because he rarely ever admits to memory lapses or doubt.

"We did a nocturnal operation one time. Forty cops. Six vehicles. Four technicians. One chopper. We captured the suspect but didn't find any drugs or money. . . . So you know what we did? We grabbed one of the detainees and began firing near his head. We said, 'Tell us where the drugs and money are or we're going to shoot you in the head.' The guy began to cry and cry and cry and cry. After three minutes, he told us where to look. We found four sacks of drugs, fifteen grand, and three machine guns. If I'm given funds to pay for an operation—food, cellphones, cars—and we don't make a capture, then I'm not going to keep getting funds."

"When we were out on operations, if the cops saw jewelry, cellphones, or cash, they would steal it. . . . Kurt told me to film them doing it, but I would never. You know why? Because they would have killed me. So what did I do? I saw it happen and let it slide. Did nothing. Didn't interest me. Why? Because my job was capturing delinquents."

He insisted that the police never killed anyone while he was working with them as part of Peace and Justice, but he did admit that he himself had homicidal longings: "I would have killed Chelito. I wanted to. I didn't do it out of respect for the rules of our institution."

As for his role in captures, which, according to him, "have always been violent," he claimed to have complied with Kurt's rules—no gun; just watch from the sidelines. But at certain moments, he seemed to sort of contradict that: "I once ripped off my balaclava and told Chelito, 'Siniestro—I captured him. Junior—I captured him. Your sister is a whore. Your father is an alcoholic. And now I've captured you!'"

And he also said this about Chelito: "My teams shot him twice. . . . I have photos of us torturing him."

Whether or not those episodes really happened that way, Cholo clearly did think that hurting mareros was warranted: "All those teenage girls that got raped, what do you think they'd say? I'll tell you what they'd say. They'd say that if their rapists were in front of them, they would kill them with their bare hands. That is what people don't get. When it comes to the delinquents, they go, 'Aw, poor baby. Don't mistreat him.' . . . But I used to say that the best medicine for a victim was hearing we captured the person who hurt them. . . . It provides a degree of spiritual and mental tranquility. People who don't work in justice don't get that."

To be clear, Cholo would have never spoken to Kurt or Carlos like this. According to Kurt, "I can remember being pissed off at Cholo and Macario for all sorts of things . . . but I don't remember either knowing or having strong suspicions that they were abusing their power."

He was probably being sincere when he said that, but one can't help but wonder whether back in the day, on his crusade to pacify the barrio, he shielded himself with some amount of wishful thinking and willful ignorance, because he knew deep down, either consciously or subconsciously, that defeating the Puchos required crossing lines he could never knowingly breach.

Carlos once happened to see a hooded Cholo—his body is unmistakable—and some cops he was with violently arrest a teenager in Nueva Suyapa. "Our personnel was not allowed to actively participate in operations," Carlos later said. "However, if our personnel wasn't there, the risks were greater . . . because the police would commit additional crimes, like taking bribes to let people go. This forced me to confront my values. Our rule was that Cholo could not actively participate in operations, but I knew he sometimes did."

What Carlos was describing there was one of the moral alibis upon which Peace and Justice was erected. All of them can be debated ad nauseum, but one of the most important ones, that sending criminals to prison was actually doing them a favor, because out on the street, they would likely be killed, had been getting corroborated by a growing pile of corpses.

Kurt and Carlos's initial understanding of the Gárgola murder, which happened back in June 2005, was that the Puchos were the ones who had crushed his head with a stone.

But that was incorrect.

Gárgola had, in fact, been killed by someone who believed he was a Pucho. And he had not been the last supposed Pucho felled by that same hell-bent hand. Two months later, Parabrisas had a chunk of his skull shot off; a month after that, Sardina was stabbed once in the abdomen, twice in the cheek, and twice in the neck; two months later, a machete was swung into Arañita's cranium; and on April 20, 2006, two bullet-ridden bodies were found near Kurt's church. They were Picudo, who, according to one of Cholo's emails, "had already been captured and let go three times," and Franklin, who had been freed after getting picked up on Peace and Justice's first big raid.

For a while, all these murders had seemed unrelated, but with the passage of time, they cohered into a bone-chilling pattern. A vigilante serial killer was on the prowl, and there were more pounds of flesh to gather.

- 11 -

SOMETIMES A PHOTOGRAPH REALLY DOES SAY IT ALL. IN THIS one, Nelson Hernández is in front of the Nueva Suyapa police post in combat boots, camo fatigues, mirrored sunglasses, and a black beret. His face is stern, his teeth are clenched, his stance is open, and each of his hands grips a skyward M16.

His father was a security guard—that is, someone known to possess a gun—and that seems to be why the Puchos bludgeoned him. At the time of that attack, Nelson was a corporal in the 1st Infantry Battalion, stationed some distance from the city, yet still, inspired by a sense of filial duty, he formed a vigilance committee in Nueva Suyapa, which, like the previous one, was known as the Encapuchados.

Their opening salvos against the Puchos were the murders of Gárgola and Sardina, both of which seemed to have occurred while Nelson was on furlough. But this was not a man who did things halfway—he would later articulate something of a personal credo on a recorded phone call: "Stupid men are only stupid because they let other men give them their wings." He deserted the military in September 2005 and, at some point, got two tattoos: an angel running away from what appeared to be a burning church on his left arm, and a howling wolf on his right.

He had an MO. He killed under the cover of night, in or close to the Diecisiete, his home turf, and his victims—to the extent they really were Puchos—were marginal ones, boys who might have done low-level tasks like collect extortion or keep an eye out for the cops. Flanked by a few Encapuchados, Nelson would snatch a victim from a public venue—Gárgola and Arañita had been at bodegas, and Sardina had been at a fiesta—and finish him off with gusto nearby.

In April 2006, however, his risk tolerance increased. Picudo and Franklin, who were taken out on the twentieth, presumably by him or his people, were not marginal Puchos but legitimately dangerous ones. And also, this was the point in time when his pace drastically quickened. Two days after that double homicide, a boy known as Moti and his cousin Ramiro were eating instant soups in front of a bodega in Flores de Oriente. In broad daylight.

Suggesting that there are gradients of evil when it comes to executing minors may be splitting hairs—Gárgola was sixteen, and Arañita seventeen—but it must be emphasized that Moti truly was a child. A thirteen-year-old with puffy cheeks, he stood just four foot eight.

Nelson, who was twenty and muscular, and two men he was with approached the bodega, a brick structure perched near the top of a steep lane. "So you must be the famous Moti," he began, seemingly in reference to the fact that the boy was said to be a Pucho button man.

"I'm not famous," Moti replied. "And by the way, we're just here to buy some things." He almost certainly knew who Nelson was and that he was in the business of exterminating Puchos. The subtext of his statement was that he was there shopping, as opposed to extorting the merchant. In other words, he was pleading for his life.

"Don't resist, or I'll shoot you," Nelson said.

The men tied Moti's hands behind his back with a length of black twine, and then Nelson told Ramiro, who was fifteen, "Follow us if you're brave enough. But if you say anything about this to anyone, I know where you live and where you would hide."

Nelson and his men then ushered Moti to the top of the lane, at which point they could have turned toward the Diecisiete, their original hunting ground, and found a discreet spot. But the barrio's new apex predator seemed eager to show everyone who sat atop the food chain. Earlier that day, he had allegedly stoned a young man at the bus terminal, one of the most trafficked places in the entire barrio, and now, as that victim fought for his life at the hospital, Nelson and his crew steered Moti deeper into Flores de Oriente, the Puchos' home base.

As their procession passed by some people near a school, Nelson shouted, "Whichever dog from Flores de Oriente snitches is going to end up like this dog." He then inched his captive, who he pushed and pulled like a plaything, past a soccer field of pinkish dirt where about twenty people had been competing. His theatrics climaxed with him leading his parade up an adjacent hillside, climbing onto a mound of dirt, gazing down at the soccer players, cocking his pistol, descending the mound, and taking his final bow.

Boom.

After the Encapuchados ran off, Ramiro ascended the hillside and wept, and so did Moti's mother, Sagrario Herrera, who lived nearby and had been alerted. According to *La Tribuna*, the distraught woman begged, "Please arrest Nelson before he kills us all!"

————

WEEKS LATER, AT FOUR IN THE AFTERNOON ON MAY 8, KURT MET up with Macario, Cholo, and two middle managers at the office. Nelson was an enemy of their enemy, but even so, Kurt didn't even consider looking the other way, and his willingness to risk his, his family's, and his employees' lives to go after someone as horrifying as Nelson felt like a vindication, concrete evidence that he was playing cops and robbers for the right reason, as opposed to, say, out of some malicious yearning to annihilate the Puchos. But capturing Nelson was easier said than done. In so many ways, he was the perfect foil to Peace and Justice.

First of all, many of the people who absolutely despised the Puchos considered Nelson to be a righteous hero. And there's a chance that Peace and Justice unintentionally helped him obtain his crime-fighting bona fides, because his maturation into a beloved marero hunter had coincided with the Puchos' accelerating demise, which the program, a tightly held secret, deserved a lot of credit for. In any case, Nelson's popularity was a wrench in the program's gears. When Cholo asked his informants for intel on him, they generally refused to help. "Don't capture Nelson; he is cleansing the neighborhood" was the sort of thing they said.

And on top of that, Nelson had gone to great lengths to silence potential witnesses. Arañita seems to have been killed for talking to the police about Gárgola's murder, and in case Arañita's relatives were considering repeating that little blabbermouth's mistake, Nelson and another Encapuchado had barged into Arañita's wake, at which point the Encapuchado kept an AK-47 trained on Arañita's thirteen-year-old sister while Nelson warned her mother, "If you denounce me, I will hear about it, and pills can't cure what I shoot people with."

In a situation like this, an investigator's best hope is that the victims' relatives will step up to testify, but Nelson's victims were either Puchos or supposed Puchos; in other words, they were the very people who Cholo and Macario had been locking up. Introducing themselves to those families and explaining what they did for a living was therefore going to be a huge risk.

And there was yet another potentially debilitating wrinkle. There were whispers that the Encapuchados were an off-the-books death squad sponsored by either the military or the police. Nelson's martial background naturally invited that type of speculation, and furthermore, the national human rights commissioner had recently released a statement from Picudo's sister claiming that Nelson and two cops without badges had crashed her brother's burial, forced the male mourners to take off their shirts, and instructed everyone to keep their traps shut. The possibility that Nelson was not a lone wolf but a proxy for the police force meant that Peace and Justice had to be very wary of collaborating with the cops.

One could be forgiven for suspecting that Cholo's allegiances would have been an additional issue here—in other words, that he would have cheered Nelson on—but for all the operative's faults and locker-room bluster, he really did seem to believe in the preeminence of judicial justice. At the meeting with Kurt on May 8, however, he did raise a serious concern: "What scares me is tracking Nelson. His gang is equipped with M16s and AK-47s. Doing this unarmed is going to be very risky."

Kurt told him that the no-gun rule stood but might change in the future, and then he urged his operative to be as careful as he possibly could be. Despite everything, the team was feeling optimistic. According to the meeting minutes, "Nelson's capture is only a matter of time."

———

THE MADURO ADMINISTRATION HAD PREVIOUSLY SET UP SOMETHING called the Death of Minors Unit, because according to the charity Casa Alianza, between 1998 and 2003, more than sixteen hundred youth were murdered in Honduras, and also because the police were presumed to be responsible for at least some of those killings. What made this unit special was that it operated outside the force's chain of command, that is, independently from its prime suspects. But due largely to a lack of resources, it hadn't even managed to make a dent in its gargantuan caseload. In its first two years of existence, it had won just seven total convictions.

The chief of the unit was under a lot of pressure to bust Nelson in particular, however, because the human rights commissioner had been waving Picudo's sister's statement around in the press. Nevertheless, when Macario and Cholo first approached him, pretty much all he knew about the vigilante was his name. He found Macario to be peculiar, and Cholo to be . . . "serious," but his unit's ten or so detectives shared just one gas-guzzling Land Cruiser, and the Peace and Justice guys were offering to provide vehicles and fuel.

The initial phase of the investigation advanced rapidly.

Cholo would enter the Diecisiete on foot and, via cellphone, direct the undercover Death of Minors agents as they took photographs of the Encapuchados' homes. They typically drove vehicles he rented, except for the one time they drove a water delivery truck.

As for the question of what sort of masochistic daredevil was going to be game to testify against Nelson, the heartwarming answer turned out to be: way more people than you'd expect. For obvious reasons, next to nothing can be said about them, but according to the agents and prosecutors who were involved in the various Nelson cases, Cholo was the one who found, recruited, safeguarded, and transported a number of the key cooperators.

By the end of May, the investigators had made progress on the Gárgola case, the Sardina case, and the Arañita case, but the Moti case was the most promising, because a lot of people had seen the death march, and because his cousin Ramiro had already given a vivid statement to the police.

Statements like that, however, were not admissible at trial. For Ramiro's recollections to matter, he would have to repeat them under oath, in front of a judge and a defense attorney who had the right to cross-examine him. Obviously, the sooner that happened the better.

"Don KURT," Cholo wrote, on May 30. "I am not good about writing but hope you have a happy vacation with your family and enjoy it a lot because when you return to this country you will come back to reality. . . . Criminal Investigation has the arrest warrant for Nelson. Macario put it together with the prosecutor in charge of the case. We will now finalize the details of the operation."

Three days later, around dawn, dozens of agents flooded the Diecisiete.

They caught three Encapuchados in one house, but Nelson was nowhere to be found.

The manhunt continued.

Two weeks later, an anonymous witness told a Death of Minors agent, "I want to state for the record that I am scared these guys are going to kill me next."

According to a police report, ten days hence, on June 23, "a fifteen-year-old named Ramiro was taken from a wake in Nueva Suyapa by Nelson. Ramiro's relatives and other witnesses say that a few minutes later, they heard gunshots, and when they went outside to see what had happened, they saw that Ramiro was dead."

– 12 –

ON AUGUST 11, 2006, A STAGE WAS SET UP ON THE DIRT FIELD in the Diecisiete so the country's new president, Mel Zelaya, could make an announcement. He was one of those politicians who cultivated a countrified persona—his signature accessory was a white Stetson, and before taking office, he had told *La Tribuna*, "I don't need security. . . . I walk around like a normal citizen. That's how it's done in other democracies. Go to Sweden or Switzerland, and you'll see prime ministers riding the bus." There would turn out to be some gaps between his rhetoric and policymaking, but he had expressed a fondness for the more tenderhearted approaches to crime control, like alternatives to incarceration, and it's safe to assume that Nelson, who was in the crowd on the field that day, wearing an AC Milan jersey and packing heat, absolutely loathed all that warm-and-fuzzy talk.

The vigilante had chosen to put himself within a stone's throw of the commander in chief even though there were five outstanding warrants for his arrest, and even though several other Encapuchados had been caught since the initial raid. And incredibly, according to someone who saw him there that day, he looked relaxed. Which was strange, because he must have known that exposing himself like this almost guaranteed an explosive confrontation.

Or maybe that's exactly what he wanted. To go out with a bang.

Someone called in a tip to the Death of Minors Unit, at which point three agents hustled east toward the serial killer and the president. They had to negotiate the city's thoroughfares, cross the barrio's entry bridge, snake up the switchback, and cruise past Genesis before arriving at the field, which, according to one of them, was packed with hundreds of people.

The element of surprise would have been nice, but in a country where the vast majority of people were mestizo and the average height was five foot three, one of the agents happened to be a six-foot-three Black man who was wearing tactical gloves and a bright red shirt. Also, he was wielding an assault rifle.

When Nelson, who was off to the side of the field, noticed the incoming agents, he fired his pistol and split. This caused the crowd to scatter into a scurrying chaos.

Then, depending on who you ask, either the Death of Minors agents or the president's bodyguards caught up to Nelson and made the arrest.

That criminals are, at heart, a sorry lot of pathetic wusses seems to be a leitmotif in Honduran-cop storytelling. That being said, both the arresting agent and his boss insist—*insist*—that at some point during the capture, Nelson literally shat his pants.

———

THE FIRST HEARING FOR THE MOTI MURDER OCCURRED SIX DAYS LATER.

In Honduran courtrooms, witnesses are the center of gravity—judges sit behind a raised wooden dais; the prosecution's table is perpendicular to the judges' bench and stage right of it; the defense's table is opposite the prosecution's; the witness box is in the middle of everything, centered on the judges' bench; and the spectators' gallery is behind it, on the other side of a wooden balustrade.

When the prosecutor attempted to introduce her first anonymous witness, Nelson's attorney harped on a technicality: Apparently, this witness had not shown a government-issued ID to the judge. The prosecutor explained that that was only because this witness didn't have one—a common problem among the poorest of the poor—but the defender would not relent.

The prosecutor asked for a brief recess and then, upon reentering the room, validated what seems to be a courthouse truism: Whether you are a victim or a victimizer, dead or alive, innocent or guilty, a sweetheart or a scumbag, there is usually one particular person you can count on to fight for you on the stand. "This witness has decided to testify with her face uncovered," the prosecutor stated. "That way, the defense can corroborate who she is. . . . This witness is very important. She is the victim's mother."

Sagrario, a middle-aged woman with a birthmark between her mouth and chin, was breathing the same air as Nelson, who, for all she knew, could have been back on the street in a heartbeat, when she declared, "A young person told me that two people had just tied up my son's hands and taken him away. I wanted to help my son, so I went to look for my uncle. But he wasn't there. That was when I heard a gunshot. . . . When I came upon Ramiro, he told me that Nelson and two others had taken Moti and murdered him. . . . And now Nelson has threatened to kill me. I am very scared. I have already moved out of the barrio."

Though undeniably courageous, her statement was also rich in hearsay, and the defense attorney seemed to have thought he struck gold in her admission that she had gone to look for her uncle. "That makes her testimony not credible," he argued. "People should protect their families, but this witness is saying that she did not intervene."

In other words, Sagrario was a bad mother, because she hadn't tried fighting the armed Encapuchados herself.

At another audience two months later, the defense attorney went after Sagrario again, except this time, he actually had a point. He presented a copy of her former employer's contract with the city, which specified that the firm's staff was supposed to sweep streets from six in the morning until two in the afternoon. He also presented a letter from her former boss stating that on the day her son was murdered around noon, she had worked continuously. "Her testimony is not valid," the lawyer triumphantly proclaimed. "She couldn't have even been at the crime scene."

The judge didn't toss out the case, in part because Sagrario's ex-boss hadn't yet given his testimony under oath. He did, however, note that the defense was going to get another crack at her at the trial. In January 2007, it was scheduled for April, for the Monday after Holy Week, which, incidentally, would fall right after the second anniversary of Peace and Justice.

Handling this final stretch of the case fell to Luis Ortiz, a pensive, soft-spoken attorney who had manned ASJ's clinics before switching over to Peace and Justice. The prosecutor was worried that Sagrario, who had gone dark, wasn't going to show up at the trial. If she were, in fact, planning to blow it off, that would have been understandable—around this time, Arañita's stepfather, who was in a very similar position as her, was murdered, almost certainly on Nelson's orders.

Cholo spent two days searching for the star witness in mid-March, but it was actually Luis who managed to get a message to her through some of her relatives. Sagrario was nervous about meeting up with a stranger but agreed to do so at the Public Ministry, and as soon as that initial get-together happened, she and Luis developed a rapport. In addition to gifting her a bag of oranges to sell on the street, he introduced her to Peace and Justice's other new employee.

Kurt had hired Ixchel Serrano, a psychologist in her early twenties, to provide therapy to the program's collaborators. As the Social Vagabond and Melanie had previously discovered, stepping into Macario and Cholo's sandbox was no easy task, but Ixchel managed to elbow her way in, and by helping to sturdy their witnesses and informants on an emotional level, she became the program's final piece, the one it had been missing. As it turned out, Peace and Justice was a triumvirate of lawyers, investigators, and psychologists. "This was a very unique and peculiar model," Ixchel later said. "Families liked to call me because I could explain what was happening in simple language, without legalese. . . . I also did psychological interventions to help people overcome trauma. . . . Prosecutors need witnesses to keep their stories well ordered, but when people have experienced trauma, they don't remember everything. It's just too painful."

Luis and Ixchel spent a good amount of time with Sagrario over the course of Holy Week. They hung out in a park, drank coffee, and, most importantly, prepped for the trial. To put a stake through her son's executioner, this shy woman was going to have to speak confidently and coherently and withstand a cross-examination by a feisty attorney who was just dying to make her look like a bumbling fraud.

The morning of the trial, a vehicle that Peace and Justice rented was used to transport Sagrario to the courthouse, where she waited in a private room with Luis and Ixchel.

Her hands were trembling.

At 10:11 a.m., a panel of three female judges called the trial to order in courtroom number 4. The defense's opening foray was a boilerplate accusation that incidentally elucidated one of the subtle benefits of Peace and Justice. He accused the prosecutor of coaching up her witnesses.

The prosecutor was able to flatly deny this. Though her response may have technically been truthful, given what Luis and Ixchel had been up to, it was also slightly disingenuous.

Sagrario took the stand after a coroner explained precisely how a bullet had traversed her child's brain. She repeated her story from the initial hearing and added that, on the day in question, her boss hadn't shown up at work, so she left at ten and rode a bus back to the barrio in time to have been there for the murder. Nelson's attorney failed to bring in her former boss to authenticate his letter, and in their verdict, the judges stated that they found Sagrario's testimony to be credible.

Nelson was sentenced to twenty-five years.

Though his guilt isn't in doubt, it is possible that Sagrario massaged the truth in order to encourage the correct verdict. As Nelson's lawyer had pointed out, mothers are supposed to defend their children—at all costs. Does that mean they ought to lie for them, too?

Months later, on August 3, 2007, Pabla Ramírez took the stand in that very same courtroom, because that was where her son Junior was being tried for murdering Pan Blanco. Unbeknownst to both her and the defendant, Peace and Justice had been handling at least two of the prosecution's anonymous witnesses.

"My son wasn't even in the barrio that day," Pabla insisted. "Before God, I am telling you, he wasn't there. He wasn't even living in Nueva Suyapa."

Under the weight of cross-examination, her testimony imploded.

Did you see Junior the day of the killing?

"He was not there."

Do you know what your son was doing that day?

"No."

Junior was found guilty. The penalty was fifteen years.

Next up was Arañita's mother, Ilda Bustillo, who headed to the courtroom in September 2007 to try putting down three Encapuchados. Nelson was off the hook for this one because, as he himself admitted, after helping to capture Arañita, he had run home to grab his machete and hadn't made it back in time to get to enjoy the kill.

According to the trial transcript, Ilda entered the witness box but then did not testify. The prosecutor soon explained why: "We all saw this woman go into a state of shock."

The case survived Ilda's paralysis, however, in large part because Peace and Justice shepherded two anonymous witnesses who did end up testifying. According to one of them, "Luis and Cholo told me, 'Be brave. You're only going to say what we tell you to. Got it?' . . . I trusted them way more than the police. With them, I felt protected."

Each of the three defendants got twenty-two years.

At a hearing for the Gárgola case in February 2008, a busload of Nueva Suyapa residents showed up to cheer Nelson on. Something that one woman previously told *La Tribuna* presumably synopsized what this bizarre fan club was feeling: "To the police, he is a serial killer, but to us, he is a hero, the only one who protects us from real delinquents, like the Puchos, who kill, rape, and assassinate honorable and hardworking people."

Nelson received thirty years for the stoning of Gárgola. When he had a chance to speak toward the end of that proceeding, what he said was, "Jehovah gives. Jehovah takes." Years later, in prison, he would meet his maker, by the blade of another man's machete.

- 13 -

EVEN AFTER THE PUCHOS AND ENCAPUCHADOS HAD FALLEN, Kurt harbored some doubts about Peace and Justice: "I'd always think, *Are we stupid? Are we crazy? In the end, is this ethical?* . . . We were arresting young kids in the poorest neighborhoods and putting them in terrible jails. Someone could say, 'They call themselves Christians, but what sort of Christians would do anything like that?'" According to the program's own accounting, between 2005, the year they got started, and 2011, they helped capture well over one hundred suspects and helped win convictions against about seventy defendants.

Kurt and Carlos believed that between 2005 and 2009, the number of homicides in Nueva Suyapa declined by roughly 80 percent. This was based on statistics Cholo claimed to have pulled from Criminal Investigation, which showed thirty-four murders in 2005, and then, across the more peaceful years, fourteen in 2008, five in 2009, and ten in 2010. These secondhand numbers—which, it should be noted, make the operative who provided them sound heroic—would obviously not be acceptable to a peer-reviewed journal. That being said, they do appear to be directionally correct.

An institute at the National Autonomous University of Honduras began recording georeferenced homicide data in 2008. Assiduously comparing their numbers to Cholo's would be tricky—to do it right, you'd have to unravel esoteric issues like how exactly Nueva Suyapa was delineated. But for what it's worth, from 2008 to 2010, the institute tabulated a sum total of thirty-two murders, and Cholo tabulated twenty-nine.

His starting-point statistic from 2005 is not independently verifiable, but thirty-four murders feels reasonable for that famously bloody year when both the Puchos and Encapuchados were active. Relative to the barrio's estimated population of thirty thousand, that equates to a homicide rate of 113 per 100,000 people. That might sound outlandish—the homicide rate in Mexico was 9 per 100,000 that year—but in reality, it made sense, because the overall homicide rate in Honduras was 42 per 100,000 people, and Nueva Suyapa was considered to be one of the most violent neighborhoods in the country.

It would be hard to conclusively prove that Peace and Justice singlehandedly caused the barrio's homicide rate to plummet, but one indication it did was that this decline, as measured between 2005 and 2010, coincided with the rest of the country's homicide rate increasing by about 75 percent. The third-in-command at the Public Ministry, who has since become a friend of Kurt's, has argued that "if every barrio with a serious security problem had a Peace and Justice, this country would be different. There were months with zero homicides in Nueva Suyapa. . . . The only way to explain that is the program."

Kurt will talk about the degree of the program's success, that 80 percent number, with an assuredness more befitting a fundraising charity executive, which he is, than a sociologist, which he also is. But to his credit, he has been willing to open up the program to outside scrutiny.

The first to look under the hood was the International Justice Mission, a Christian organization that takes on labor slavery and human trafficking worldwide by, for instance, working with Thai cops and prosecutors to rescue children from brothels. IJM used to be one of ASJ's largest donors, and in launching Peace and Justice, Kurt and Carlos had more or less reformulated IJM's model and applied it to gang violence. According to one of that organization's executives, "Based on hard data, like the number of murders and the reported instances of extortion, and also based on anecdotal evidence, like conversations with community members, I can attest to the reduction in violence. . . . No one can tell me that their work wasn't real, because I got to see it firsthand."

One sign that the program really did have a massive impact was that as early as 2007, it began running out of things to do in the barrio and started working on sexual violence cases nationwide. That year, Kurt told his contacts at IJM about something that happened in Olancho, a rural state in eastern Honduras where ASJ had recently set up one of its clinics: "A thirteen-year-old girl was raped by a sixteen-year-old neighbor. Awful story, and the police did nothing for two months. The girl and her grandma came to the clinic and got the case going. An arrest warrant was issued recently, but apparently, the boy's family heard about it and sent him to the United States. Yesterday, however, someone affiliated with our clinic saw him and heard he wasn't leaving until Sunday. At two p.m., they called us and asked for help, and that afternoon, preparations were made. The ASJ investigator left Tegucigalpa at three a.m., arrived in Olancho by seven with the warrant and two police officers, and arrested the young man by nine. Pretty cool to see justice happen."

In late 2013, three grad students from Princeton's Woodrow Wilson School of Public and International Affairs traveled to Tegucigalpa to study Peace and Justice, which, by then, was operating in two more barrios in the capital. One of the students' reports noted that the program's success in Nueva Suyapa "illustrates that swift enforcement can be effective at curbing homicides and reducing crime." And they also added that "MS-13 and Barrio 18 have sporadically operated in Nueva Suyapa but have struggled to gain a foothold, possibly because ASJ's Peace and Justice program keeps these violent groups at bay." They stopped short of anointing the program as the proven remedy to the region's crime epidemic, however, because they first wanted to see it tested in more places and for it to be subjected to a formal evaluation.

At the time, the ultimate proving ground for any anticrime initiative was arguably San Pedro Sula, the mercantile city located four hours north of Tegucigalpa that was widely reported to have had the highest homicide rate of any non-war-zone city on earth. In 2014, Peace and Justice used funding from the US State Department to deploy one attorney, four investigators, and two psychologists to Rivera Hernández, the most notorious barrio in that city.

In the ensuing years, the Open Society Foundation, which was an ASJ donor, paid scholars from the State University of Rio de Janeiro to evaluate Peace and Justice. By the time they completed their study in September 2017, the program was operating in a chunk of Rivera Hernández that encompassed an estimated 44,000 people and in a swath of Tegucigalpa that encompassed an estimated 140,000.

The researchers compared the average number of homicides per month before the program arrived in a neighborhood with the average number after. The only barrio they excluded from their analysis was Nueva Suyapa, because those early-year statistics were not verifiable. Across the other Tegucigalpa barrios, however, they found that once the program started up, the average number of homicides per month halved. To put some concrete numbers behind that, in the largest of those barrios, there were eighty-five murders in the thirty-one months before the program began, and just seventeen in the twenty-nine months after. That is a 78 percent decline. And across the Rivera Hernández areas, the equivalent decline was an almost-as-impressive 67 percent.

To determine if the program was responsible for those improvements, as opposed to other factors, the scholars compared the barrios the program operated in with a control group of similar ones. According to their calculations, after adjusting for the other factors that might have contributed, the program itself caused the homicide rate to decline by 32 per 100,000 in the Tegucigalpa areas and by 101 per 100,000 in the Rivera Hernández areas. The Rivera Hernández result is on moderately weaker footing, because the program hadn't been operating there for as long, and because the population estimate wasn't rock solid. But even so, all things considered, both of those results are extraordinary.

The scholars also took the time to interview twenty-six of the program's collaborators—witnesses, informants, and relatives of victims. According to their report, "These beneficiaries feel enormous gratitude for the support they received, above all for assistance in changing homes when that was necessary, and also for the psychological therapy, which many would not have had access to if it weren't for Peace and Justice."

Kurt hoped to eventually see the program replicated abroad, and that seems to be one of the reasons why, in 2017, he submitted an op-ed titled "What Chicago Can Learn About Violence from Honduras" to the *Chicago Tribune*, the paper he and Jo Ann had read as undergrads. "I grew up on Chicago's South Side," he wrote, "before the area became synonymous with rampant crime. . . . In 2016, the University of Chicago's crime lab reported that only 26 percent of Chicago homicides and just 5 percent of shootings resulted in charges. Through the organization we founded, the Association for a More Just Society, my wife and I and a group of Honduran friends decided to see what we could do to mend the gap in trust between citizens and the police. . . . We operated our strategy by faith and a shoestring budget, and after years of hard work, we saw incredible results. . . . If this message from Honduras is anything, it's that we can turn the tide of violence."

The newspaper did not publish his piece.

- 14 -

O N VALENTINE'S DAY 2012, 856 MEN AND A WOMAN ON A
    conjugal visit were inside Comayagua Prison, a one-story
    structure designed to hold just 300 inmates. The building
was packed with triple-stacked bunk beds made of wood; there were
no smoke detectors, sprinklers, or fire extinguishers on the prem-
ises; and the only set of keys was in the possession of a guard who
was stationed outside the gates. Above the prison's front entrance
was a famous old maxim: "Let justice be done, though the world
may perish."

Chelito had been transferred there from Renaciendo when he
turned eighteen. According to a social worker who met with him,
"Elvin is maturing emotionally and mentally. . . . He says his stay
at Renaciendo was one of the worst experiences of his life, because
the personnel there harassed and abused him. . . . He says he has
undergone a positive change due to the better treatment at Comayagua. . . . He feels like his whole life has been a disaster but also rec-
ognizes the extreme harm he has caused. . . . He knows he will leave
prison someday and worries about what he will do on the outside."

Around 10:30 p.m., a mattress somehow ignited.

When the guard with the key chain noticed the blaze, his reaction was to drop it and run away.

Some inmates managed to bash through the metal roof panels, and hundreds more made it out alive thanks to a convicted murderer who worked in the infirmary, and who, incredibly, scooped up the ditched key chain and opened as many modules as he could. But despite his valiant effort, this was the deadliest prison fire ever. Three hundred sixty men and one woman were consumed.

Amid the fiery bedlam, some prisoners had managed to escape, and by the time it petered out, many of the cadavers were too charred to be recognizable. The process of trying to identify the cremated remains was more like an archaeological dig than a crime scene investigation. It dragged on for weeks. Ultimately, officialdom did list Chelito among the dead, but to this day, there are many people in Nueva Suyapa who do not believe that. What those skeptics do believe is that Chelito started the fire as a way to break free, and that the yo-yoing hell-raiser pulled off his signature magic trick, this one last time.

BOOK TWO

FEAR AND ANGER

– 1 –

UNTIL CONSTANTINE THE GREAT LEGALIZED CHRISTIANITY, Christians were martyred for bearing witness to their faith. In Greek, the language of the New Testament, the word "*martyr*" actually means "witness," and even after it seeped into English unaltered, "martyr" remained, for a time, intrinsically linked to the act of bearing witness. "Nor is it the death of the witness," the seventeenth-century philosopher Thomas Hobbes wrote, "but the testimony itself that makes the martyr: for the word signifieth nothing else, but the man that beareth witness."

When Kurt talked about the Bible, he could almost sound like a teenager hyping up a comic book. He was in awe of the early Christians' into-the-lion's-den bravery, and he used certain verses to psyche himself up, such as his favorite, 1 John 4:18: "There is no fear in love, but perfect love drives out fear." On the basis of that, he saw love and fear as shoulder-angel-like forces that were locked in a zero-sum battle to alter one's capacity for courage. Said another way, if he *loved* his neighbors wholeheartedly, as the Bible commands, then he would be able to manifest a virtually limitless courage in the name of protecting them from harm, because that love would overpower whatever *fear* he had for himself.

He felt like part of his job at ASJ was making this love-conquers-fear ethos contagious, which, as a practical matter, entailed pushing his staff to do the dangerous work he and Carlos architected with the expectation that they, in turn, would embolden their beneficiaries to take risks like testifying against mareros in court. According to Luis, the Peace and Justice attorney, "When I got scared, or when my friends told me to cut this shit out, Kurt could inspire me. . . . I didn't live in Nueva Suyapa. He did. My wife didn't live in Nueva Suyapa. His wife did. My kids didn't live in Nueva Suyapa. His kids did. Seeing his passion for delivering justice to those people and watching him be an extraordinary human being inspired me to do something with life-and-death consequences."

The forum where Kurt most explicitly used the Bible to inform what the charity did in the here and now was its weekly Monday morning devotional. For the one on December 4, 2006, he and his staff of about sixteen crammed into the windowless conference room on the second floor of the office. Sitting beside him was Dionisio Díaz García, a chubby forty-three-year-old lawyer with sleepy eyes and a tuft of gray near the front of his full head of hair. Kurt considered him to be one of the nicest people he had ever met; he meant that as a compliment, but in the context of ASJ's inherently confrontational work, it was also something of a critique.

What mitigated that particular shortcoming of his was that his direct supervisor, a journalist named Dina Meza, was just about everything he wasn't: skeptical, stubborn, tough as nails, and unflinchingly lionhearted. To somebody unfamiliar with Honduras, their initiative, which was called the Labor Project, would have sounded benign, like something that didn't require such hard-edged qualities. But it did, and right now, Dina, a single mom in her mid-forties with brown eyes and a bob cut, worried that something awful was about to happen to either her or Dionisio, who, despite his contrasting personality, was a dear friend. She had had reason to feel that way even before the previous week, when one of their colleagues received an anonymous text message in broken English: "The life of Dionisio, could be in danger!!! take care, look for someone closer to your enemies!!!!!"

The Labor Project's primary beneficiaries were, believe it or not, private security guards. In Honduras, they were seemingly in front of everything—restaurants, supermarkets, gas stations, parking lots, warehouses, schools, hospitals, mansions, and hotels. At a superficial level, this invasion of the mall cops was mildly comedic, but what wasn't so funny was that working as a security guard absolutely sucked.

Many were forced to work inhumane twenty-four-hour shifts; some earned less than the minimum wage of $100 per month; and benefits like healthcare, sick days, maternity leave, vacation, and severance were typically not provided. And furthermore, nobody guarded the guards—here are some real examples of a type of headline that frequently appeared in Honduran newspapers: "Outlaws Kill Guard for Shotgun," "Zoo Guard Robbed and Killed," "Guard with Bullet in Head Holds On for Twenty Days," "Guard Commits Suicide," and "To Be a Guard Is to Have One Foot in the Grave."

Much of this exploitation—the marathon shifts, the poverty wages, the lack of benefits—was illegal, but that counted for nothing, because Honduran labor law went almost entirely unenforced. One reason why was that the Labor Ministry, the institution in charge of enforcing it, was a farce of Kafkaesque proportions. Its inspectors usually didn't have access to vehicles, so if a worker wanted his claim to be investigated, then *he*—a person likely on the brink of starvation and default—had to cover the costs of transporting the inspector. And financing that would probably prove futile, because the ministry was both toothless (the maximum fine it could levy was $265) and compromised (for example, a deputy minister of labor concurrently ran a private security firm).

Kurt and Carlos wanted to eradicate this type of white-collar law-breaking about as much as they wanted to eradicate gang violence in Nueva Suyapa, and just as Peace and Justice was their response to the inadequacies of the police force, the Public Ministry, and the judiciary, the Labor Project was their surrogate for the Labor Ministry. Dina had been investigating private security firms and exposing their illicit HR practices in *Revistazo*, ASJ's online magazine, while Dionisio had been suing them in court.

When dreaming up new endeavors, Kurt and Carlos had a tendency to oversimplify and defang the world, and out of the gate, they had homed in on the Labor Project's philanthropic potential, on how profoundly it could help the type of guards they and everyone else encountered on a day-to-day basis. But in getting so excited about that, they had failed to seriously contemplate a certain piece of common knowledge: The private security industry had a dark side.

———

DURING THE COLD WAR, THE HONDURAN MILITARY HAD BEEN VERY entrepreneurial, and one of its main sidelines was selling security services to corporations. In the mid-nineties, the country aggressively demilitarized, which meant hordes of soldiers suddenly found themselves out of work. Inevitably, some of them founded private security firms, and many others joined their ranks.

It was the perfect time to be setting up shop. A single superpower now sat atop the global world order, and in accordance with its wishes, free-market economic policies were implemented throughout Latin America. The Honduran government privatized a number of state-owned enterprises and also established zones where factories could manufacture and export apparel without much in the way of taxes, tariffs, or regulations. But the country was not a safe place to do business in, nor was it a safe place to be rich. Mareros regularly assaulted banks and delivery trucks, and according to police statistics, in 2000 and 2001 alone, about $4.5 million of ransom money was disbursed to kidnappers.

Obviously, counting on the Honduran National Police to protect your person, property, staff, and kin was a very stupid thing to do, and while the poor sometimes found themselves turning to vigilantes for protection, the wealthy typically outsourced theirs to the burgeoning number of private providers. And as of ASJ's unforgettable devotional in late 2006, private security had become something of a mass-market product. Guards could be found not just in front of topiary hedges and multi-ton gates but also middle-class subdivisions and even some barrio bodegas.

The United Nations was so concerned about the industry's boom that it dispatched something called the Working Group on the Use of Mercenaries to Honduras. The mission's report would soon note that in a country with twelve thousand cops, there were likely somewhere between twenty thousand and seventy thousand guards, and also that, beyond the 123 registered security firms, there were more than 280 operating illegally, about which "nothing is known: who owns them; who works for them; how they choose employees; what their backgrounds are; what weapons they use; and who supplies them."

The registered firms self-reported that their armories contained machetes, pistols, shotguns, AK-47s, Uzis, bayonets, silencers, grenade launchers, explosives, bulletproof vests, infrared goggles, radars, and satellite communication systems. And it was an open secret that some of the firms, whether they actually provided security services or not, were arms-trafficking outfits. A political scientist from Brooklyn College named Mark Ungar concluded that many Honduran cops were enhancing their incomes by laundering the weapons they seized through the firms.

And that was just one of the many ways in which the police force and the security industry were inappropriately intertwined. Lots of retired, fired, and suspended officers went to work for the firms, and the Zelaya administration had recently announced that guards could participate in police operations. What made this coziness especially problematic was that the force was part of the Security Ministry, and the Security Ministry was supposed to be regulating the industry. Unsurprisingly, it hardly did.

Back in 2003, the United Nations Development Programme had lobbied for a reform that would have forced the ghost firms to actually register. According to Ungar, however, that proposal was quashed after a group of cops threatened to murder the chief of police.

"In Honduras," the UN mission on mercenaries explained, "there exist, in truth, 'tiny armies' to which the state has ceded part of the monopoly on the use of force. The authorities cannot control them."

———

DELTA SECURITY SERVICES' CORPORATE LOGO WOULD HAVE LOOKED at home atop a buccaneer's mast—inside a black triangle, two golden short swords crossed behind a golden globe.

Much about this firm was murky and unverifiable, but for all intents and purposes, Richard Swasey was its owner and boss. Because of his European-sounding name, many people assumed he was a gringo, but in actuality, he was a Honduran from Roatán, a fingerlike island located thirty miles out into the Caribbean Sea. It was said that he had made a fortune in the seafood business before building Delta into a leading security firm. Accomplishing that must have required a lot of hard work, but he clearly knew how to play hard, too. Before setting out to compete in Honduras's most recent National Sport Fishing Tournament, he had told a reporter, "I'm ready to chase first place like a wolf at sea."

Dina had chosen to target his firm in particular because it was both a prolific violator of the labor code *and* a major winner of the security-services contracts that federal agencies doled out to watch over its buildings. In other words, Swasey was making boatloads off a government whose laws he was brazenly disregarding.

Throughout this whole saga with Delta, which had been going on for years now, Kurt and Carlos maintained a tunnel vision around the upside scenario. If the Labor Project actually managed to force Swasey to grant benefits, put workplace protections into effect, and meet the minimum wage, then his roughly one thousand guards would have less strenuous days and more money to put toward essentials like medicine, meat, and textbooks for their kids. And if Dina and Dionisio could make an example of the worst-of-the-worst company in the worst-of-the-worst industry, then there was no reason they couldn't also help the guards working for other firms, as well as the janitors mopping floors, the cooks flipping burgers, and the cashiers counting change—that's hundreds of thousands of mistreated workers nationwide.

Because that endgame sounded so glorious, Kurt and Carlos refused to be daunted by the many obvious reasons to be afraid of Swasey: He was a fat cat in an industry known to be infested with criminal activity; he had somehow won a cornucopia of lucrative contracts from a notoriously corrupt government; he was a seagoer in a part of the world (between Colombia and the United States) where nautical activity aroused a certain specific type of suspicion; and he had made it clear that he was extremely annoyed about what ASJ was trying to do to his business.

Up until now, disregarding danger had led Kurt and Carlos not to excruciating pain or total annihilation but to altruistic feats, so like riverboat gamblers on a once-in-a-lifetime run, they had come to greatly discount risk and to treat fear like a largely unhelpful impediment that stood in the way of them helping the poor. What allowed them to break through that roadblock, they believed, was their love-your-neighbor spirit, but a few others had been wondering if love was also making them blind.

A few months earlier, Melanie, the social worker who previously resigned, sent Kurt a critique that she had clearly written in the spirit of trying to help a charity she would remain a loyal donor to. After laying out what she disliked about Peace and Justice—its association with the police, for instance—she provided an analysis written by a Chicago-based therapist who had once been Kurt's student. The clinician hypothesized that what was really behind Peace and Justice was Kurt and Carlos's "need to prove themselves strong and courageous in the face of a threat they have internalized as threatening their own identity and sense of control." She then went on to recommended "the support and guidance of someone with more perspective, to work through that and get to the place where the analysis and work can be about peace and justice instead of fear and anger, however righteous that anger might be."

She seemed to be suggesting that Kurt and Carlos were motivated not by radical selflessness or credos from an ancient age, but by a juvenile hero complex and a garden-variety machismo. Is attempting to save others vainglorious? And justice, that pillar of modern civilization—to what extent is it just ol'-fashioned payback dolled up with robes, gavels, and wood-paneled walls?

This critical email from an ex-employee and an ex-student did not shake Kurt and Carlos to their core, but because Dina's foreboding was about to prove prescient, they were soon going to have to self-reflect like never before. In addition to the abovementioned questions, they would have to grapple with another: What do we, the living, owe to our martyrs?

– 2 –

RIVERS THAT BEGIN IN HONDURAS'S CENTRAL HIGHLANDS meander through fertile valleys before colliding with the Caribbean Sea. The Humaya and the Sulaco meet in a pine forest between Tegucigalpa and San Pedro Sula. Back in the sixties, the Harza Engineering Company of Chicago identified a box canyon near their confluence as a potential site for a hydroelectric dam. Normally, before investing hundreds of millions of dollars in one of those marvels of modern engineering, you'd want to see well over fifty years of localized rainfall data in order to be able to predict the future reservoir's maximum and minimum levels. No such data existed for this watershed. Nevertheless, the Honduran power authority came to the conclusion that building a dam was worth doing, partly based on a feasibility study that was commissioned, audited, and updated by Motor-Columbus of Baden, Switzerland, a firm that was poised to earn tens of millions of dollars in fees should the project go forward.

Motor-Columbus drew up blueprints for what would be one of the tallest and most cutting-edge dams on earth. They wanted to build *that* . . . in Honduras!

The Honduran Society of Civil Engineers felt that the design was way too grandiose, and another group of local engineers argued for five small dams instead of one single behemoth. What if something went wrong? Should an impoverished country really saddle itself with an oppressive amount of debt and then bet everything on an architectural experiment dreamed up by foreigners?

The military men running the country and the international financiers backing the project dismissed the naysayers. At the time, 80 percent of the country's power was being produced archaically, by burning wood, charcoal, or diesel, and a big chunk of the population didn't even have access to electricity. That gigantic problem could be solved, in one fell swoop, by one gigantic solution.

Construction began in 1980. To seal off the floor of what was going to become the reservoir, a consortium of European firms—Impregilo of Milan, Züblin of Stuttgart, and Losinger of Bern—poured cement over the surrounding valley. They also erected a herculean wall that stood even taller than the Hoover Dam's. A second consortium—Motor-Columbus, Astaldi of Rome, and Codelfa of Tortona—built the underground powerhouse where four Swiss-made turbines were going to convert the captured river water that rushed by them into an overabundance of electricity.

The reservoir started filling up, and by 1986, its surface was high enough above the intakes on the dam wall that the pressure in the tubing that ran down from them was sufficient to run the turbines in the powerhouse. The Cajón Dam was finally in business.

That was the good news.

The bad news—the very bad news—was that the reservoir's floor had cracked, and the water seeping through it was putting upward pressure on its intact portions as well as eroding the foundation of the dam.

Motor-Columbus and the Honduran power authority, which was known by the acronym ENEE, scrambled to fix this. They drilled a drain hole through which the subterranean water could escape; it led to a pit in the powerhouse that was emptied downstream by electric pumps. And in an effort to actually seal off the floor of the reservoir, Cementazioni e Sondaggi of Milan injected concrete into its fractures. These remediation efforts were completed in 1990, and from the outside, they appeared to have worked.

Over the next few years, however, another potentially catastrophic issue reared its ugly head. There wasn't enough rain falling in the catchment area, which meant that the reservoir was receding, and consequently, that the pressure in the tubing was declining. It eventually got so low that the turbines could operate at only three-quarters of their designed capacity. In February 1994, ENEE had no choice but to start rationing electricity nationwide, which, of course, pissed everyone off. One handyman told the press that in a single week, he had been called to fix over a hundred televisions that had been short-circuited by the rolling outages.

And to make matters worse, despite the Milanese contractor's efforts, the fractures in the reservoir's floor had not been successfully plugged. That April, cloudy water was pouring into the powerhouse's pit at a rate of one residential swimming pool every single minute. The pumps could barely keep up with this torrential inflow, and given that water corrodes rock with the passage of time, the cracks in the floor and the fissures beneath it would inevitably expand until the deluge outpaced the pumps, flooded the powerhouse, fried the turbines, and enveloped much of a nation in an antediluvian darkness.

There was seemingly no way to stave off that calamity—one of the consortiums had been injecting different mixtures of cement, sand, and gravel into the fissures, but headwater would just push them out before they had a chance to harden. And there was no backup to Cajón—the country's now-out-of-use diesel generators had been badly damaged by rust.

Toward the end of June, ENEE paid an American aviation company $60,000 a day to spray silver iodide and salt into the clouds above the catchment area. This geoengineering did stimulate some rain, but only enough to reduce the reservoir's rate of decline from twenty centimeters per day to ten. Once it became clear that this Hail Mary effort wasn't going to prevent the inevitable, ENEE had to warn a populace already dealing with five-hour outages each day to brace themselves for twelve-hour ones.

By the end of that month, the reservoir's surface had sunk to twenty-seven meters above the intakes, the lowest point at which all four turbines could function.

On July 2, one of them stopped spinning.

Across the country, churchgoers were praying for precipitation just like their ancient ancestors once prayed to a rain god called Chac. But the pressure in the tubing still kept dropping, and one month later, a second turbine seized up.

Within weeks of that, ENEE decided to proactively take a third one offline, which meant that just one turbine remained active.

Soon thereafter, however, came a gift from the gods: Heavy rains started falling. And then, finally, in late August, the reservoir began to rise.

But Cajón was not yet out of the woods, because the water leaking through the reservoir's floor still threatened to destroy the turbines.

Having tried all the remedies proposed by the Europeans, Cajón's chief geologist decided to give it a go Honduran style. His team fanned out across the region, purchased every toy ball they could find, and injected 8,650 of them into the underground fissures.

As hoped, the plastic ones, which they had filled with concrete, sank to the bottom of the cavities, while the wooden ones floated up to the top. But to the engineers' dismay, the balls didn't create a tight-enough seal, so the grout they injected flowed out before it could settle—the same problem as before.

The balls did, however, provide buttressing for the next piece of the puzzle. The engineers inserted twenty-five thousand rolled-up polypropylene feed sacks, the type used by campesinos, into the fissures, and all that everyday material stuffed in there proved to be the proverbial finger in the dike. The grout could now stay in long enough to harden. By April 1995, the gushing flow into the pit had become a negligible trickle, and electricity rationing was no more.

Three and a half years later, a massive hurricane called Mitch swelled Honduras's rivers. There was another dam perched above Tegucigalpa, and when panicking officials decided to open up its floodgates, out of concern that it would collapse under the weight of its bloated reservoir, an aqueous avalanche barreled down into the city and sheared a number of densely populated neighborhoods into oblivion.

The eye of the storm passed over the watershed around Cajón, downriver from which one-third of the country's population resided.

Throughout the tempest's landfall, 1.3 trillion pounds of stormwater, a weight far greater than the combined heft of the entire human race, pressed up against the backside of Cajón and down against its reservoir's rubbish-filled foundation.

Yet incredibly, it held strong.

Mitch was exceptionally deadly and destructive, but it has been estimated that Cajón reduced the peak flow of water downriver, which is what causes the most fatalities and devastation, by a full 80 percent.

———

CARLOS IS NOT GOOD WITH DATES, BUT SOME TWO AND A HALF YEARS before ASJ's unforgettable devotional in December 2006, he, Bernarda, and their two sons drove northwest in Bernarda's car, an archaic sedan they jokingly called the Time Machine. They were going to go check out Cajón, an awesome sight that was taller than the tallest building in Tegucigalpa. But they were running behind, and by the time they arrived, the site was closed for the day.

The couple tried sweet-talking one of the security guards on duty, and amazingly, out of the kindness of his heart, he let them break the rules. He rode with the family down the access road to the dam and, at some point, mentioned how his employer treated him.

That security firms essentially spat on their staff was not breaking news to either Carlos or Bernarda, given that many of their neighbors in Nueva Suyapa toiled in that field. But for some serendipitous reason, this man's commentary proved to be a spark. On the family's three-and-a-half-hour drive back home, Bernarda said that ASJ should do something to help the guards, and soon thereafter, Carlos mentioned the idea to Kurt.

The gringo liked it; he liked it a lot. His father had been the principal of his middle school, and Mr. Harley Dale Ver Beek was considered to be a strict administrator—even the man's name was intimidating. Because of that, once Kurt got to high school, some of the older kids busted open his binders and dunked his head in the toilet. Though he was now in his late thirties, nightmares still brought him back to those awful school days, and whenever he witnessed bullying in real life, he reacted viscerally. For example, when picking up his son at school one day, he snatched the class bully, lifted him up, and let his feet dangle.

The situation the guards were in pulled on his picking-on-the-little-guy trigger, and his North Star, the Bible, contained some motivation for trying to help them: "Look! The wages you failed to pay the workers who mowed your fields are crying out against you. The cries of the harvesters have reached the ears of the Lord Almighty."

The biggest hurdle to working on this was presumably going to be finding someone who had the guts to go after private security firms. But in that department, Kurt lucked out.

The formative event of Dina's life had been the disappearance, in 1989, of her brother, an activist accused of being a guerrilla, into what she described as a clandestine government prison; according to her, she was the one who organized the group of agitators that secured his release, and that was when her lifelong commitment to fighting for human rights was forged.

Though she had a degree in journalism, she rebelled against some of that industry's norms. For instance, she felt she could be an activist and a reporter at the same time, that there was a sweet spot between heartless objectivity and hysterical pamphleteering where she could fight for the oppressed while still being fair-handed with their oppressors. *Revistazo*, a publication inside of a charity, was the perfect place for that type of unorthodox approach, and in July 2004, Kurt brought her in to run it. He didn't like it when she showed up at the office in her pink Juicy sweatpants but was wise enough to keep his trap shut.

At the time, Dina's life was in turmoil—it had been only a month since she left her husband and took their three kids to another house. Yet she still threw herself into the Labor Project, which, at this stage, was a largely journalistic endeavor. Delta fell into her crosshairs as soon as she started poking around the Labor Ministry. To be able to expose the company, however, she knew she was going to have to recruit some whistleblowers.

All over Tegucigalpa, day and night, Delta guards stood around in their epauletted button-downs with the firm's logo on the sleeve and caps that read PRIVATE SECURITY. As it turned out, these bored-out-of-their-minds men were generally happy to chitchat with an attractive woman who approached them off the street, and in time, dozens sat for tell-all interviews.

Dina learned a lot.

Some had been forced to sign a prewritten resignation letter with the date field left blank, so that when Delta fired them, it could fill in the date and use the phony document as grounds to withhold their legally mandated severance. The company also nickel-and-dimed its workers with a hodgepodge of different deductions, which could be as nitpicky as the cost of delivering their paychecks, and which could have the effect of reducing their take-home incomes to well below the minimum wage.

All in all, the guards earned something like $115 a month to commute to a post and do next to nothing for twelve or twenty-four hours straight. Check your clipboard. Move a traffic cone. Pace. Say "good morning" to a passerby. Pet your shotgun. Relieve yourself in a bucket in a shed. Politely wave to your supervisor as he swings past to supervise you. Sit down. Stand up. It's 7. It's 8. It's 11:09. It's 11:41. It's midnight. Seven more hours to go!

Shoulders sore. Eyelids heavy. Mind mush. You can yawn, but *do not* fall asleep, because that supervisor might return at any moment, and because, who knows, there might be some mareros eyeballing your firearm.

Sunrise, finally. Your reliever arrives. Go back to the barrio and try to sleep even though it's bright and hot, even though your wife needs you to fix this, that, and the other thing, and even though you still haven't found time to get your blood pressure checked. Because in less than twenty-four hours, your next twenty-four-hour shift will begin. You will be there, no matter what, and don't you forget, not even for a second, that you are expendable, and the tiniest error will likely get you fired and show your children what malnourishment feels like.

You have a job. You are one of the lucky ones. So shut up and get back to work.

The labor code stipulated that a company could extend the standard eight-hour workday by up to four additional hours—not *sixteen*—only if it paid overtime (ha!), and only if the job were not dangerous (ha!).

That regulation and a bunch of others were very clearly on the books, but daring to mention any of them to Delta's management was not going to go well. A gray-bearded guard told *Revistazo* that after three years on the job, he finally worked up the courage to request the overtime and bonuses he was legally owed. In response, his supervisors asked him to surrender his radio and revolver. When Dina went to visit this unemployed man at his home, she noted that "the tiny cornfield that surrounds his house provides his family with shade. Also, it is the only food they have left."

Dina was planning to publish a series of damning articles about Delta under *Revistazo*'s logo, a blue eye with a stylized indigo-and-yellow lid. But before doing so, she felt obligated to do something very few reporters would have had the courage or decency to do: She was going to confront Swasey herself, in person.

- 3 -

LA CEIBA IS A SMALL TROPICAL CITY WEDGED BETWEEN THE Caribbean Sea, the Cangrejal River, and the Nombre de Dios Mountains. Starting in the late nineteenth century, bananas were brought there from nearby plantations and quickly loaded onto steamships so that faraway Gilded Age consumers could enjoy this sweet, nutritious novelty product before any brown dots sullied its skin. Around the turn of the century, a gringo fugitive hiding out nearby, who published stories under the pen name O. Henry, coined the term "banana republic" to satirize how a handful of American corporations completely dominated Honduras. Nothing would encapsulate that more than the events of 1911 to 1912, when Sam "the Banana Man" Zemurray, one of the most audacious businessmen in American history, dispatched a mercenary by the name of Lee Christmas and a private army he had mustered in New Orleans to Honduras, where they managed to replace the president of the country with Zemurray's pliant ally.

The level of inequality between the gringo tycoons and the local campesinos was astronomical, and that is what inspired about thirty-five thousand farmhands and dockworkers to go on a sixty-nine-day wildcat strike in 1954. Against all odds, they succeeded in getting the Honduran government to enshrine a fairly progressive labor code that mandated overtime, eight-hour shifts, and paid vacation.

Fast-forward a half century, however, and enforcing this code fell to people like the chief inspector of the Labor Ministry's outpost in La Ceiba, a middle-aged man with an angular mustache. He was supposed to investigate firms like Delta, which, in the prior three years alone, had had about a hundred complaints lodged against it. But there was no indication that he had been doing that, and it's safe to assume he was surprised when, on September 16, 2004, Dina and her colleague, Eda Velásquez, a lawyer with feathered bangs, showed up at his office and informed him that he was going to have to do . . . his job. They had brought along a writ they procured at the Labor Ministry's headquarters in Tegucigalpa, which instructed this bureaucrat to immediately conduct an inspection of Delta.

Waltzing into a private security firm was a frightening thing to do, even for an inspector with the legal authority to do it, and letting two private citizens come along was certainly not by the book. But Dina and Eda, who felt they had to be there to make sure it happened, insisted.

Delta's office was a brick house located near a golf course and a Masonic Lodge; inside were tile floors, printers, wall-mounted trophy fish, hefty men in open-chested shirts, and wooden shelves lined with the black binders that presumably contained the personnel records the inspector needed to review. According to Dina, Swasey, a large pot-bellied man whose cheeks sometimes flushed, wasn't rude, but during their brief conversation, he casually placed a pistol on his desk. Also, he refused to let the inspector scrutinize his records.

A week or two later, Dina and Eda returned with three inspectors from Tegucigalpa. They were denied entry, but when they tried again three days after that, for some reason, they were welcomed with open arms. Swasey took Dina and Eda to a nearby Applebee's to congenially break bread, and then, over the course of the next month, he more or less gave the charity and the ministry carte blanche to examine his records and interview his guards.

He even sat for an interview with Dina himself. In a sea-blue Hawaiian shirt, he explained why he had recently decided to settle with some of the complainants: "Many things motivated us, including your visit, and the information you provided. I was uninformed about certain things. I just didn't know."

Dina saw something Machiavellian behind all this noblesse oblige, so whenever she went to La Ceiba, she acted like she was behind enemy lines—for example, she switched hotels every night and received routine check-in calls from relatives.

But Delta kept playing nice. Toward the end of November, it signed a highly unusual agreement with ASJ and the ministry whereby, going forward, the company would let the charity audit its compliance with the labor code. Then, in April 2005, it allowed the charity to host a weeklong seminar on the top floor of its office for the approximately 150 Delta guards who worked in the capital; the purpose of this was to make sure they all knew what the labor code entitled them to.

At the opening ceremony for that seminar, Kurt, who was wearing khakis and a cheap sport coat, addressed Mario Castro, the firm's jolly-faced regional manager. "We are very happy," Kurt said, "and we expect that, in the end, this process will not be something sad for you but something good for you." What Kurt—whose private-sector experience consisted of stocking shelves at a supermarket in high school—seemed to be suggesting was that clients would value Delta's newly elevated corporate conscience, and therefore, that the significant costs of complying with the labor code would be offset by it winning more contracts.

Carlos, who was in a gray short-sleeved button-down, then declared, "We have to recognize the company—its openness, its enthusiasm, its wanting its guards to enjoy the benefits granted by the law." He handed Castro a Certificate of Recognition, an unframed printout, and as he did, the two men beamed.

———

WITHIN A MATTER OF MONTHS, SWASEY'S "OPENNESS" AND "ENTHU-siasm" would come to look like nothing more than a strategy of evasion and delay—he and his executives were avoiding Dina, and his guards continued to report labor-code violations.

When Dina and Eda finally managed to get a meeting with Castro, on July 8, 2005, most likely in ASJ's conference room, he complained that his workers had become unruly because "they think you can yank us by the ears." Their conversation didn't become uncivil, however, until the two women brought up Tomasa Turcios.

For the first four or so years Tomasa worked for Swasey, she had felt satisfied with her job and proud of her performance in a male-dominated profession. According to her, everything changed when her bosses took her firearm, accused her of stealing it, and then, to recoup the cost, docked her salary for five straight months. During the period when those subtractions occurred, she and her three daughters were forced to get by on not much more than tortillas with salt.

The company had since reimbursed her for half of the deductions—which, in and of itself, seemed to substantiate her story—but it was refusing to pay out the other half unless she withdrew a complaint she made to Criminal Investigation; it alleged that she had been falsely accused of theft.

Tomasa's main takeaway from the ASJ seminar was that the first step toward obtaining your rights is having self-esteem, so not only would she not retract that complaint, but within the past few weeks, she had submitted another, this one to the Labor Ministry, demanding the overtime and bonuses she was legally owed.

This woman was, from management's perspective, a royal pain in the ass. Castro became visibly irritated upon hearing her name and soon dared Dina and Eda to sue the company. That challenge was technically a fair one to make, as claims left unresolved by the Labor Ministry's administrative process were supposed to get duked out in court. But Castro was likely assuming that a cash-strapped charity representing impoverished clients on a pro bono basis would desperately want to avoid the costs and hassles inherent to a trial. In other words, his blustery volley was likely an attempt to force his interlocutors to retreat.

The meeting minutes don't specify which woman responded, but it was almost certainly Dina who held their ground. If Delta backed out of this mediation, she warned Castro, "lawsuits would start raining down."

The affronted regional manager stood up as if to storm out of the room, only to then gather himself and sit back down. It was in the company's interests to avoid litigation, too, because unlike the ministry, the courts could make sizeable judgments.

With a legal battle possibly on the horizon, it seemed like Eda was about to become the charity's vanguard. Immediately after this meeting, however, she emailed Kurt, "I need some time off because of my flu and tonsilitis."

And that would be it for her; she would never again work at ASJ. Her abrupt exit was never explained, but according to a former colleague, "Dina and I thought she was going crazy or something. She had been hearing gunshots in the office. Stuff like that was happening that made no sense."

DINA HAD USED DIONISIO TO GET CHILD SUPPORT FROM HER EX-husband and thought he was the most empathetic lawyer she had ever met. That quality and the others that shone right through him—his sweetness, his politeness, his humility, his silliness—did not suggest he belonged on the front lines of a bellicose charity alongside Kurt and Carlos's band of swashbuckling eccentrics. That being said, he had been wanting to do more pro bono work than he could afford to as the sole proprietor of a one-man private practice, so in September 2005, he began working for the Labor Project half-time.

Dionisio was a man who had a hard time saying no, which meant his schedule was often bursting at the seams with an unmanageable surplus of meetings, audiences, and favors he had agreed to do. His wife, Lourdes, who he had married in his late thirties, was trying to help him get better organized, but that was very much a work in progress, and his first weeks at ASJ were characterized by him missing deadlines and him forgetting commitments.

After he kept a group of Delta guards waiting for over two hours on September 20, he leveled with Dina, told her that he couldn't handle this job on a half-time basis. He suggested she replace him with someone else.

This was going to become a pattern: Dionisio gets overwhelmed, Dionisio almost quits, Dionisio does not quit. The thing was, he felt a lot of compassion for the guards, ASJ was realistically the only place where they could get assistance, and the charity was in desperate need of his legal acumen, especially right now, because that very same day, Delta decided to escalate the feud with Tomasa.

At this point, it would have been hard to legally fire her—to a judge, that would have looked like retaliation for her two complaints, and since she was newly pregnant, she benefited from certain special protections. The firm had previously tried to get her to quit, it seems, by reassigning her to a graveyard shift in an inconvenient part of the capital. But she had been managing to endure those two-hour commutes to the middle of nowhere and those scary nights all alone in the dark because they amounted to nothing less than a test of her capacity to mother—after all, that was how she earned money to feed her kids and unborn child.

So the company went ahead and used a cheat code: It notified her and five other guards that, effective immediately, their posts were going to be in La Ceiba, a city located more than six hours away. Obviously, there was no way Tomasa could uproot her life on a dime.

Ten days later, Kurt and Castro met up in ASJ's conference room to try to resolve this. The company had recently been attributing its recalcitrance to Dina and her "malevolent purposes," and as if she were trying to prove their point for them, in the middle of this meeting, which was ostensibly a last-ditch peace summit, she barged in with a labor inspector, who served Castro with a citation he had apparently been avoiding.

This provocation was, in the grand scheme of things, probably ill-advised, and Kurt did sometimes worry about Dina's instinctive belligerence. But his charity wasn't in the business of ladling out soup to homeless people or doing arts and crafts with the elderly, and one of the ways he and Carlos gauged the potential utility of whatever they were up to was whether or not it pissed somebody off. Therefore, in his mind, the company's distaste for Dina was an indication that she was doing a very good job. He did sometimes feel the need to pull her off the warpath, but at the end of the day, he'd rather his staff be too gladiatorial than too meek, which, incidentally, was the issue with her new partner.

Castro agreed to reverse three of the cross-country transfers but not Tomasa's. That meant that she was now unemployed, and a courtroom clash was set to begin.

– 4 –

HAVING AGAIN DETERMINED HE WASN'T CUT OUT FOR THIS, Dionisio was planning to stick around just long enough to train Saúl Bueso, a more aggressive attorney. But once again, he didn't end up leaving. On November 4, the tag-teaming lawyers sued Delta on behalf of Tomasa for the equivalent of $3,606, and between then and December 15, they would demand $10,683 for thirteen other guards. Though those sums, in and of themselves, weren't material to a company that was going to be earning over half a million dollars from the state telecom company that year, these lawsuits still posed a threat, because if Tomasa and the others were ultimately victorious, a new precedent would be set for its entire workforce.

In November, Dina, Dionisio, and Saúl drove to what they thought was Delta's office in La Ceiba, but they were surprised to see that the signage now referred to SETECH, another Swasey-controlled private security firm. Soon thereafter, Delta guards started reporting that they were being forced to switch over to SETECH.

These shell games presumably had several purposes. First of all, serving subpoenas cost money, so it behooved a defendant to make himself as unfindable as possible—in La Ceiba, the Labor Project trio had been informed that Delta was now headquartered on the island of Roatán. Second of all, if Swasey transferred all of Delta's assets and contracts to SETECH before the trials concluded, then any judgments won would be against an essentially bankrupt entity.

The labor court in Tegucigalpa was on the third floor of the Supreme Court of Justice building. On February 1, 2006, Saúl went there to request an embargo, and on March 14, a judge ruled favorably, which meant Delta could not sell, transfer, or borrow against eight of its vehicles. This was a big win, because the value of that rolling stock significantly exceeded the litigants' claims.

During this heady period when the Labor Project solidified and gained ground—not just against Delta, but also against some fast-food chains, janitorial service providers, and other security firms—Dionisio would burst into the dull confines of the labor court with a bunch of coffees-to-share in hand while singing out, "Good morning, good morning, good morning." He and Dina would bring Tomasa gifts to help her get by, and he once spent an entire weekend helping a fired guard move houses.

That type of high-touch altruism was not something that Kurt sought out or regularly engaged in at this point in his life; the gringo instead sought to maximize his philanthropic impact by managing his staff and schedule according to the advice of corporate gurus like Peter Drucker. Dionisio, on the other hand, was all about the up-close-and-personal. In order to defeat Delta, however, he was going to have to exit his comfort zone, especially once Saúl resigned in May 2006 and he became the Labor Project's full-time attorney.

On July 18, Dionisio convinced a judge to assign a *guardian ad litem*, a court-appointed defense attorney, to represent Delta, which would allow the trials to move forward even if the truants never emerged. And incredibly, the *guardian ad litem* named was none other than Luis, the Peace and Justice attorney. That a judge would allow an ASJ employee to represent Delta was patently absurd, and that Dionisio had somehow finagled this was a clear sign that he was finally playing hardball.

Exactly one month later, he got the court to upgrade the existing embargo, to order that those eight frozen vehicles actually be seized. In another country, a diktat like that might have activated a series of bureaucratic pulleys and gears that seamlessly spit out the desired outcome. But this was Honduras, so Dionisio was essentially going to have to impound the vehicles himself.

Since confiscating property from a private security firm was obviously far outside his wheelhouse, Kurt asked Cholo to help him out. The operative quickly did his part by locating what his colleague was looking for.

In the early evening, on August 22, Dionisio drove a judicial official to a dead-end street in central Tegucigalpa, where he pulled his maroon pickup truck behind a parked Kia Towner, a tiny commercial vehicle that resembled a bug—flat face, bulbous cabin, low-slung bed. Though it had a SETECH logo on it—two lightning bolts around a silhouette of Honduras—and though it was in front of SETECH's satellite office, Dionisio knew that Delta actually owned it.

After a guard there made a phone call, two of the company's representatives argued with Dionisio and the official, but eventually, they did hand over the keys.

The official drove the Towner behind Dionisio for about fifteen minutes, until they reached Plaza San Pedro, a down-market strip mall where Dionisio owned a small retail property and was thus entitled to use a few spots in its open-air parking lot. Regarding their decision to escrow the Towner there, Kurt later said, "Dionisio asked us in advance if it was OK. . . . The other option was to put it in the Supreme Court's lot, but they charged like 50 or 100 lempiras a day"—about $2.50 or $5.00—"and this whole process could have taken a year."

Dionisio lived in a middle-class subdivision with a top-down view of the capital. He got home around nine, which wasn't abnormally late for him, and as soon as he saw Lourdes, he handed her the keys to the Towner and said, "Guard these as though they were your own eyes."

She really wished her husband would work less but also appreciated how being a hard-charging do-gooder made him feel happy and fulfilled. To justify his extreme level of dedication, he liked to say, "You chop wood today so you're not hungry tomorrow." As for what that "tomorrow" might hold, his dream was to one day work with Lourdes, who was pursuing a law degree, and he had promised his five-year-old that he would take him to Disney World, someday in the future, once more wood was chopped.

———

DINA RECORDED THE UNEXPECTED CALL SHE RECEIVED THE NEXT afternoon. It followed a basic structure: She would calmly ask a question—"Why don't you let the court subpoena you so you can explain that to a judge?"—and Swasey would respond with a hysterical, wide-ranging, semi-inscrutable diatribe. His voice indicated that he was extremely irritated, as did some of the things he said, such as: Dina stole the Towner, her team destroyed his business, her team was getting itself mixed up in a problem, and he was a person who had tentacles.

That night, seven armed men drove up to the entrance of Plaza San Pedro in a gray van and another vehicle, all of them in plain clothes except for a stout guy in a yellow polo that had the SETECH emblem on it. The shopping center was being watched by a teenager named José Adolfo Ramos, the same security guard who had let Dionisio and the judicial official enter the lot the night before. The yellow-shirted man told Ramos that he was going to be taking the truck with the insignia that matched his shirt.

The teenager could tell that these were the type of people who you couldn't say no to, so he let the man and a mechanic he was with enter the lot. The two of them managed to push the Towner out onto the street and to get it started without the key.

The following day, August 24, Dina and Dionisio broke the news to Kurt at his desk on the third floor. The gringo's mind immediately jumped to a financial concern—Was the charity going to have to pay to replace the Towner?—but Dionisio's main worry was of a different type.

A brazen crime had been committed in defiance of the court, and it therefore felt like their opponent's true colors had finally come into view. Predictably, Dionisio's instinctive response was to throw in the towel. When he and Dina stopped to chat on their way down the stairwell, he told her, "I'm out."

Dina was built to handle this sort of situation and believed her friend could too, so, standing there on the tiled stairwell, between its peach-colored walls, she silently challenged him by reaching down and cupping her hand in front of her crotch.

What she was trying to say was, *Have some cojones, man.*

———

SIX DAYS LATER, CHOLO AND MACARIO ESCORTED DIONISIO TO THE Villa Adela police station. By now, the Peace and Justice guys had become virtuosos at manipulating the police force, but in this case, things did not go smoothly. The station's complaint reception desk refused to receive their complaint, and its Vehicle Theft Unit informed them that the Towner's disappearance did not qualify as a vehicle theft. It was all a bit mystifying.

Cholo, Macario, and Dionisio then drove into a noisy warren of clogged one-way streets downtown, and at the police station there, they managed to submit their complaint. Filed under record number 8113–06, it included a copy of the embargo order, a statement from Dionisio, and a notarized testimony from Ramos, the teenage security guard, which was something Dionisio had previously arranged for.

An explanation as to why they had encountered resistance at Villa Adela walked into this station before they left. It was three of Swasey's men.

Dionisio had dealt with two of them before, but the third was unfamiliar. Roger Medina had thick wrists and broad shoulders; as it turned out, he used to work for Criminal Investigation; and according to a dossier ASJ would later produce, he now served as Swasey's "iron fist."

Professional thugs know that direct talk is completely unnecessary and instead rely on a surrealistic form of communication that is known, in Honduras, as subliminal messaging. It is saying ordinary things in a strange way or strange things as though they were ordinary; it is a slightly overwrought concern for someone else's safety; it is an intonation, a stance, a pause, a glint in the eye. The goal of this stagecraft is to unbridle a target's imagination, to send it galloping off into the most nightmarish wastelands of his mind. Done right, it can avert the need for much messier business like breaking kneecaps or kidnapping kids.

"My man, I've seen you before," Medina said to Macario.

The ponytailed attorney played along by asking whereabouts.

"I don't remember, but it doesn't matter, because I just filmed you walking out of Criminal Investigation"—as in, he had just filmed them leaving the other station, Villa Adela, and then followed them here.

The ASJ group got the hell out of there, at which point Medina filed a complaint under record number 8114–06. It falsely claimed that no embargo order existed and, therefore, that Dionisio was a carjacker.

Which of the two dueling complaints Criminal Investigation was going to prioritize became apparent two days later when Roque Martínez and another detective showed up at ASJ's office and questioned Dionisio in a tone that suggested he was not a victim but a suspect. Cholo observed that the two cops arrived in a beige Toyota 4Runner with plate PBN-7649, the same truck he had clocked as belonging to Medina outside the station downtown.

And according to Macario, when he soon went back to that station, he was informed that they did not have a complaint number 8113–06 on file.

It was starting to look like Swasey really did have as much sway over the government as his bounty of state contracts implied. Cholo had even heard whispers that one of Delta's vehicles was in the possession of Carlos Zelaya, the president's brother, who, it should be noted, was widely rumored to be a shady guy. "During Mel's presidency," a narco later told a journalist, "Happy Hour was the time of night when the radars got shut off and people tight with Mel's brother could enter the country freely."

Dina, in typical Dina fashion, had actually had the gall to call up the first brother herself on August 25. He had denied knowing anything about Delta but asked for its number, and a few minutes later, a SETECH executive called Dina and told her to leave him alone. Obviously, there was nothing even remotely conclusive about this exchange, but in time, there were going to be additional indications that Swasey was somehow linked to the Zelayas.

ASJ's next move was to submit the contents of 8113–06 directly to the Public Ministry. According to Macario, however, when he later followed up on it, "The file contained not what we presented but, to the contrary, an accusation that Delta had made against Dionisio."

And to make matters worse, the media ran with the company's version of events, some outlets with such fervor that one couldn't help but wonder if Swasey's "tentacles" were at play. On September 5, a radio host said, in a tone that implied the charity's behavior was the moral equivalent of dumping chemicals into a well, "It is important to urge all sectors of the nation to stay alert to the activities of entities like this, which, contrary to the spirit with which they are supposed to operate, involve themselves in disrespecting authority and violating the law."

On September 11, ASJ presented its side of the story at a press conference it organized in a hotel ballroom. Behind a table topped with goblet-style water glasses sat Dionisio in a dark suit, Dina in a brown T-shirt, and Tomasa with her baby boy on her lap—the infant, who had been in and out of the hospital with lung and heart problems, did not appear to be healthy.

For a previously under-the-radar charity, dealing with a smear campaign was a major burden, but Kurt tried to keep his people on offense, too. The day after the press conference, Dionisio argued Tomasa's case in court, and after Luis, the *guardian ad litem*, said almost nothing in Delta's defense, the judge announced that a verdict would be coming in two weeks' time. Given the one-sidedness of the debate, however, it felt like a foregone conclusion. In other words, Dionisio seemed to be very close to delivering a jackpot to Tomasa and striking a precedent-setting blow against the firm.

Now they just had to wait.

ASJ's office was sandwiched into a row of wall-to-wall houses on a sloping side street. Dionisio was accustomed to needy workers swinging by without notice, so at two p.m. on September 19, a day that topped out at eighty-six, when one of his colleagues let him know that someone was asking for him out front, he probably thought nothing of it.

He headed down the stairs, and in case he had to take notes, there was a pen in his shirt pocket. What was waiting for him outside the front door, however, was not what he would have expected—a guard, a janitor, or a cashier—but two Delta lawyers who wanted to chat.

Dina, who had been out and about, soon arrived and saw the three lawyers talking outside. Then she saw Swasey emerge from an unplated green sedan with tinted windows. He was wearing a black golf shirt and leather boots, and he was accompanied by at least seven associates, some of whom looked like businesspeople, and some of whom, including Medina, looked like toughs.

It was one of those supercharged moments when it felt like just about anything could happen, so an ASJ employee started taking photographs. In one of them, Medina stares at the camera without any discernible expression; in another, he is cracking up through a

Cheshire grin. And as had been the case at Plaza San Pedro, only one member of the posse was wearing the yellow SETECH polo; he was burly, and when the ASJ photographer tried to take a head-on shot of him, he turned his face away from the camera.

Everyone coalesced around Dina and Swasey. The irate mogul had about eight inches on her as well as the high ground on the sidewalk, which meant she had a direct line of sight to the ready-to-pop pimple that was located just beneath his lip. According to her, the gist of what he had to say was, *Let's resolve this*, and the gist of her response was, *Let's do that in court.*

At one point, he leaned forward, angled his arm like an Egyptian dancer, and extended his index finger toward Dina's forehead. She was well aware that a woman's body could speak volumes, so it was no accident that in her kitten-heeled boots, fitted gray bowler shirt, and chandelier earrings, she looked remarkably at ease.

Dionisio's body language was the antithesis of Dina's. Swasey and his menagerie eventually left without incident, but during their visit, Dionisio had gazed shyly at the ground and leaned awkwardly away from the argument's ground zero, as though he were sick and tired of these hostilities, as though he could not tolerate them for a single second more.

– 5 –

ONE WEEK LATER, IN THE SMALL HOURS OF THE NIGHT, DIONI-
sio and Cholo drove north with an embargo order in hand.
Once they arrived in La Ceiba, they impounded a Delta van
in collaboration with the local police, at which point Dionisio signed
the official form documenting this with the signature that had become
part of his comedic routine at the labor court—the two *D*'s in Dionisio
Díaz García, which stretched way above the rest of the runic characters, looked like a pair of an old-time cartoon character's eyeballs.

He and Cholo stored the van at a local police station and then
elected to suffer a second six-and-a-half-hour drive in a single day
rather than risk sleeping in what they thought of as Swasey's domain.

Throughout October, Dionisio continued to make strides. On the
third of the month, he sued SETECH on behalf of an employee who
claimed to have been improperly fired; this was an important mile-
stone, because that firm had been Swasey's safe haven, and because
the lawyer had several more cases against it in the hopper. And he
soon received an indication that those cases were eventually going to
prevail. On the twentieth, a judge, after having postponed the verdict,
ruled in Tomasa's favor.

This victory ended up being provisional, however, because five days later, a Delta attorney finally crawled out of the woodwork to submit an appeal.

At this point, the Labor Project was still mainly a Dina-and-Dionisio thing, but as the conflict with Swasey's firms intensified, Cholo and Macario got more and more involved. In early November, the two Peace and Justice guys made dinner plans.

Cholo arrived at the shopping mall first, and through the window of the Pizza Hut he was heading to, he saw Medina sitting with another man. According to the operative, this was unexpected, but that defies credulity. It seems much more likely that a get-together had been arranged without Kurt or Dina's say-so, especially since Macario, who soon arrived, happened to know Medina's companion, Carlos Aguilar, aka Cuervo, "the Crow," a young man with a shadow-like mustache who had once dated his cousin, and who now worked for SETECH in some capacity.

The four men chatted about their mutual interests, macho stuff like motorcycles and rock 'n' roll, and then Medina got down to brass tacks. "The time for dialogue is nearing an end," he warned.

He also offhandedly mentioned that Dina's daughter was "a hot-tie." As intended, this raised a number of alarming questions, such as, How did he even know what she looked like?

Cuervo meanwhile played the good cop. He insisted that ASJ could still negotiate with Swasey, and Cholo and Macario agreed to propose that to their colleagues.

Kurt was no longer open to settling, however, especially since his understanding of what Cuervo was referring to was a truce between ASJ and Swasey, not his companies fundamentally altering their approach to human resources. "The only person who ever wavered about that kind of stuff was Dionisio," Kurt recalled. ". . . Everyone else—Macario, Cholo, me, Dina, Carlos—thought these guys are just proving more and more that they're bad people, and we can't give in."

A day or two later, without telling anyone, Dina took a taxi to the public hospital, which was one of the many government buildings that SETECH guarded. She somehow knew that Medina would be there, and according to her, after she approached him in front of the building, she shook his hand and said, "You deliver that message directly to me. My daughter is a hottie, huh? If she so much as trips, you're going to get blamed for it."

———

THERE WAS A COMMENT SECTION UNDERNEATH EVERY *REVISTAZO* article, and ever since Dionisio confiscated the Towner, an army of trolls had been posting eerie things. Around the time of the Pizza Hut summit, "Mauri" wrote, "In the coming days, this novel of terror will come to an end."

That same day, "Richard Swasey" wrote, "I am a businessman who doesn't use bodyguards, not even a chauffeur. . . . I lament the psychological warfare this publication is waging." That comment was posted from a computer with the IP address 205.211.194.221, the same device used by eighteen other digital creatures, including "Mother of 2 boys," "Angry Honduran," "mauri," "The Finger," "Alejandra," "alejandra," and "Alejndra."

A flurry of posts landed in early November, many from "Hannibal" and "Roger Medina," but then, on the ninth of that month, the trolling just suddenly stopped.

A week or two later, around half past noon, Macario was eating at a Wendy's while keeping an eye on his motorcycle outside. According to him, at one point, he looked up and saw Cuervo sitting on it.

The young man then entered the restaurant with a smile on his face, at which point Macario said, "I guess they have you following me, you son of a bitch."

"Nah, I'm not following you," Cuervo replied. "This is a coincidence."

"You're following me."

"No, I'm not."

Cuervo soon cut to the chase: Was there going to be a negotiation or not?

Macario told him that there would not be, and when Medina showed up ten minutes later and repeated Cuervo's question, Macario repeated his answer.

It was clearly final.

Soon thereafter, on November 27, Macario received an anonymous text message: "The life of Dionisio, could be in danger!!! take care, look for someone closer to your enemies!!!!!"

In a blast email, the charity asked its donors to pray for Dionisio's safety and also for "God to change the hearts of the owners of Delta and SETECH." But at its Monday morning devotional a week later, the truth is that Kurt didn't feel particularly concerned. For some reason, perhaps his habituation to successfully ignoring danger, he thought they were several lengths away from the end of the rope, that at worst, their opponent's next salvo would be something like shooting up one of their houses—a potentiality which, coming out of his mouth years later, sounded like it would have been almost tolerable.

Carlos wasn't in attendance that morning because of a conflict, but he had met with Dionisio over the weekend, and from his perspective, all the subliminal messaging had come across not as a red alert but as a panicking punk's bluster. And to his point, Delta really was against the ropes—the grand finale of Tomasa's case, the appeal hearing, was scheduled for that afternoon.

Cholo and Macario went out to grab a quick breakfast, and when they returned, they saw Dionisio carrying a bunch of files toward his pickup. He normally wore slacks, but he was on his way to court, so he was dressed in a light gray suit.

At various moments throughout this saga, Dionisio had clearly felt afraid, but recently, he had been telling his colleagues that he didn't think anything bad would happen to him because he hadn't done anything wrong, as though fairness were a force of nature. He liked to listen to romantic music, but as he motored west on Boulevard Fuerzas Armadas, he had his radio tuned to the morning news.

He soon drove past the Francisco Morazán National Pedagogical University, a campus of brick buildings where, earlier that year, he had attended a seminar on human rights; at one point, the teacher had made each of the attendees answer a profound question out loud— How do you want to be remembered?

Roadwork was blocking a lane up ahead, as it had been for several weeks now, so as could have been predicted, the boulevard's high-speed flow of two-lane traffic bottlenecked into a single glacial line. The attorney wedged his truck between a blue car and a white taxi, with no room to maneuver in either direction. He would have been able to see workmen filling potholes, a vendor at a roadside stall, and a barren mountainside off in the distance.

It was sunny.

Dionisio wanted to be remembered as a happy person.

- 6 -

KURT RUSHED TO THE SCENE—NO STOPLIGHTS, A SIX- OR seven-minute tear—thinking there must be some way to fix this because he was the type of person who could always find ways to fix things. After he passed through the police tape cordoning off Boulevard Fuerzas Armadas, however, he got to see what unfix-able looked like: The man he had just prayed with was leaning over his center console, his left cheek laced with drying blood, his right hand tightened into a cadaverous clutch.

This was a professional job, no doubt about it. Two men on a motorcycle had pulled up to the lawyer's window; bullets had struck his neck, face, and ear; nothing had been stolen; and no one else had been harmed.

There is a lot of mythology about *sicarios* in Honduras, and one thing said about elite hitmen is that they plant undercover lookouts to keep an eye on the immediate response to their handiwork. That was why Cholo, who was standing under a tree on the shoulder of the boulevard, was already in Cholo mode, photographing the group of rubberneckers lingering on the median, among them a lanky guy in a tank top and a muscular man holding a radio.

Another thing said about the slyest sicarios is that they time and position their killings so that an allied detective will get assigned the case. Dionisio happened to have been murdered within the jurisdiction of Villa Adela, the station where he, Cholo, and Macario had been unable to submit a complaint, and the detective now surveying the crime scene was Agent Martínez, who, according to Cholo, had previously shown up at ASJ's office in a SETECH vehicle.

The lawyer's corpse was later brought to a mortuary for the wake. Because Dina had been the one who recruited him, she felt like some of its attendees silently blamed her for what had happened. Nevertheless, she still spent the entire night on the floor of the funeral parlor.

At the cemetery the next day, Carlos and five other pallbearers carried a lacquered wooden casket to the edge of a rectangular hole. He didn't like the idea of ranking deaths by their atrociousness, but he couldn't help but think, *Of everyone, why did it have to be Dionisio?* That the sacrificial lamb had been the cheerful pacifist felt blackly ironic and surgically cruel, as though this were an Olympian deity's diabolical act of revenge.

The dead attorney was covered up in soil, and then, as the mourners festooned his burial mound with a kaleidoscopic assortment of flowers, his young son ate an ice cream cone.

Kurt, who was wearing a black turtleneck in the bright midday sun, felt anger, so much anger, toward the man who, in his mind, had undoubtedly orchestrated this. And he also felt guilt, a lot of that, too, because this tragedy was undeniably a byproduct of his Gospel of Courage. For the time being, however, he was largely repressing those painful emotions, because he could not assume that this was a one-off attack. In other words, his guard was up.

A security expert with the International Justice Mission sent him some recommended safety precautions, and at an all-hands-on-deck meeting the following day, he relayed them to his shell-shocked staff—be suspicious of door-to-door salespeople; switch up the timing and route of your commute; drive circuitously to determine whether you are being followed; and angle your car seat so that your head is aligned with the steel rod in the window framing.

Toward the top of the list of ASJ people presumably now in danger was Carlos. Though, on paper, he was just a board member, in reality, he was more than that, and at ceremonious events like that training seminar, he was basically presented as the charity's leader, in large part because Kurt thought it was inappropriate for a gringo to be running a Honduran organization.

Given the circumstances, it probably would have been prudent for Carlos to leave the country or at least relocate to a well-guarded building, but he didn't do anything like that. The reason why was that he felt safest in Nueva Suyapa, not because it was objectively safe, but because, having devoted his life to the place, he believed it would protect him from harm.

If the barrio really did possess karmic powers, then arguably, nobody deserved to benefit from them more than Carlos. Weeks before Dionisio's assassination, he had gotten to experience the sublime joy of announcing the names of his first batch of Genesis grads as they received their diplomas on a stage; incredibly, the majority of them would be going off to college.

And that was just one of his many philanthropic feats. His microlender had grown to serve about five hundred borrowers. One woman who initially took out a loan to start hawking candies on the street was now running a restaurant, and according to a man whose parents borrowed to expand their bodega, "If it weren't for Genesis, we wouldn't be here. Of my seven siblings, the oldest three are lawyers, the next is a doctor, the next is a dentist, and the other two are doctors."

Carlos's large portfolio of responsibilities meant he had no choice but to get on with his life, despite the possibility of a follow-up attack. Three days after the assassination, he began descending the barrio's switchback on a scooter he borrowed to be able to weave through the inevitable morning traffic. A friend who needed a lift was holding on to him, and about halfway down the descent, Carlos noticed that a motorcycle with two men on it had fallen in behind them.

He kept going.

On the one hand, Two Men on a Motorcycle was essentially the real-life manifestation of the Honduran Grim Reaper; on the other, two men on a motorcycle, doing whatever harmless thing they happened to be doing, was a ubiquitous sight in the city.

Carlos crossed the entry bridge, looped three-quarters of the way around a traffic circle, and then headed west on a boulevard, presumably wondering, as he nervously checked his mirrors amid a cacophony of rumbles, honks, and exhaust, whether he was imagining things, and if he wasn't, what the hell he should do about it.

He dropped his passenger off and then, about ten minutes later, parked on the cobblestones in front of the post office, a neoclassical building with a corner-facing entryway. After he went inside to retrieve a package, he came back out and saw that the same riders were there. Now he was completely terrified. And calling for help wasn't an option, because he had forgotten his cellphone.

He hopped on the scooter and sped off, believing that to stop was to die, that right now, locomotion was his guardian angel. But unfortunately for him, up ahead, in front of the public hospital, a red light was shining.

Screw it. Carlos ran the light, veered into a parking lot, darted into a Dunkin' Donuts, and locked himself in the bathroom.

Alone with the toilet smells, time ticked by.

About thirty minutes later, he went for it, burst out of the store, and then he rode all the way back to Genesis, where he found his cellphone on his desk.

It soon vibrated. A text message in English had come through. "You are next because you are the heat," it read, that last word seemingly a misspelling of "head," as in the head of ASJ.

Those eight words hit Carlos like a poison. He managed to keep himself glued together long enough to complete some urgent tasks, like recording his testimony at a government agency called the National Commission for Human Rights. But when he got back home later that day, a cocktail of panic, impotence, and rage melted him down into hysterics. And on top of all those horrible feelings, there was a kicker: As he came to realize that his tear ducts were selfish—for he had not wept for Dionisio this intensely—he also felt ashamed.

The next day, many of his neighbors came by. A group of teenagers, some of whom had taken full advantage of his hospitality over the years—the free dinners, the mattresses on the floor, and the like—informed him that, for the time being, they were going to be following him around. Even they knew the sicario folklore, knew that assassins preferred to strike when their targets were alone. For the next few days, whenever Carlos mobilized, a caravan would form, with a couple of his neighbors driving in front of him, a couple more driving behind, and the teenagers riding in the bed of his pickup.

A LINCHPIN OF KURT AND CARLOS'S SHARED IDENTITY HAD LONG been a blasé attitude about safety and a not-so-subtle contempt for the privileged people who cowered behind gates and guards. But now that there was a dead employee on their ledger, they had to accept that their daredevil era had come to a close.

The normal way to protect a workforce was to hire private security, but that was costly, and furthermore, ASJ had been an antagonist to that entire industry. Therefore, the best solution would be to get assigned official police protection. Whether or not that happened would come down to the whims of the éminence grise who helmed the National Commission for Human Rights, Dr. Ramón Custodio. Unfortunately, he and Dina were at odds.

Their beef began before the assassination. Dina had notified his commission about Delta and SETECH's threatening behavior, with the expectation that it would get the charity set up with a retinue of police bodyguards. But the commission hadn't done that, so at a press conference the day of her friend's burial, a weeping Dina had accused Custodio of malpractice.

From there, things had only gotten worse. Dina had been the one to escort Carlos to the commission right after the motorcycle chase, and according to her, while there, Custodio pulled her aside and said that because of something he knew about Swasey's companies but could not elaborate on, ASJ should back off. This comment was ostensibly helpful, but the eminent man who had seen it all should have known that in a country where friendly heads-ups and hostile threats were often syntactically indistinguishable, it would hit Dina like a total mindfuck.

Four days later, on December 11, she, Kurt, Carlos, and Luis, the Peace and Justice lawyer, went to the commission's headquarters, a two-story glass building. Dina meant business—unbeknownst to her two bosses, she had hidden a recording device on her person.

After chairs screeched into place, Kurt, in an uncharacteristically hesitant voice, explained that they had come to request police protection and to find out what Custodio knew about their adversary.

It happened to be the elder statesman's seventy-sixth birthday, but as he responded in a drowsy and lugubrious manner, it became clear that he was not in a festive mood. "Kurt," he said, "you know the Honduran reality. They"—as in, Kurt's Honduran colleagues—"are the ones being victimized. You are not. And neither is this security business. . . . One Honduran has already died. You are not going to die. Nor will the director of this security business."

"I understand that, doctor," Kurt replied, "but Dina says you intimated that you know more—"

"I don't have to intimate anything. Nor should she overinterpret. I cannot say more."

"Something about these people being responsible for some sort of massacre, that you know something about his business associates, and that that can help us—"

"I can't go any further than that. I am now repeating myself."

There was a pause, and then Kurt said, "I guess that's all then."

"If she, you, or he"—Custodio pointed at Dina, Carlos, and Luis, deliberately excluding the gringo—"requests *my* protection, then I will give it. But I am not going to get involved in a conflict when I don't understand all the implications."

"Your request for protection has been made. . . . Any other questions?" Custodio's colleague interjected, clearly hoping to bring these unpleasantries to an end.

Dina had had enough. "Yes, I have a bunch of questions," she said. "But the doctor is not going to answer a single one of them."

Custodio shot back, "I don't want to get involved in a conflict I have already warned you about."

"Doctor," Dina replied, "if you were sitting where I'm sitting, and I was the commissioner, how would you feel?"

"I don't know how you should feel. Honestly, I'm just trying to do my duty as humanely and ethically as possible."

"If I were in your position, I would provide information to a fellow Honduran whose life is at risk."

"I am saying—"

"You could give us more information but are choosing not to. In my opinion, that is irresponsible."

"I appreciate that. I'll have it officially documented that she thinks I'm not fulfilling my duties as a public functionary and a human being. Consider it noted."

"Great. And I'll repeat that anywhere I want."

"And I'll repeat, once again, that you, you, and you"—he again left out Kurt—"have my protection. . . . Is that understood?"

"Yes, understood."

"Good. That's what I like. Speaking clearly and precisely. I don't want to discuss this anymore."

Kurt, Carlos, Dina, and Luis marched toward the exit of the building, and the instant one of them opened the front door, they all burst into laughter—intense, uproarious, childlike laughter. Kurt tried saying something about "the little old man" but was unable to complete a full sentence. The fact that this bewildering curmudgeon was responsible for their safety was utterly outrageous, and for now, gallows humor was all they had.

———

DESPITE EVERYTHING, ASJ WANTED TO STAY ON THE ATTACK. IT HAD to be cautious with its words, however, because in Honduras, the punishments for slander, defamation, and libel were severe.

In the days after the Custodio standoff, the charity paid to run a spread in *El Heraldo* and *La Prensa*; it included a photo of Dionisio, a photo of Swasey, and the observation that the assassinated lawyer "defended the labor rights of security guards who worked for SETECH and Delta Security Services, among other companies." At the bottom of the ad, in bold capitalized letters, the charity implored the government to suspend all its contracts with SETECH, which, by its estimate, added up to over $3 million per year.

On December 20, three of Swasey's executives appeared on the country's preeminent morning talk show, *Frente a Frente*, to rebut the allegation implicit in the charity's spread. In their defense, one of them said, "I received training in human rights law at the International Human Rights Court in the Hague. I would never advise someone to violate a human right." And in general, they presented themselves as the good guys. "ASJ should meet up with us because we also don't want the murder of a lawyer to remain in impunity," one of them added.

The following day, one of Swasey's lawyers reached out to an ASJ attorney, and after the two of them met up, the latter told Kurt that the other side still wanted a rapprochement. "Swasey told his lawyers that what has been happening is hurting his business's reputation and impacting his finances," the ASJ lawyer wrote to Kurt, before adding a detail that, through the lens of subliminal messaging, sounded quite sinister: "They also talked about knowing who Dina is."

At this point, it would have been hard to fault Kurt and Carlos for waving the white flag. The world is an unpleasant place when the subtlest attributes of your day-to-day surroundings—expressions, postures, bulges, shadows, accelerations—could be split-second warnings of your forthcoming demise. And frightening things had happened almost every single day since the assassination. For instance, a man on a motorcycle had asked someone in front of Genesis where Carlos lived, and a security-industry insider had written to Kurt, Carlos, and Dina, "You have some serious adversaries who want to harm your people."

Some of the charity's employees were thinking about quitting, and all the unexpected expenses—the funeral, the newspaper ads, the bars on the office windows—meant the charity was going to have a tough time making payroll. Carlos was having nightmares, and Kurt was having difficulty sleeping.

The only release of whatever was brewing inside the gringo seems to have been an incendiary email he sent to, of all people, a group of Jo Ann's relatives: "I am writing this without Jo Ann's permission but I have been saddened by your lack of communication during this very hard time. . . . It reminds me of several years ago when Jo Ann was in the hospital for three days and in bed for over a week with pneumonia. We were very worried and never heard from any of you either."

His provocation unearthed a gripe that must have been festering for a while. "HOW ABOUT YOU SEND MY SISTER & MY NIECE & NEPHEW BACK TO THE STATES ON A PLANE RIGHT NOW!" one of Jo Ann's siblings replied. "I AM CHILLED AS I

READ THE EMAIL ABOUT SOMEONE BEING KILLED WHO YOU WORKED WITH SO CLOSELY."

"Honestly, an email or phone call in which you say 'Get on a plane' would be way better than silence," Kurt fired back. "Don't think we have not considered it. Also don't think that I am in control (that I could put Jo Ann on a plane or am keeping her from doing it.) . . . ASJ is a part of who we are and what we believe God is calling us to do. If Christians do not stand up for the victims of abuse, robbery, rape, murder, then who should?"

Soon thereafter, Kurt wrote again, "Well, I just told Jo Ann about this email and she is not too happy. And I think she is right. . . . I can blame the stress and tiredness, but in the end, I am sorry I did it the way I did. . . . I also know that it is not always easy to know what to say or how to say it and that you don't always understand what we do and why."

Everyone needed a breather.

A few days before Christmas, a pile of luggage was strapped onto the roof of a fifteen-passenger van, and sixteen people and a stool were loaded inside of it—four Ver Beeks; four Hernándezes; Dina plus her three kids; and Macario, his partner, and their two children. They drove all the way through Nicaragua to a coffee-growing region in Costa Rica, where a friend of Kurt's owned a cabin that overlooked a mountain meadow.

Being outside their theater of combat gave them a chance to feel what they needed to feel and to clearheadedly discuss some big-picture questions, such as, Should they go after Dionisio's killers? The charity happened to have a homicide-solving operation in-house, but Peace and Justice's purpose was broad and philanthropic—it was about making entire neighborhoods safe. This pursuit felt different. What would hunting down Dionisio's murderers really accomplish? And to what extent would doing so just be an externalization of their "fear and anger"?

The turkey they had intended to cook on Christmas Eve was spoiled, but that didn't stop them from creating the carefree evening they all desperately needed. Carlos's ultraconservative church considered dancing to be a borderline sin, but after someone placed a radio on the porch, he got in on the action anyway. As the adults danced and sang along to "La Bilirrubina," a *bachata* track about lovesickness, Carlos's elder son, Carlos Daniel, could sense that they had an emotional breakthrough.

The four families toured around Costa Rica for a few days, and whenever they were about to do an activity, a jokester among them would say, "You, you, you, and you can participate," while pointing at some people but not Kurt. Carlos, meanwhile, wouldn't stop complaining about how overrated the country was. "These beaches have nothing on Honduras's," he kept muttering.

He was entitled to his own opinion, but relative to the rest of Central America, Costa Rica was, in fact, a laudable anomaly, a safe, middle-income, highly literate country that citizens didn't flee en masse. It even ranked as one of the happiest nations on earth!

The worthwhile project of trying to make Honduras more like Costa Rica was currently well beyond the frontier of Kurt and Carlos's sphere of influence, but just as the murder of Javier, Fidelia's husband, once shunted them toward Peace and Justice, the murder of Dionisio would eventually lead to a drastic enlargement of their dreams. But that would come later. As for what to do in the here and now, there was, of course, only one place to find the answer.

The New Testament, the Christian half of the Bible, is known to promote a fairly unnatural response to being victimized—namely, you are supposed to turn your cheek and love your enemy. But Nicholas Wolterstorff, the philosopher Kurt admired, has jumped through all sorts of hoops to argue that meting out justice to victimizers is also scripturally valid: "The quizzical lawyer asks Jesus, 'What is the essence of the law?' Jesus then quotes the Old Testament—doesn't just summarize it, actually quotes Leviticus 19 . . . which culminates with the injunction to love your neighbor as yourself. Preceding that is a long list of examples of love, and one of them is: When your neighbor does something wrong, you shall reprove him, or you will incur guilt yourself. Now that's really striking. The right kind of punishment is an act of love."

That type of love was precisely what Kurt and Carlos aimed to show Dionisio's killers.

– 7 –

A NUMBER OF CHARACTERS WHO SEEMED TO HAVE WALKED OFF the pages of a spy novel started feeding Kurt and his people gossip about the assassination. This flock of little birdies included several Honduran spooks, a person Cholo nicknamed the Wizard of Oz, a French mercenary, and an American military vet who instructed Kurt, the first time they met up, to go to a hotel and look for a man with a newspaper. Who were these people really, and what were they after? Were they kind souls helping a charity in duress? Greedy exploiters angling to get paid? Or double agents attempting to misdirect? That ambiguity was one of the problems with this ecosystem of back-channel rumormongering; it was undoubtedly awash in conjecture, hyperbole, gamesmanship, and lies, but ASJ still felt like it had to tap into it. One message that emerged, loud and clear, from various sources, was that Swasey was even dodgier than previously imagined.

A little history.

Cocaine originally got to the United States via speedboats and airplanes that hopscotched across the Caribbean Sea. Starting in the early eighties, the American antinarcotics apparatus spent billions of dollars on a quasi-military operation to intercept those vessels, and eventually, it did succeed in all but shutting down this gateway. But as seems to be the golden rule of the War on Drugs, this had little impact on the availability of cocaine in the United States, because the narcos simply shifted their routes westward, to a path with less resistance.

The easternmost section of Honduras's Caribbean coastline is the northern edge of Mosquitia, one of the densest jungles on earth, and southwest of that is the vast ranchland of Olancho. Turboprops packed to the gills with plastic-wrapped kilos would take off from Venezuela at night and buzz an hour or two across the pitch-black airway to Mosquitia and Olancho, while additional product was shipped aboard boats camouflaged with dark blue paint. The Honduran narcos were the connective tissue between the Andean cartels, which handled manufacturing and that first leg of the journey, and the Mexican cartels, which handled most of the overland movement to the United States. These intermediaries would truck payloads from, say, a landing strip in Mosquitia to Honduras's border with Guatemala. That short transit route was freakishly valuable, and right in the middle of it was La Ceiba, the small city where Swasey resided.

The impresario has never been charged with any narcotrafficking-related crimes, but that didn't stop the little birdies from claiming he was a heavy hitter. That innuendo alone would have scared most anyone off his scent, and additionally, throughout January 2007, the ASJ staff experienced a series of hard-to-interpret incidents: When the receptionist walked past a parked pickup truck on the eleventh, a window rolled down halfway to reveal a man she recognized as Swasey; Macario noticed that a green sedan with no license plates followed him on the fourteenth; after two employees got into a bizarre traffic altercation on the nineteenth, the charity ran the plates of the SUV involved in it and discovered that it was registered to Carlos Zelaya, the president's brother; and finally, on the twenty-fourth, a neighbor saw a man in a black vehicle photograph the compound where Kurt and Carlos lived.

If Swasey actually was a mafioso, then it was going to be next to impossible to convict him of anything, because Honduras's justice system was generally too frail and venal to cope with extremely rich criminals.

Kurt had been hoping that the International Justice Mission, which supported ASJ with donations and advice, and which courageously took on sex traffickers and slave owners across the world, would help them out with this case. In February, however, an IJM executive wrote, "We feel that the danger far outweighs the possibility of success with regard to Delta/SETECH. We do not believe the case is doable. We are concerned about the safety of your staff, their families, and your own. . . . We fear that this case is beyond your capacity as well as ours."

THERE IS A BASIC ARCHITECTURE TO A PROFESSIONAL KILLING: A mastermind orders it, intermediaries plan it out, and assassins do the deed. For obvious reasons, the sicarios tend to be the most exposed portion of the conspiratorial structure, and in Dionisio's case, they were remarkably exposed, because neither had worn a helmet or a mask when they committed murder on a busy boulevard in broad daylight. According to Cholo, this almost unbelievable nonchalance can be explained by the country's almost unbelievable level of impunity; in other words, the assassins probably weren't worried about getting caught.

By the end of January, the charity had identified a number of persons of interest, including some suspected sicarios, a handful of Delta and SETECH employees, and five crooked cops. Then, on February 16, a little birdy proffered another one directly to Kurt.

At the time, this suspect, César Amador, didn't stand out, but he should have, because as the charity would later learn, he was the camera-shy, yellow-shirted man who had shown up at its office with

Swasey. He also happened to be a poster boy for the revolving-door relationship between Criminal Investigation and SETECH. He was currently an active-duty detective, but while serving out a seven-month suspension for committing what was described in a court record as "the crime of bribery," he had gone to work for SETECH.

Because there was so much intermingling between the company and the force, the official investigation into Dionisio's murder felt like a sham from the start. The leadership of Criminal Investigation had rejected Cholo's plea to yank Agent Martínez off the case, which meant the operative had no choice but to work with a detective who, in his mind, was a SETECH lackey. Nevertheless, the two of them got to it.

Cholo located the home of a woman who had been selling *baleadas* on the side of the boulevard the day of the murder—as the taco is to Mexico, and the pupusa is to El Salvador, the baleada, or "the woman who was shot," is the quintessential Honduran dish, a pillowy flour tortilla folded over refried red beans, runny cream, and crumbly cheese. This vendor, whom the charity code-named Baleadas, admitted to having seen two men kill Dionisio and to hearing one of them scream, "We got that son of a bitch!"

The next step was going to be showing her photos of the persons of interest. Kurt worried that Cholo would focus exclusively on his own pet theory—those five crooked cops—so on February 17, he urged the operative to also make sure to show her the other suspects, including Amador.

Soon thereafter, Cholo and Agent Martínez met up with her. After looking through the photos they brought along, she informed them that the sicario who piloted the motorcycle was not Amador but Junior Grandes, a SETECH employee who had previously worked in Criminal Investigation.

With that identification made, it had to be assumed that Baleadas's life was in jeopardy, so on February 22, a judge approved the Public Ministry's request to hold an anticipatory statement hearing, which was permitted when a witness might not survive for much longer.

Later that afternoon, Cholo drove Baleadas, Agent Martínez, and a prosecutor to the courthouse. According to Cholo, just before the hearing began, Baleadas had some unsupervised alone time with Agent Martínez.

Once she took the stand, the prosecutor asked what he thought was a rhetorical question, "Can you recognize and identify the culprits?"

"I didn't see them," she replied. "The motorcycle was moving fast."

This contradicted what she had said before. "What about the photo album the detective showed you?" the prosecutor said, in an attempt to salvage this.

"The riders were little fat guys—light-skinned and stocky."

"Was this man on the motorcycle?" the prosecutor asked, as he showed her a photo of Grandes.

"I don't know. I don't remember."

Soon thereafter, the defense attorney went in for the kill: "Would you be able to recognize those guys if you saw them again?"

"No."

The hearing was over in ten minutes.

———

THE CHARITY HOPED TO PINCH MEDINA, SWASEY'S "IRON FIST," FOR an easier-to-solve crime in the hopes that that could be used as leverage to get him to squeal about the assassination. He and a man who was now a senior official in Criminal Investigation had once been accused of carjacking in the eastern city of Danlí. That sounded promising, but in Honduras, the only record of a crime could be inside a manila folder next to an easy-to-intimidate civil servant, and Medina, who used to work in Criminal Investigation himself, seemed to know how to play the bureaucracy like a fiddle.

After Cholo traveled to Danlí, he wrote to Kurt, "THE

RECORD IS LOST THAT IS TO SAY IT WAS NOT FOUND IN THE ARCHIVE. . . . SO THIS PERSON CANNOT BE CAPTURED."

Medina's remaining vulnerability was Ramos, the teenage parking lot guard who, back in December, had told Cholo and Agent Martínez that Medina was one of the men who had taken the Towner. The ten-to-fifteen-year sentence he could have gotten slapped with for that sounded like a lot of potential leverage, and that was why Cholo and Macario had been urging the Public Ministry to arrange for Ramos's testimony to get recorded at one of those anticipatory statement hearings. As of March 2007, however, that still hadn't happened.

This was indicative of ASJ's general sense that the ministry was slow-playing the case and stonewalling them. The prosecutors' excuse for this was that they wanted to avoid the perception that the charity was tampering with the investigation. Fair enough, but the charity was allowed to tamper with other homicide cases, so one couldn't help but wonder if there were "tentacles" influencing things behind the scenes. After Cholo finally managed to speak to the prosecutor handling the auto-theft cases, on March 8, he shared his exasperation with Kurt: "She was very clear in affirming the following: 'I am in the middle of a training course and don't know how the vehicle investigations are going.'"

The following night, Cholo noticed an unplated 4Runner with aftermarket spotlights fall in behind his station wagon. He accelerated, swerved, gained some distance, turned down a dirt lane, and shut off his lights to dissolve into the darkness.

When Kurt heard about this, his initial reflex—even now—was to assume that it was a coincidental road-rage incident, but it must have made him a little nervous, because twelve days later, on March 21, he entertained something that had previously been off the table: negotiating. "What do you think about the idea of us looking for . . . someone neutral to open a dialogue with someone at SETECH?" he wrote to Carlos, Dina, Macario, and Jo Ann.

Four days later, Ramos, the teenage parking lot guard, was hanging out with eight people in the eastern half of the city. A white van stopped in front of them, and the man who jumped out of it shot Ramos. Just him, nobody else.

———

ONE OF THE GREAT MYSTERIES ABOUT SWASEY WAS HOW HE MANaged to win *so many* government contracts. It almost certainly wasn't because his firms were especially adept at providing security. Two years earlier, *El Heraldo* reported that the Health Secretariat had chosen to renew SETECH's contract for the public hospital in Tegucigalpa even though, in recent months, gear had been stolen from Pathology and Orthopedics, a fire had broken out in Oncology, and two people had been murdered on-site. And these revelations had not rectified the problem; since then, *La Tribuna* had run the following headlines: "Mareros Invade Hospital to Murder Burned Youth," "Perverts Infiltrate Rooms in Maternity Ward," and "Unstoppable Misdeeds at Hospital Escuela."

Swasey being a narco would go a long way toward making sense of his bounty of federal contracts, because Honduran narcos were known to launder money through licit front companies that bribed politicians in order to win bids. This made Swasey's supposed relationship with the first brother look extremely fishy. "When Carlos and Mel Zelaya go to La Ceiba," one little birdy claimed, "they go out on his yacht." And according to another one of the charity's sources, "Carlos Zelaya has been going from ministry to ministry threatening ministers not to cancel SETECH's contracts."

If Swasey truly was an organized crime boss, then it was unlikely that any witnesses, including his underlings, would ever dare to testify against him, even if juicy plea deals were on the table. That is why roundabout maneuvers have often been the only viable way to topple kingpins. For example, what brought down Al Capone wasn't his role in the Saint Valentine's Day Massacre but an audit conducted by the Internal Revenue Service, and what ended the reign of Juan Matta Ballesteros, Honduras's greatest narco—who, funny enough, owned a private security firm himself—was an illegal rendition to the United States.

Kurt pushed Cholo to trace how cash had been flowing into and out of SETECH in the hopes that they'd find evidence of money laundering, bribery, or tax evasion. In order to get that financial information, however, entities like the Finance Secretariat and the Superior Accounts Tribunal would have to cooperate, and simply put, there were certain personages that your average bureaucrat was never going to go near. None of this went anywhere.

———

ONE OF THE ONLY POSITIVE DEVELOPMENTS FOR THE CHARITY WAS that its security situation had improved. It had installed barbed wire and a heavy-duty door at the office, and because of Dr. Custodio, the crotchety but true-to-his-word commissioner, an elite police unit called the Cobras had assigned a team of agents to protect Kurt, Carlos, Macario, Dina, and another *Revistazo* journalist.

This free contingent of around-the-clock bodyguards was a blessing, all things considered, but it was also a source of stress. "Suddenly there was this big guy, completely bald, looked like the Rock, riding around in our car with us," Carlos's son, Carlos Daniel, remembered with great annoyance. Carlos and Dina worried that their guards would sell them out; Jo Ann hated the optics of Kurt being shadowed by a chaperone; and when the charity learned that the Honduran National Police was paying the Cobras a measly amount and also not reimbursing them for their work-related expenses, it decided, in order to not be hypocritical, to voluntarily supplement their salaries, even though its coffers were far from flush.

The charity had raised about $50,000 right after Dionisio's assassination, but most of that money had already been spent, and on April

14, Kurt was notified that at the end of the month, ASJ's sister charity in the United States—the shell through which most of its funding came—would have only a few thousand dollars left in the bank.

Another pressing problem was that Cholo hadn't been assigned any Cobras. "I'm really worried about him," Macario wrote to Kurt and Carlos, on April 18. "Unlike us, the homie has no protection. . . . Maybe divine protection, but I wouldn't count on that."

That night, the mother of Cholo's son received a call from a stranger whose voice sounded muffled. "You take care of yourself," the caller said, multiple times.

Two days later, a *Revistazo* journalist noticed a car with unusual antennas parked near the office, and three days after that, a man approached two ASJ interns at a bank and asked if they knew Dina and Macario.

Kurt had seen enough. He tried getting Cholo a visa to travel to the United States, but the American embassy didn't come through, so around May 1, the operative decamped to Guatemala City, where the International Justice Mission, which had an office there, got him set up with a room in a theological seminary. It was a perfectly comfortable hideout, but he was eager to get back on the hunt. While he waited for his bosses to decide whether or not they were going to let him do that, he read books, visited art museums, and went to the zoo, where he got to see a giraffe and a hippo for the first time in his life.

With Cholo deactivated, the murder investigation was on ice, and the Labor Project was back to the basics. A lawyer named Félix Cáceres had assumed Dionisio's job back in February, and he was now representing about thirty SETECH guards. That he had been willing to fill a position whose prior occupant had been killed in the line of duty indicated that he was an exceptionally brave attorney, but everyone has their limits. On May 18, he informed Kurt that he was resigning because of an anonymous text he had received: "Back off SETECH or we will leave you like Dionisio."

Now *everything* was either at a standstill or dead in the water, and there was also a sense among some of the charity's staff that the organization was rudderless and out of control, that Kurt, who frequently traveled around Honduras with his students, and Carlos, whose day job was still running Genesis, didn't quite qualify as full-time leadership. A consistent source of blowups at the office was the tension between Dina, who ran the Labor Project, and Cholo and Macario, who refused to keep her in the loop about the investigation.

Even Tomasa, who was poised to receive a windfall should the charity just nudge her case through appeals, knew it was time to surrender. According to her, she told her contacts at ASJ, "So that there's no more death, let's just drop this."

Shutting down her case was one thing; completely backing off SETECH and the investigation, across all fronts, was another. But as it happened, Kurt was about to be offered that type of all-encompassing out by none other than the man, the myth, the legend: Richard Swasey himself.

The tycoon was suing Kurt for defamation on the grounds that ASJ's newspaper ad had insinuated that he was responsible for Dionisio's murder; his suit also made sure to point out that the charity had been calling him the owner of SETECH when, in reality, his son was.

This litigation posed an existential threat to ASJ, because a large judgment could have brought about its financial ruin. That was why, when Kurt and Macario headed to the courthouse to attend a mandatory mediation on May 22, the gringo could feel fear and apprehension in his stomach. And then there was also just his general nervousness about finally coming face-to-face with Swasey, who, in his mind, was an angry and homicidal crook.

At a table with a judge presiding, Macario and Swasey's attorney sparred about the merits of the case, but to Kurt's surprise, throughout the mediation, he found Swasey, who was wearing a loose button-down and a seaman's watch, to be calm, reasonable, and somehow sort of trustworthy. Kurt's understanding was that the executive would drop the suit if he publicly apologized for linking him to the assassination, and more broadly, that what his opponent was really putting on the table was a total armistice.

Kurt had not gone there that day prepared to accept anything like that, but for a reason so mysterious he would later wonder if he had been brainwashed, he now felt open to cutting a deal. He and Macario agreed to send their counterparts a proposed settlement agreement by June 5.

That same day, Cholo, who was back in town, and who obviously wanted to do the exact opposite of settling, asked Kurt if he could reengage with Agent Martínez. "I think I should do it but need you to give me the go-ahead," the operative wrote.

When Kurt got home that night, he caught up with Jo Ann. Though she didn't have day-to-day responsibilities at the office, she sat on the charity's board, and Kurt considered her to be a full coconspirator in his and Carlos's locuras. He would even sometimes forward her work-related emails with questions like, "Any good ideas on how to work our way through this tomorrow? I love you! Me."

So naturally, he told his wife all about the chance Swasey was giving them to put this whole debacle in the past, to finally be done with the dead-end investigation, the stifling bodyguards, the financial stress, and the constant deathwatch.

"You're not seriously considering that—are you?" Jo Ann asked.

"No," Kurt replied. "But—"

"No, but?" Jo Ann cut him off.

Two weeks later, on June 5, the deadline for a settlement offer, Macario informed the court that one would not be forthcoming.

– 8 –

THE CHARITY WASN'T GOING TO FORFEIT, BUT OUT OF RESPECT for the Public Ministry's concerns about tampering, it did take a step back from the investigation. This gave Kurt and Carlos a few months to focus on a related initiative.

If the person they suspected of masterminding the Dionisio hit was actually at fault, and if that individual was as politically formidable as alleged, then the government was going to punish him and his underlings only if the charity acquired clout and used it to apply pressure.

ASJ tried to do that in a number of ways, such as by organizing demonstrations and press conferences, but in truth, the real action happened abroad. As of August 2007, Carlos had met with congressional staffers in Washington, DC; he and Dina had met with parliamentarians in London; and he and Kurt had met with Congressman Vernon Ehlers in Grand Rapids, Michigan. What they were trying to do through all that was tap into a certain transnational power structure: Rich-world politicians can influence their countries' far-flung diplomats, and those diplomats can, in turn, influence officials in aid-dependent nations like Honduras.

Carlos was the charity's primary dignitary, both at home and overseas, not just because he was Honduran, but also because he could simplify a situation and demarcate its moral topography in a way that made him a far more compelling public figure than Kurt, the slightly hokey sociologist who adored lists, slideshows, and graphs. But that doesn't mean Carlos enjoyed this role. In fact, telling Dionisio's story over and over again pained him, in part because he had the self-awareness to know that by using it to pull on heartstrings, he was incidentally marketing *himself* as some kind of courageous, worker-protecting hero. That side of this made him feel icky, and in combination with the grief, the guilt, the fear, the migraines, and the incessant international travel, he was having a tough time.

He started taking Lexapro, an SSRI used to treat anxiety and depression. Though he didn't mention that to Kurt, soon thereafter, the gringo told him that *he* was taking the exact same medication. Jo Ann had persuaded him to go see a psychiatrist because there were mornings when he couldn't get out of bed.

One bright spot in their world was that Dina had received Amnesty International UK's Special Award for Human Rights Journalism Under Threat, a prize given out to one reporter in the world each year. To celebrate her accomplishment, the charity threw a reception on August 7, in a ballroom in Tegucigalpa, and over two hundred people, some of whom were diplomats and government officials, showed up. This was Dina's night, but it was also an opportunity to canonize Dionisio in front of a powerful audience, so on a stage adorned with a banner that conferred upon the fallen attorney a moniker worthy of a saint, "the Lawyer of the Poor," Carlos gave an eleven-and-a-half-minute speech that put his assassination in a broader context.

When, in 1948, the United Nations enshrined the Universal Declaration of Human Rights, the objective was to eradicate barbarity. But there was no enforcement mechanism attached to it, so throughout the Cold War, when various Latin American militaries tortured people and committed a whole slew of other atrocities the declaration supposedly prohibited, the burden of trying to bring it to life fell to emergent groups of local activists. Carlos recited a prayer attributed to one of the most famous ones, Óscar Romero, the Salvadoran archbishop who was shot through the heart after criticizing that country's military junta.

Honduras had its own catalog of martyred human rights defenders. According to a charity known as CODEH, there were 218 political assassinations and 110 disappearances in Honduras between 1981 and 1984. And during that period of time, the annual amount of aid the United States sent to the Honduran military increased from $9 million to $77 million, even though the American ambassador was aware that a military unit called Battalion 3-16 was in the business of kidnapping and murdering civilians.

In 1987, a CODEH executive named Miguel Ángel Pavón testified about some of the disappearances before the Inter-American Court of Human Rights. Three months later, he was paid a visit by Two Men on a Motorcycle. "Miguel Ángel Pavón's family, his colleagues at CODEH, and former members of the military attributed the killing to Battalion 3-16," Amnesty International reported.

And the fall of the Berlin Wall did not bring the country's martyrology to an end. Jeannette Kawas, who is said to have saved hundreds of plant and animal species by stymieing logging and development, was assassinated in February 1995. Germán Antonio Rivas, whose regional television network was known to expose corporate misconduct, was gunned down in November 2003. Within weeks of Dionisio's killing, the Environmental Movement of Olancho lost two compatriots, and just a few months before Carlos's speech, Donny Reyes, the treasurer of an LGBT organization in Tegucigalpa, was arrested for no clear reason and then diabolically thrown into a cell with fifty-seven mareros, where he was subsequently beaten, gang-raped, and left to reflect on that experience in a puddle of urine and feces.

Many of the region's martyrs have been elegantly memorialized—Jeannette Kawas lives on as the name of the national park she once defended; Miguel Ángel Pavón is a neighborhood in San Pedro Sula; and Archbishop Óscar Romero stands in white limestone above Westminster Abbey's Great West Door, between Martin Luther King Jr. and the anti-Nazi dissident Dietrich Bonhoeffer.

But what matters more to the martyred, being commemorated or getting revenge? Hopefully not the latter, because in virtually all of the emblematic human rights–defender cases in Honduras, none of the sicarios, intermediaries, or masterminds have ever been caught.

Dionisio sacrificed his life in the name of Articles 23 and 24 of the Universal Declaration of Human Rights, which mandate decent wages, humane working conditions, and adequate rest for laborers. He thus unequivocally belonged on the country's roster of martyrs. That being said, Kurt and Carlos weren't yet ready to let him become just like the others, an unavenged bust, plaque, or day of the year. They were done waiting around for the Public Ministry, and in short order, their homicide investigation would be back on.

———

WHEN KURT WOULD REACH OUT TO THE AMERICAN EMBASSY, HE could usually speak only to what he described as "third-level people." But those subordinates had been assuring him that the big cheese, the ambassador, was mentioning Dionisio's case to Honduras's president, security minister, and attorney general. And this high-level nudging did seem to have a trickle-down effect. Starting in August, the Public Ministry's third-in-command began accepting meetings with Kurt again, and less than a week after Dina's soiree, the ministry forced Criminal Investigation to replace Agent Martínez with a detective Cholo trusted.

This was a huge deal. Agent Aracely Cruz, a female on a force that was about 95 percent male, had a stellar reputation and was willing to intently pursue a case that clearly had the potential to implicate her own department. She knew for a fact that there had once been a Dionisio case file in Criminal Investigation's archive, but according to her, "When I went to retrieve it, it wasn't there. . . . It had disappeared. How bizarre. Obviously, I suspected my colleagues."

It didn't take long for the charity's adversaries to realize that it had restarted its investigation—or so it seemed. On August 19, Macario found his gray basset hound dead in his yard, and three days later, one of Dina's Cobras saw a man in a van photograph ASJ's office.

These events were unsettling, but they did not discourage the charity, which soon managed to push through another crucial personnel change. The Public Ministry reassigned all the Dionisio-related cases—the Towner theft, the assassination itself, and the murder of the teenage parking lot guard—to Juan Carlos Griffin, a prosecutor Macario went to college with.

Griffin, who earned his stripes by prosecuting organized crime cases in San Pedro Sula, had worked with Agent Cruz in the past. She had made such an impression on him that now, when her bosses offered to assign him as many more detectives as he wished, he passed, because he knew that reliability was far more valuable than manpower.

"WE NOW HAVE THE ELEMENTS TO GET TO THE ARREST WARRANTS," Cholo wrote to Kurt, on October 31. "THAT IS MY GOAL BY THE END OF THE YEAR. . . . WE ARE NOT LIKE THE OTHER NGOS THAT JUST COAST AND MAKE PLANS THEY DO NOT ACCOMPLISH."

———

IN THE WEEK LEADING UP TO THE ONE-YEAR ANNIVERSARY OF ASJ's darkest day, the staff hung "Lawyer of the Poor" banners all across the capital, and other charities put out supportive press releases. On the anniversary itself, December 4, 2007, Carlos led an open-air press conference in a square downtown. Dionisio's widow, Lourdes, who was onstage with him, felt grateful that he and Kurt were still fighting tooth and nail for her husband.

In the days around this press conference, Kurt and Carlos were able to meet with the Spanish ambassador, the German ambassador, the Swedish ambassador, the security minister, and the attorney general. His Royal Highness the American ambassador wouldn't see them, but his minions said that he had recently talked up Dionisio's case to Vilma Morales, the president of the Supreme Court, and two days after the anniversary, she met up with them.

Morales was a very important potential ally, because she could influence how the judiciary handled the case. Though there was a plethora of unsolved murders she could have chosen to devote her special attention to, there was a reason why she might have wanted to focus on Dionisio's in particular.

The headline *La Tribuna* had run for his assassination was "Sicarios Attack Again: Liquidate Another Lawyer." The words "again" and "another" were selected because in the two weeks leading up to that, four other attorneys had been killed. This spate of murders was extremely concerning, because it has been known, for a long time, that when lawyers drop like flies, society cannot function—"The first thing we do, let's kill all the lawyers," said one of Shakespeare's ruffians. And Dionisio's death had not marked the end of this particular type of bloodletting. "In 2007," wrote the authors of *Bribes, Bullets, and Intimidation*, "on the very day when the Honduran College of Lawyers was holding a vigil in front of the San Pedro Sula cathedral to protest the killing of fifteen lawyers that week, hit men ambushed and killed Judge Alba Leticia Bueso."

It almost seemed like Justice Morales's profession was under attack, and arguably, the Dionisio case, which was well publicized domestically and of interest to the international community, was the perfect opportunity for her to take a stand.

Kurt operated under the probably somewhat unfair assumption

that anyone as powerful as her in Honduras had done at least a few shady things, but he and Carlos found her to be understanding and enthusiastic about the case. Presumably, she told them what she had already told the American ambassador, which was something one of his third-level people relayed: "She needs witnesses."

If only that were so easy.

The refreshed detail—Agent Cruz, Griffin, Cholo, and Macario—didn't have any witnesses yet, but at least they had made some other inroads.

Why they were so keenly focused on two particular suspects, Agent Amador, the yellow-shirted man, and Ramón Solís, a SETECH employee, cannot be revealed, because that would compromise sources, but they did feel confident that they had their marks. Word on the street was that Solís, alias Oso, or the Bear, was a sicario. He had been arrested in June 2006 on a murder charge, but four months later, a judge in Roatán had released him on his own recognizance. That pretrial-detention decision may have been totally legitimate, but it's worth mentioning that Swasey was rumored to have major sway in Roatán, and that Oso was liberated just six weeks before Dionisio's murder, at a moment when the ASJ-SETECH feud was red hot.

The detail's suspicions about those two men were going to remain nothing more than that, however, unless they found a witness who was willing and able to corroborate them in court. Cholo had already spoken to several people who had been on the boulevard that day; some would admit to having seen Two Men on a Motorcycle, but besides Baleadas, who had identified another culprit, and who hadn't held up on the stand, none of them would admit to having seen their faces, as though these sicarios possessed the power of Medusa.

On December 13, Cholo, Griffin, and Agent Cruz went on a long drive in order to question a witness who previously had nothing that helpful to share. But as their luck would have it, asking a second time paid off. This man, who, going forward, would be known to the outside world as Z, claimed not only to have "eagle eyes" but also to have seen the sicarios' faces.

The detail, realizing that they may have just struck pay dirt, immediately rushed Z to a police station in San Pedro Sula, where they showed him a photo album they had previously prepared. With what he described as 100 percent certainty, he identified Agent Amador as the motorcycle driver, and Oso as the shooter. Since his signature would have given away his identity, he authenticated the two Photographic Identification Certificates with his fingerprint.

Z also gave the detail a clue as to why he had changed his mind about cooperating. In the immediate aftermath of the assassination, some of the bystanders on the boulevard had speculated about what *type* of lawyer Dionisio was. Because many Hondurans couldn't afford attorneys and had only seen them do sleazy things like weasel guilty mareros out of trouble and file spurious land-title claims against barrio properties, someone standing there on the street, observing a lifeless lawyer, may have very well thought, *Did that son-of-a-bitch have it coming?*

But according to Z, because of all the news coverage, he had since come to appreciate that the Lawyer of the Poor was not a money-grubbing shark but a beloved mensch, and that was why he was now assuming the immeasurable risk of putting this entire case on his back.

KURT CELEBRATED CHRISTMAS IN MICHIGAN AND WAS PLANNING TO stick around for a few more weeks in order to teach a seminar at Calvin. But his mind kept straying south.

He worried that the sicarios would take out Z, or that the mastermind would take out the sicarios. These were not paranoid concerns— weeks before a trial was set to begin against the cops who illegally detained Donny Reyes, the LGBT activist, the prosecution's star witness was shot dead in her home.

"Do you feel like the prosecutor is slow-playing the process of requesting the warrants?" Kurt wrote to Carlos, Macario, and Cholo, on January 3, 2008.

"We've already waited a year for this," Cholo replied, in an effort to calm his boss down. "Why not give it five to eight more days to make sure the case is well polished?"

The detail raced to do that by, for example, proving that SETECH once owned a motorcycle similar to the one described by witnesses. This sort of information certainly had the potential to bolster the prosecution's case down the line, but taking time to gather it now risked tipping off the company, which, by its very nature, had eyes and ears all over the place.

As always, Carlos was in charge while Kurt was away, and with the yearlong investigation climaxing under his watch, he was clearly worried about screwing things up. "I had a dream about you and Dina last night," he wrote to Kurt, on January 9.

"That's nice," Kurt replied. "Good things or bad things?"

"You're an angel! . . . I dreamt that you came back, got angry, and fired everyone at ASJ."

"First you say I'm an angel, then you say I got angry and fired everyone—mmmmm :)"

On January 18, Cholo and Macario finally sent Kurt and Carlos a plan for the arrest operation. Apprehending a cop and an alleged hit man simultaneously in two different cities—Amador lived in Tegucigalpa, while Oso lived in La Ceiba—was going to be tricky, especially since they didn't want to loop in too many officers, lest one of them tip off their targets.

Kurt peppered Cholo with questions about their plan, but the operative wasn't looking for tactical guidance from a sociologist. What he was looking for was cash to pay for rental cars, fuel, and hotel rooms. In many countries, bankrolling a police operation would be seen as unethical, but in Honduras, ponying up was often the only way to make one happen.

Now it just came down to execution.

"A single small error can undo a long and arduous endeavor," Kurt reminded Carlos and Macario.

"We've spent every single day working through the issues," Macario replied. "We've talked through everything multiple times. We've analyzed this from every different angle."

———

ON SUNDAY, JANUARY 27, KURT AND CARLOS MET UP WITH JUSTICE Morales, and three days later, a judge she trusted in Tegucigalpa issued arrest warrants for Amador and Oso. Macario immediately emailed copies of them to Cholo, who had already deployed to La Ceiba with five agents from an elite organized crime unit. The first two internet cafés he went to didn't have legal-sized printer paper, but the third one did.

The next morning, that squad of agents blockaded the entrance of a local barrio with traffic cones, and as soon as Oso stopped in front of them, they sandwiched him with two vehicles and made the arrest.

In their operational schematic, Cholo and Macario had predicted that "the bosses of these security companies will not be imprudent enough to react violently or publicly defend the two suspects." But as it turned out, that was wrong.

Soon after Oso was allowed to make a phone call at a police station in La Ceiba, Swasey showed up with one of his attorneys. According to an American embassy cable that would later be obtained by WikiLeaks, the two of them then "tried to stop the arrest."

But that didn't happen. Instead, Cholo and the agents transported Oso to Tegucigalpa, where, earlier that morning, Amador had been captured, too.

Busting two alleged assassins in a human rights–defender case sounded like a triumph, but according to Agent Cruz, her boss's immediate reaction was to reprimand her for not letting him know what had been coming down the pike. "Some of my colleagues wouldn't even look at me," she recalled. "Some of them booed."

Clearly, the detail had had good reason to be cautious about who they looped in, but because of that reticence, raids that should have happened simultaneous to the arrests were delayed until the following day.

A search party composed of a judicial official, two prosecutors, multiple Criminal Investigation agents, and several other functionaries broke through the door of Oso's tiny house. All they found inside, however, were two teddy bears and a handful of other objects. It seemed like the house had just been emptied.

Meanwhile, a separate search party ransacked SETECH's office in Tegucigalpa. "The computers didn't have a single datum on their hard drives," their report read. "The manager claimed that they had been reformatted the day before because of a virus."

Those searchers did, however, come upon some very interesting physical documents. A letter dated a few months before Dionisio's assassination described a loan SETECH made to Oso's mother, and attached to that was a letter from Swasey explaining that the interest payments were going to be deducted directly from Oso's salary. This begged a number of questions. First of all, at the time the loan was made, Oso was in jail on a murder charge, so why was he still on SETECH's payroll? Second of all, why did an executive who was infamous for chiseling his workforce lend about $10,000 to the parent of an employee?

Cholo and Griffin were there for the scouring of Amador's modest house in Tegucigalpa, where the most meaningful discovery was two plastic bags that contained a large number of objects and documents, some of which were irrelevant, some of which were incriminating, and some of which were downright chilling.

There was a hard-to-decipher note about Oso, which indicated that the two men had some sort of connection to each other.

There was a list of five people who worked on human rights–related issues.

There was a bank receipt dated one month after Dionisio's assassination, showing a deposit into Amador's account of about $2,650, which, ballpark, was what a sicario job was said to cost.

There was a second bank receipt from that very same day, showing that Amador transferred all he had just deposited to a prosecutor who previously worked in Mosquitia—said prosecutor would soon disappear, as would the last person who ever saw him.

Finally, there was a SETECH document with a handwritten scribble on the back: "DIONISIO DIAZ GARCIA—ASJ (ASSOCIATION FOR A JUST SOCIETY), TELEPHONE 239–44 and 382–7202, Trapiche, block D25, house number 2497."

– 9 –

AMADOR AND OSO'S INITIAL AUDIENCE WAS CALLED TO ORDER on February 5, 2008. Though both men were working class, they were being jointly represented by José Marcelino Vargas and Olga Suyapa Irías, which was eye-catching, not just because those attorneys were assumed to be very pricey, but also because Marcelino Vargas had been representing Swasey in his slander lawsuit against Kurt, and Suyapa Irías had been with him when he showed up at ASJ's office.

And the presence of those lawyers wasn't the first indication that SETECH had a vested interest in this case. The day after the defendants were arrested, the company released a statement declaring itself to be a victim of the "tendentious, treacherous, and malicious" claim that it had something to do with the murder of "Dionisio Ramos." Swasey, who had signed the statement himself, apparently did not know that that was not Dionisio Díaz García's name. And what made this error even more cringeworthy was that it seemed like it might have been a self-incriminating slip of the tongue—after all, the other murder victim in this saga was a teenage parking lot guard by the name of José Adolfo Ramos.

Since the case against Amador and Oso seemed strong, Kurt worried that the trial would somehow get subverted. There were a whole bunch of precedents for that. For instance, the judge who had been assigned to Archbishop Romero's case had had to flee El Salvador after home intruders attempted to kill him, and much more recently, the three key witnesses to a Honduran environmentalist's murder were taken out. Those types of spectacular scenarios felt like real possibilities, but during Amador and Oso's initial audience, a far more conventional form of defense arose—Amador had an alibi.

He and three of his colleagues from the Villa Adela station—Agent 728, Official K-11, and a second official—separately took the stand to collectively explain what Amador had done the day Dionisio was murdered around half past ten. According to them, at half past nine, Agent 728 drove Amador, Official K-11, and two anonymous witnesses from Villa Adela to the courthouse, which took them about twelve minutes. Amador and Agent 728 then spent many hours inside the courthouse, watching over those two witnesses, who were there to testify about the robbery of a delivery truck. The second official, who came to the courthouse separately, and Official K-11 were there to testify in defense of two cops who had been charged with corruption—in other words, they were there to defend their own. At three in the afternoon, Agent 728 left the courthouse with the two anonymous witnesses, but Amador stuck around in solidarity with the officers on trial. Finally, at five p.m., Amador and Official K-11 departed.

The defense was able to reinforce this alibi with some physical evidence. One of Villa Adela's logbooks showed that on the day in question, Agent 792—that was Amador—and Official K-11 had left for the courthouse at 9:32. And another logbook, one dedicated to anonymous witnesses, showed that that same day, Agents 792 and 728 had been guarding witnesses for the delivery-truck case.

This exonerating tale would have felt airtight if it weren't for the fact that the notations in those logbooks were handwritten, and that both of them had been administered by Official K-11, Amador's direct commander and brother in arms. And some inconsistencies were already apparent. For instance, while the alibi bards were claiming that Amador, Agent 728, and Official K-11 had left Villa Adela together, that first logbook didn't show Agent 728 leaving with the other two. And Griffin was able to muddy these waters even more by introducing a third Villa Adela logbook, which, it should be noted, the Public Ministry got from someone who didn't work directly with Amador, and which, it should also be noted, the defense vociferously tried to suppress. This logbook showed no record of Amador leaving Villa Adela at any time between 7:40 a.m. and 4:10 p.m., even though it was supposed to have documented his comings and goings.

For all these reasons, his alibi wasn't yet solid enough to override Z's compelling testimony, so the judge decided that the defendants would remain behind bars while the judicial process against them advanced.

———

IN THE YEARLONG LEAD-UP TO THE TRIAL, THE TWO SIDES JOCKEYED for advantage, both at various audiences and, apparently, behind the scenes, too. ASJ kept diplomatic attention on the case; Cholo kept Z in one piece; and Kurt strategized with Griffin's bosses. The judge who handled this interim phase of the proceedings later admitted that, on the one hand, government officials were letting him know that the eyes of the international community were on him, and that, on the other, someone sent him death threats via text.

Once Griffin found time to study Amador's alibi more closely, he discovered that that delivery-truck audience had happened not on the day Dionisio was murdered, as the bards had claimed, but three days prior, on December 1, 2006. Nonetheless, there were two separate entries about that audience in the anonymous-witness logbook, one on "12/01/06," when it actually occurred, and another, directly beneath it, on "12/04/06." And bizarrely, in the column to the right of those dates, one of the two defendants in that case was matched up with "12/01/06," while the other was matched up with "12/04/06."

It seemed like the logbook had been doctored, so at Griffin's request, on June 19, 2008, a court-appointed handwriting expert forced Amador to write out a bunch of words, numbers, and dates.

This technician later concluded, based on the way Amador constructed characters—the flourishes, the proportions, the angles, and the pressure of the writing instrument—that he had made a notation in one of the logbooks at 3:20 p.m., which contradicted his claim that he had stayed at the courthouse until five.

Poking that hole in the alibi did do some damage to it, but not that much, given that Dionisio was killed in the morning. And the handwriting expert's report didn't even address Griffin's most burning curiosity: Had the logbooks been tampered with?

On September 24, Griffin's team asked the court to order a second handwriting analysis.

In a major blow to their case, this request was denied.

————

JUST BEFORE LUNCHTIME ON FEBRUARY 18, 2009, THE FIRST DAY OF the trial, a bailiff opened the door behind the judges' bench, and Carlos walked through it. As he passed by Amador and Oso, who were sitting with their arms crossed at the defense table, he nudged his glasses up his nose.

He then sat down in the witness box where, over the roar of the air conditioner and the stenographer's clickety-clack, he walked the three black-robed judges through this multiyear odyssey—the initial agreement with Delta, the seizure of the Towner, and so on.

He was on the stand for about thirteen minutes.

The following day, that same door behind the judges' bench was opened, except this time a bailiff backed through it to roll into the courtroom a wooden box on casters that looked sort of like an indoor phone booth. He left it in front of the witness box. It was immovable wood all over except for a darkly tinted window on the side now facing the prosecutors' table, and a closed wooden door on the side now facing the judges. The bailiff proceeded to open that door so only the judges could see the figure inside—it was a person cloaked head to toe in one of those burqa-like robes. Meanwhile, all the defendants and their attorneys could see was a solid side of the booth and the front side of the open door.

Z removed his hood before delivering his testimony. He spoke timidly, sometimes inaudibly, with long awkward pauses between words and phrases, as though he were a petrified hostage being forced to reveal top-secret information at gunpoint. It often seemed like he was on the verge of a Baleadas-like capitulation, but when one of Griffin's colleagues asked him, point-blank, if he would be able to recognize the sicarios, his answer was "Of course."

That was the bailiff's cue. He shut the door of the booth and spun it 360 degrees so Z could observe the entirety of the courtroom through the tinted window. This was the moment of truth, and Z came through. He declared that the defendant in the long-sleeved shirt, Oso, was the triggerman, and the defendant in the short-sleeved shirt, Amador, had been driving the motorcycle.

That right there was Z's most critical duty, but he wasn't home free yet. He still had to survive a cross-examination, and in this case, the word "survive" wasn't purely metaphorical, because there was a risk that he could accidentally reveal his identity with his words. In fact, it seemed like he had already fudged some ancillary details in order to avoid doing just that. For instance, he had explained his presence at the crime scene like this: He was riding a bus to either—he provided different explanations at different times—go to work or attend to a personal matter, and when he saw all the traffic on the boulevard, he decided to bail on his commitment; it was then, he claimed, after he hopped off the bus and was crossing the boulevard to catch another, that he saw a cold-blooded murder occur.

Marcelino Vargas, who had been one of Griffin's professors at law school, asked Z questions about what he was doing that day. Griffin persistently objected to this line of inquiry on the grounds that it could trick Z into verbally unmasking himself. The judges overruled him, but his annoying interruptions did seem to deter the defense attorney from digging too deep.

But Marcelino Vargas was paid the big bucks for a reason, and as it happened, he was about to use the obscurity around anonymous witnessing to his own clients' advantage.

The person tasked with setting up his forthcoming attempt at a knockout punch was Agent 728, who took the stand and said that he goofed at the initial audience, that on second thought, he was now remembering that on the day of the murder, he and Amador had been watching an anonymous witness not for the delivery-truck case but for one in which the crime was—wait for it—the theft of cheese. Implicit in that was the following: A police force that often did next to nothing about rapes and murders had devoted personnel to a transgression that belonged in the plot of a Disney movie, and furthermore, those sinister dairy larcenists had scared whichever poor soul happened to have witnessed their macabre deeds into seeking statutory anonymity.

This second draft of the alibi sounded absurd, but Marcelino Vargas brought in someone who could corroborate it: the man who, supposedly, was the anonymous witness in that cheese case.

The prosecutors were outraged that the judges decided to admit him, because at this stage in the game, they weren't going to have enough time to verify that he was who he claimed to be. Which was a shame, because long after this trial was done and decided, the prosecutors would discover that no anonymous witnesses had testified at the cheese audience.

Yet now, a young man claiming to have done just that entered the courtroom, not in the wooden booth, where vulnerable witnesses were supposed to go, but on his own two feet. Then, with his face exposed and real name stated, he assured the judges that at the precise time Dionisio was being murdered, he had been with Amador inside the courthouse.

And he was as certain as Z—100 percent.

KURT THOUGHT MARCELINO VARGAS HAD OUTFOXED GRIFFIN, SO when he sat down in the spectators' gallery on Monday, February 23, the day a verdict was expected, he was feeling pessimistic. At this point, all he could do was silently pray for the result he wanted, and to his surprise, he got an immediate response from up above—he felt God tell him that something miraculous was about to happen.

And in short order, something miraculous did happen, though it wasn't the type of miraculous Kurt was hoping for.

An officer of the court announced that the trial was being postponed, because one of the judges had been stung by a bee, and that had caused him to go into anaphylactic shock. In light of Swasey's supposed powers, this was obviously extremely suspicious, and if a conspiracy to derail the trial truly was afoot, then that implied that a guilty verdict had been coming.

Carlos and an ASJ attorney immediately reached out to four ambassadors—the American, the German, the Spanish, and the Swedish—asking each to contact the president of the Supreme Court, who could hopefully thwart whatever chicanery was going on here.

But sometimes an allergic reaction to a bee sting is actually just an allergic reaction to a bee sting, and after the stricken judge was discharged from the hospital, and a brigade of firefighters removed hives from the walls of the courthouse, the trial resumed, four days later.

The attorneys summed up their arguments, and then Lourdes

made the simplest of statements: "My husband's death cannot remain in impunity. All I am asking for is that justice be done."

Amador got to say his piece, too: "I am also asking for justice. . . . The Public Ministry is unethical. They were just looking for someone to blame."

After that, the three judges left to deliberate.

When they reentered the courtroom, one remarked on how incredibly packed it was. Many ASJ employees had come to hear the verdict, including Deisy Ordóñez, the receptionist. "I was sitting next to Erica, one of the *Revistazo* journalists, and Hilda, who handles food at the office," she recalled. ". . . We were all frozen. Our hands were sweating. It was such a heavy moment. We cried. Hilda and I were holding hands, and she said to me, 'My dear, pray that there will be justice.'"

In their ruling, the judges noted that though Amador may have gone to the courthouse at half past nine, as that one logbook suggested, that didn't mean he stayed there long. They also observed that there were no notations about a cheese case in the anonymous witness logbook. As for Z, they felt his testimony was in such tight accordance with the ballistics and autopsy that he really must have seen what he claimed to. Therefore, they convicted Amador and Oso of premeditated murder, a crime that carried a sentence of twenty to thirty years when done for hire.

As soon as Kurt was able to, he got up and hugged the prosecutors.

"This was one of the few cases of a murdered lawyer that actually got closed," one of those prosecutors later said. ". . . If ASJ hadn't been involved, if they hadn't guarded the anonymous witness, we wouldn't have been able to win the conviction."

According to one of the American embassy's third-level people, "Whether it was pressuring us or the government, Kurt was the most amazing advocate. . . . I wouldn't have expected the leader of a charity to do all the things he did after an employee got killed. . . . He's a hero in that way."

Kurt, Carlos, and one of their colleagues soon sent a letter to the various diplomats who helped them out, primarily to say thanks, but also to remind them that there were bigger fish to fry. "We are determined to achieve a yet more historic conviction," they wrote, "against the individuals responsible for hiring these hit men. This will send an even stronger message to the Honduran people that their justice system can work, and to those participating in organized crime that their days of impunity are numbered. However, given the wealth, power, and connections of those thought to be behind Dionisio's murder, we expect convicting them to be exponentially harder."

– 10 –

ACCORDING TO THAT AMERICAN EMBASSY CABLE OBTAINED BY WikiLeaks, which was written right after the sicarios were arrested in February 2008, the security minister had informed the American ambassador that "the police were intent on arresting Swasey as well."

But as of March 23, 2009, that still didn't even seem close to happening, so Macario concluded a memo about this issue with some serious sass: "Out of respect for our thesis that the government can function on its own, I have been staying at arm's length. This has led to things taking way too long and to me suffering emotional torture on a grand scale."

He was making a dig at one of Kurt and Carlos's emerging core values, which was that even as their employees tried getting the government to do what they wanted it to do, they should do so in a way that strengthened the government's ability to function without them. Sometimes that simply meant not just immediately doing bureaucrats' work for them.

Macario clearly had had enough of all that and was eager to dive headfirst into the mastermind investigation. The following day, Cholo wrote out some potential avenues they and the Public Ministry could pursue, such as figuring out who the obvious suspect had called in the lead-up to the assassination.

These investigative ideas could have theoretically led to concrete evidence, but as Kurt soon explained in a letter to his board, the country's frothy political climate likely meant that the obvious suspect was virtually invincible. "The current president is carrying out a variety of efforts to change the constitution," he wrote, "presumably to make it possible for him to stay in power longer. ASJ has heard that the president's brother and possibly the president himself have received financial support from Swasey." His point was that in a country where politics and the law were not entirely walled off, and at a moment when the administration needed the support of its allies more than ever, locking horns with a deep-pocketed loyalist was a losing proposition.

And whether Kurt liked it or not, he was already engaged in just that type of battle. The charity had tried to get Swasey's slander lawsuit dismissed, but soon after the sicarios' conviction, the Constitutional Chamber of the Supreme Court had shot down its final appeal, which meant that there was now nothing stopping a trial from beginning. According to the ASJ lawyer who had been working on this, the chamber's decision was not objective. "Carlos Zelaya, the Honduran president's brother, has been helping SETECH with the judiciary," she wrote at the time.

When Kurt showed up for the first day of the slander trial in February 2010, however, a surprise was in store: Marcelino Vargas announced that he had not heard from his client in months. Because of that, the trial was postponed, but Kurt felt like it was never going to happen, and he was right—it never did.

The charity had meanwhile been incessantly urging the Public Ministry to go after the mastermind, and it continued to do so throughout 2010. But with time, other priorities arose, and without there being any last-man-standing clash, or even a memorable moment of surrender, the war with SETECH eventually faded to black. One explanation for this surprisingly benign conclusion was that the charity's most bellicose staff members were no longer there.

Dina was long gone. She had gotten upset when she heard that Amador and Oso were about to be arrested, not from her colleagues, who she expected to keep her informed, but from somebody else. Kurt recalled what happened next: "Carlos, Dina, and I sat down in my office, and she said, 'I know you want to fire me. Just fire me. You are trying to avoid having to pay me severance.' And we said, 'Dina, we don't want you to quit. You just can't keep doing this crazy stuff.' For example, when we put up security cameras in the office, she held up a sign in front of them that said, 'You Are Abusing My Human Rights.' Everything was just so over the top with her."

Less than a week after that conversation, Dina resigned. "They wanted me to start wearing a suit," she later said, "but I did a lot of interacting with victims, so I told them, 'I am never going to change. I will always be the same Dina.'"

Later on, as the mastermind investigation slowly slipped into nothingness, Kurt and Carlos began transforming ASJ into a more professionalized, less ragtag operation, one that would have the credibility to receive large grants and the proficiency to affect Honduras at a national scale. As part of that institutional skin shedding, they fired Macario, because foul language, snide emails, and chair throwing were no longer acceptable at ASJ. "He was deeply, deeply hurt," Kurt later said. "He had finally come to trust us, and he had stuck his neck out and done all this stuff for us, and then we fired him. He knew he could be a pain in the ass, but I don't think he ever thought we'd go that far."

There is no taming a man like Cholo. He could make gestures toward accountability and the other corporate mores, but he was a lone ranger at heart, and his natural habitat was always going to be the dark edge of the gray area. As part of a Peace and Justice manhunt, he bought drugs for an informant. To test out the armed security detail stationed at the office, he once secretly arranged for a gunman to storm through the front door; shockingly, this exercise didn't result in anybody getting shot, but it still wasn't funny, because Deisy, the receptionist, who was six months pregnant at the time, literally fainted in terror.

According to Kurt, he fired Cholo; according to Cholo, Cholo quit.

The Labor Project was not a zero. By the charity's own accounting, in the five years leading up to February 2010, it provided free labor-rights training seminars to about seven thousand workers in the security, janitorial, and fast-food industries, and it won 135 legal cases on behalf of exploited workers. "With the money I was awarded," one of the successful litigants said, "I was able to fix up my house, which had been about to fall down."

But relative to Kurt, Carlos, and Dina's initial aspirations, the Labor Project was inarguably a failure. A survey the charity conducted in 2010 indicated that the great majority of SETECH's guards still didn't receive overtime, social security benefits, or their legally mandated bonuses. And disregarding the labor code like that remained the norm—around then, the Labor Ministry estimated that 63 percent of companies were not in compliance with the minimum wage law.

Kurt felt bad that they didn't come through for the country's low-income workforce, and part of him wondered if their grand victory—helping to put the assassins behind bars—was nothing more than horse trading, Swasey tossing them a charming little win that had no material impact on his life as a way to bring this whole annoying saga to an end. Maybe the charity never had any chance of getting him to comply with the labor code; maybe in Honduras, which was one of the most unequal countries on earth as measured by the Gini coefficient, that teeny tiny circle of ultrawealthy individuals could not be made subject to the law.

Over the years, a few wisps of information about Swasey have seeped into the public domain. For example, in 2012, a narcotrafficker tried justifying his wealth to a Honduran court by presenting a contract for a $2 million loan he had received from a Swasey corporation. And then, in 2016, after a radio station called Stereo Ceiba reported that Swasey had been arrested for possessing "commercial firearms," *La Prensa* reported that he was "being investigated for the assassination of an ex-soldier who used to run La Ceiba's prisons."

One indication of how much power he had back in the day has been the success of his various representatives. In early 2009, Suyapa Irías, the lawyer who defended the sicarios alongside Marcelino Vargas, joined the prestigious commission that got to choose a short list of nominees to become the country's next Supreme Court justices. One of the justices ultimately appointed through that process was Jacobo Cálix, who had been Delta's legal counsel when the Labor Project first began. But the ultimate middle finger to the charity came in early 2010, when a SETECH executive was made second-in-command at, of all places, the Labor Ministry.

If this story had ended here, it would be sad enough, but unfortunately for everyone who loved Dionisio, more heartbreak was yet to come.

———

MARCELINO VARGAS AND SUYAPA IRÍAS HAD FILED A CASSATION claim, a type of appeal, soon after Amador and Oso were sentenced, and after a three-year wait, on May 15, 2012, the Penal Chamber of the Supreme Court of Justice published its unanimous ruling. Jacobo Cálix, who was one of the three justices on that chamber, did not recuse himself, despite the apparent conflict of interest.

Cassations are supposed to be about violations of law or procedure, not about reassessing evidence, especially oral evidence, because while the three trial judges had been able to factor in the between-the-lines details they personally observed, such as the witnesses' facial expressions, the three justices had merely gotten to read a transcript of the proceedings. This meant they had no clue, for instance, that upon being asked a simple question, the cheese-case mystery man had sheepishly looked toward Marcelino Vargas, as though he were needing to be told what to say.

In their ruling, the justices went after Z. Even though the Photographic Identification Certificates he fingerprinted in San Pedro Sula specified that he had picked Amador and Oso out of "photo albums," and even though, later on in court, he clarified that he had been shown eight to ten different images, the justices worried that he had not been shown a "plurality of photos." And more broadly, they just doubted that he could have remembered the sicarios' faces after a little over a year had elapsed.

On the flip side, however, they "encountered no rational reason to doubt the exculpatory testimony" given by the cheese-case mystery man, despite the fact that he had performed the exact same feat of memory as Z, namely, recalling that over a year in the past, he had seen Amador's visage at a particular place and time.

The defense had made their cassation on two separate grounds, the first being that their clients had not benefited from the presumption of innocence, and the second being that the trial judges had shown poor judgment. Which of those two claims the justices applied their ruling to mattered a great deal, because while a favorable ruling on the former would have triggered a retrial—a retrial at which the prosecutors would have likely been able to debunk the cheese-case mystery man—a favorable ruling on the latter would have led to a far more conclusive outcome, Amador and Oso getting freed without the possibility of retrial.

And that's exactly what happened.

And that was it—The End. There was no higher court to appeal to.

Years later, on a Friday night in Tegucigalpa, a twenty-nine-year-old woman was walking to a candy shop when a stray bullet struck her fatally. According to a vague *La Prensa* article about this, two men had been arguing nearby, one of them recklessly fired his gun, and Amador was arrested with the murder weapon.

By then, Dionisio was commemorated in a billboard-sized mural on the top floor of ASJ's office, his painted face surrounded by polychrome swirls, a couple of doves, a row of security guards, his wife and son, and the biblical passage that had become the charity's war cry: "By this we know love, that he laid down his life for us, and we ought to lay down our lives for our brothers and sisters."

Lourdes, Dionisio's widow, died of natural causes in 2021, which left her college-aged son, Mauricio, with no living parents. Before her health deteriorated, however, she made it clear that she didn't have any hard feelings toward Kurt, Carlos, and their team. "I have never felt that at any moment," she said. "They are the ones who helped us move forward. They are our second family. They helped me raise Mauricio."

"We try to keep Dionisio's memory alive, even now, after all these years," Carlos recently said. "In part, this is a form of therapy, a way to drive off feelings of guilt. . . . We also use his memory to strengthen our own passion. He offered his life for something that I think was right. But to be honest, it was our locura."

To memorialize Dionisio is one thing, but if justice is what the martyred want most, then Kurt and Carlos have failed their fallen comrade.

For a long time, whenever Kurt saw a headline about someone dying in La Ceiba, his eyes would jump down to the body of the article, where he was hoping to see, in his heart of hearts, the name of the man he holds responsible.

And when he was informed, via WhatsApp, that according to La Ceiba News—a Facebook page with about seven thousand followers that identifies itself as a "Media/News Company"—Swasey passed away in August 2020, his immediate response was, "Great news."

BOOK THREE

A Higher Level

— 1 —

CARLOS JOINED ASJ FULL-TIME IN JANUARY 2011. "GENESIS WAS a necessary learning experience," he later said, "but I got to a point where as a professional, a human being, and a Honduran, I felt ready for a higher level."

Getting to work with your best-friend-slash-next-door-neighbor as an equal partner may sound unequivocally awesome, but Jo Ann worried that this co-director setup could somehow damage their relationship. Kurt and Carlos, however, were confident they could make it work; they shared the same values—extreme courage, extreme optimism, extreme faith, extreme frugality—and they almost never fought.

Nevertheless, in agreeing to this, Carlos was signing up to be judged according to certain deeply ingrained racial stereotypes, like that it must be the gringo partner who was pulling the strings. "Sometimes stuff like that doesn't bother me, and sometimes it does," Carlos later admitted. "Some of our employees feel like they need to treat me one way, and Kurt another. . . . I've learned to live with this, and honestly, part of ASJ's strength is the combination of our two cultures. . . . Kurt is more schematic. He's one, two, three this, and one, two, three that. Me, no. I'm like *psh*. More emotional, more creative.

I come up with ideas, and then Kurt puts them into that one, two, three structure. . . . Also, I don't care if our staff clocks in at eight a.m. What matters to me are results. Kurt is different. He wants people to sign in on time."

From their offices up on the third floor of ASJ's building, which were separated by a wall with a glazed louvered window, they jointly ran a substantial charity with about fifty employees, dozens of volunteers, and a million-dollar budget. Yet neither of them took a salary—Kurt and Jo Ann lived off what they made from the Calvin semester-abroad program, while Carlos and Bernarda got by on her teaching salary.

ASJ had come into its own by taking on individual cases, and it still did that. According to its annual report, in 2011, its three clinics provided psychological counseling to 2,340 people and legal counseling to 3,276; its land team helped 3,700 homeowners get titles to their properties; Peace and Justice helped capture 27 suspects; and a Peace and Justice spin-off that focused on child sexual abuse helped capture 14 more.

A lot of these efforts amounted to pinch-hitting for the government, but realistically, the charity could only do so much of that, so Kurt and Carlos, who wanted to help not just thousands of Hondurans but millions, were now aiming to revamp the government itself.

As of 2011, the charity's transformation into an anticorruption organization had begun. Kurt and Carlos had people diagnosing the public health and education systems, but what they wanted Honduras to have, above all else, was a functional criminal justice system. In other words, just as they once set out to make their barrio safe by replicating the work of cops and prosecutors, they were now setting out to make their country safe by rehabilitating the Honduran National Police, the Public Ministry, and the judiciary.

That ambition—to make justice reign across an entire nation— would have sounded quixotic pretty much anywhere, but in Honduras, it sounded especially idealistic, not just because those three institutions seemed to be well beyond salvation, but also because the country's violence problem had reached an almost apocalyptic level.

Nothing captured this better than the bare-bones homicide statistics, which, thanks to a sociologist named Julieta Castellanos, were now compiled by a reliable, nongovernmental source. According to the institute she founded, the Violence Observatory, whereas back in 2005, there had been 2,417 homicides in Honduras, in the three most recent years, 2008, 2009, and 2010, there had been, respectively, 4,473, 5,265, and 6,239. And in October 2011, her observatory forecasted that Honduras was on track to have the highest homicide rate on earth for the second straight year—its final tally for 2011 would be 7,104 murders.

It would be hard to conclusively prove why the annual number of homicides in the country nearly tripled in a seven year-span, in large part because the vast majority of those killings have never been solved. But a few factors likely contributed.

For one thing, the antimara crackdown of the early aughts, which entailed locking up scores of young men in prison modules that were ruled by either MS-13 or Barrio 18, had been followed not by those maras disintegrating but by them getting even stronger. For another, Honduras had gone from being one of the places cocaine passed through to becoming its primary way station. According to what some US officials would soon tell *The Washington Post*, perhaps one-third of the entire world's cocaine supply was flowing through the country.

And there was another factor, too.

Back in early 2009, Mel, the Stetson-capped president of Honduras, had announced a convoluted plan that would let the populace decide, through two separate referendums, whether they wanted there to be a constitutional convention. This was presented as an effort to, among other things, encode special protections for historically oppressed groups, but many assumed that what it was really about was Mel trying to cling onto power.

The thing was, Honduras's constitution prohibited presidents from serving more than one four-year term; other leftist presidents in the region, including Venezuela's Hugo Chávez, had obliterated their term limits through somewhat similar maneuvers; and Mel did seem to have a certain degree of affinity for Chávez, who was a pariah in much of the West. This was the basis for the conservative establishment's allegation that Mel's plan was step one in his scheme to turn Honduras into his own little Venezuelaesque pinko autocracy.

At the level of animal intuition, that allegation may have felt spot-on, but one flaw with it was that the constitutional convention Mel was proposing wouldn't have occurred until *after* the upcoming election, which he couldn't even legally run in. Nevertheless, the powers that be allied against him; both the National Congress and the Supreme Court deemed his dual-referendum plan to be illegal.

But the cowboyish Mel intended to defy those checks and balances by going through with the first referendum anyway, on June 28, 2009. That never came to pass, however, because before the crack of dawn that day, hundreds of soldiers stormed his house and put him on a plane to Costa Rica.

In response to this coup d'état, a deluge of protesters, some of whom hadn't even been fans of Mel, poured into the streets. And once the illegitimate interim government deployed cops and soldiers to suppress them, public spaces became battlegrounds, and the country descended into a semi-anarchic state. This likely impacted the homicide rate, because amid the roiling pandemonium, mareros and narcos could essentially run amok.

Through it all, Julieta's observatory systematically converted the country's cesspool of violence into concrete numbers; that being said, she was much more than just a bean counter. Over the course of her career at the National Autonomous University of Honduras, whose flagship campus was located at the foot of the Montañita, she had published many works about crime, policing, and armaments. And it seemed fitting of the times that someone with that particular area of expertise was rector of the entire national university system. Because Julieta held that prestigious position, she was a nationally known, quasi-political figure. And she wore her power well, as she typically donned silk scarves, pearl earrings, and half-rimmed spectacles, and typically communicated in declarative bursts separated by deep-in-thought pauses.

She, of all people, had no illusions about the other factor that was contributing to the country's astronomical homicide rate: the Honduran National Police. Not only did the force do a miserable job of preventing murder, it also allegedly added to the kill count itself. Julieta, of course, knew all about this; after all, she had literally written the book on it, *Honduras: Police Reform and Citizen Security*. But researching and writing can yield only so much understanding, and within excruciating pain, there lies a more primal type of knowledge.

On October 21, 2011, a little over a week after her observatory released its forecast, Julieta lent her champagne-colored RAV4 to the youngest of her three sons.

It was a Friday night in Tegucigalpa.

THAT HER SON RAFAEL AND HIS BEST FRIEND, CARLOS DAVID RODRÍguez, both undergrads at the national university, even drove to a classmate's apartment and celebrated her birthday into the small hours of the night was, in and of itself, a small act of merry rebellion in a city where nightlife had been greatly diminished by the many perils innate to the moonlit world.

When they left her place around half past one, they weren't quite ready to call it a night. There was a karaoke bar nearby, but as they tried driving into the shopping center where it was located, the security guards stationed there stopped them, because the venue was about to close.

Rafael protested. In another country, this classic brand of joie-de-vivre dispute might have been a lighthearted matter, but here, it was necessarily tensioned by the ambient fear of violence. After several minutes of arguing, a police pickup happened to drive past, and one of the guards, having had enough, whistled loudly. At that point, M1–92, a blue-and-white truck with SERVE AND PROTECT on the side, came to a halt in the half light of some lampposts.

An aficionado of comic books, which he liked to draw in his spare time, Rafael surely knew that fleeing from the law was an inflammatory thing to do; nevertheless, he immediately hightailed it. Maybe he did so with his blood-alcohol content in mind, or maybe this was simply his knee-jerk survival instinct. Because encountering the police at night was scary, anywhere in Honduras, but especially here, within the jurisdiction of La Granja, the most notorious station in the city.

A car chase ensued through the desolate streets that were made to flicker red and blue by M1–92's strobing beacons. Three officers were in the cabin, and it was the fourth one, up in the bed, who opened fire. After a bullet drilled through the side of Rafael's abdomen, the RAV4 drifted to a stop.

The cops then did what cops were rumored to do in such situations. They carried the bleeding Rafael into M1–92, forced the uninjured Carlos David into the back seat of the RAV4, and drove both vehicles south—away from the hospital, away from the jail, away from the illuminated city.

The two friends must have known exactly what was about to happen to them. And what is one supposed to do in such a dreadful situation? Your limited options include begging, fighting, weeping, praying, and gazing up at the stars.

The cops eventually turned off the highway and rumbled two miles down a dirt road to a dumping ground known as Little Ovens.

Despite the fanciful name, it was nothing more than an outcropping of stones in the middle of a forest.

———

THE BODIES OF THE TWO UNDERGRADUATES WERE DISCOVERED the following morning.

If one of them hadn't been the rector's son, the police "investigation" would have likely ended before it even started, and the press would have likely parroted one of the force's go-to clichés for dehumanizing victims: *Oh, they were just cannon fodder in gang warfare*, or *Oh, they were part of a drug deal gone bad.*

But this was not going to be business as usual, because Julieta was a senatorial force of nature who could get any politician on the phone, who could get herself airtime on the talk shows that swayed public opinion, and who would soon have thousands of people demonstrating in solidarity with her. In other words, she was the new Honduran pietà.

On Monday, the fleet manager at La Granja noticed that M1–92 was spick-and-span clean, as though it had just come off the lot. But even so, this wasn't going to be a whodunit for long. A witness had seen the cops carry Rafael into M1–92, and on Wednesday, the Public Ministry raided La Granja. According to Griffin, the prosecutor who worked the Dionisio case, when he got there that morning, the station's main hallway was lined on each side by a row of masked cops. Walking through that gauntlet was, as intended, exceptionally intimidating, but the prosecutors still managed to seize a lot of potential evidence.

Immediately thereafter, one of the ministry's technicians found a bloodstain on M1–92's tailgate. The cleaners had missed a spot.

This case looked to be open-and-shut, so much so that on Thursday, the brass preemptively detained the four M1–92 cops in a station downtown. According to the force's internal regulations, the officers could be held in that limbo state for up to eight days, which seemed like more than enough time for the judicial machinery to handle the next steps: confirm that the blood came from Rafael, file charges, issue warrants, and formally incarcerate the culprits. But just three days later, on Sunday afternoon, a journalist called Julieta.

Apparently, on Friday, the four M1–92 cops had been freed from that station on the condition that they voluntarily return by Sunday at noon. They hadn't done that, and as it turned out, it was the perfect time for them to go AWOL. That day, the Public Ministry's forensic laboratory signed off on a dictum stating that they were 99.99999999999999 percent certain that the blood on the tailgate was Rafael's.

The vanishing of these cops was a masterstroke of bureaucratic sleaze in which a multitude of officials did just the right amount of obfuscating, equivocating, and finger pointing to ensure that this effrontery was not easy to attribute to anyone in particular. The brass could say that they went out of their way to preemptively detain the cops, and that the Public Ministry should have moved faster; the lab could say that it issued its dictum in record time; and the attorney general could say that his prosecutors had needed that dictum in hand in order to file charges. All those excuses sounded at least somewhat convincing, but in reality, the force could have held on to the cops for several more days; Julieta heard a rumor that the lab deliberately delayed its dictum; and at least a few people inside the Public Ministry felt that the attorney general subtly postponed the indictment by nonsensically shifting prosecutors on and off the case.

This debacle was impenetrably labyrinthine, but even so, it functioned as an earsplitting alarm announcing, once and for all, that the country's criminal justice system was rotten to the core. If these institutions would do this to the rector, under the brightest of spotlights, then what had they been doing to everyone else, invisibly in the shadows?

Julieta now possessed not just an academic's expert authority and a rector's positional authority but also a victim's moral authority, which meant she bore a cross, a duty to lead the charge against the institutions of criminal justice.

"This is a caricature of a country," she declared on *Frente a Frente*, on October 31. "We, the citizens of this nation, do not deserve to be subjected to these institutions. . . . They are monsters that feed on the blood of our youth, monsters that fill up their own bank accounts to the brim. . . . So I am telling you this: Even though I am still dealing with the severe pain of losing my husband three years ago, and even though, before I could finish mourning him, I had to begin mourning another member of my family, I'm going to give everything I have to this fight. If I lose my life along the way, so be it."

THE DAY AFTER THE UNDERGRADUATES WERE MURDERED, KURT emailed Carlos, "Should we offer to help?"

Julieta wanted two things: to capture her son's killers, and to cleanse the country's institutions of criminal justice. Kurt and Carlos had been wanting to fix those institutions, too, but unlike her, they didn't have enough pull to seriously even attempt to do it. What they did have, however, was Peace and Justice, perhaps the most competent murder-solving outfit in the country.

It sounded like a match made in heaven.

Kurt and Carlos tried getting in touch with her, but Julieta was busy, grieving, and famous, so they were unable to get a meeting.

While they were sidelined, someone else stepped up to help lead the charge against those institutions.

Alfredo Landaverde, a seventy-one-year-old with a square chin and a salt-and-pepper mustache, originally came to prominence when he founded an alternative political party built around a Catholic brand of altruism. But what he was most known for was calling out the police. Unlike most naysayers, however, throughout his career, he had been willing to get his hands dirty. For example, he previously worked for both the Security Ministry and the Public Ministry on the battle—the losing battle—against narcotrafficking.

In his willingness to take on David-versus-Goliath fights, in his Bible-suffused focus on criminal justice, and in his commitment not just to critiquing but also to helping remediate, he was, in so many ways, an exemplar of what Kurt and Carlos hoped to become. But role models can easily become cautionary tales, and on *Frente a Frente*, on November 1, Landaverde broke an unwritten rule: He named names.

Next to an on-screen photograph showing the pale face of the chief of the Honduran National Police, General Ricardo Ramírez del Cid, Landaverde declared, "Ramírez del Cid knows who is in charge of organized crime. . . . Ramírez del Cid knows who runs the maras. . . . Ramírez del Cid knows which cops are in gangs."

Watching him say that on live television was as stomach churning as watching a climber scale a cliff without ropes, because in a country with such stiff defamation laws, he was getting as close as he possibly could to a stinging j'accuse against a man with an extremely unsavory reputation.

Landaverde knew he was risking it all—his own brother had gotten the Two-Men-on-a-Motorcycle treatment back in the eighties—but he still felt like he had to speak up, because in his mind, the police force was pushing his beloved country into an abyss.

In other media appearances that month, he delved into another verboten topic, the 2009 assassination of his friend Julián Arístides González, who, at the time, had been the country's drug czar. That case had been ice cold for a while, but Landaverde was now alleging that police officers were responsible. On November 28, he gave a statement about it to the Public Ministry.

A little over a week later, he and his wife, a Venezuelan sociologist named Hilda Caldera, drove off to run some errands. They had originally met at a library in Caracas in the late seventies, at a time when Landaverde believed that by studying abroad, he could learn how to fix his homeland. But after spending the bulk of his life attempting to do that, he was now driving through a country that the Peace Corps was about to abandon due to "security concerns," a country where, as Landaverde himself explained, "nine congress-people have been machine-gunned to death," and a country where, two days prior, the offices of *La Tribuna*, the newspaper that first linked police officers to the undergraduates' killing, had been shot up by unknown assailants.

Hilda, who was in the passenger seat, put on some lipstick, and then, right when they stopped at a red light, she saw a flash and felt a burning sensation on her back.

Hoping to make sense of these baffling phenomena, she looked left, only to see her husband's head tilted back, and his mouth ajar.

As she was trying to process that, Two Men on a Motorcycle rode away across a bridge.

Years earlier, her husband had written her a letter that said, "I want to die by your side."

———

LIKE MOST EVERYONE ELSE, KURT AND CARLOS WERE DEEPLY DIS-turbed by the news about Landaverde, but they also knew that the tragedy had the potential to get them to the woman they had been pursuing. In order to finally reach Julieta, however, they were going to need a ghost from the past.

If you were to have heard Cholo claim that he and Landaverde were dear friends, you probably would have raised an eyebrow. But it was true. "My husband and he were very, very, very tight," Hilda, who survived her wounds, later said.

Kurt and Carlos thought long and hard about the pros and cons of reimmersing themselves in the Cholo Experience, but when you needed it, you *really* needed it, so inevitably, Kurt reached out to his former operative, on December 20.

Soon thereafter, Cholo brought Hilda, who had been wearing a black-and-white shawl to symbolize her grief, and who was dead-set on hunting down her husband's killers, to meet Kurt at ASJ's office. Since she knew Julieta—they were both sociologists who studied crime—she was able to make the subsequent arrangements.

On January 25, 2012, Kurt, Carlos, Cholo, and Hilda went to meet Julieta in the rectory, a large office with peach-colored walls, a cluttered desk, and an antique coffee table surrounded by chairs. "I felt very grateful that these people, who didn't even know me, sought me out," Julieta later reflected. ". . . Normally, people tell you to drop the case, to just let God take care of it."

This small group of people decided to jointly wage a Double Fight. They were going to try to punish whoever had a hand in killing the undergraduates and Landaverde, and they were going to try to remake the institutions of criminal justice. That second part was going to be mind-numbingly multifaceted, but from the start, their number one goal was to purge the police, to replace the bad cops with ones that were better. It is hard to convey how dangerous that was going to be— according to a specialized publication called *InSight Crime*, corrupt cops in Honduras had a much more direct role in criminal activity than their counterparts in Mexico and Colombia.

The force's mothership was a campus of pale yellow buildings on a hill in downtown Tegucigalpa, and this facility's name, Casamata, somehow said it all. Though that word is technically an old-fashioned term for a bunker, because *casa* means "house," and *mata* can mean "it kills," the headquarters of the Honduran National Police sort of sounded like "The House of Murder."

And it truly was. Unbeknownst to the outside world, the force's internal inspectorate had already determined that within those jaundiced grounds, General Ramírez del Cid and about two dozen other cops had conspired to assassinate Arístides González, the drug czar.

The inspectorate had actually written up a detailed report about that, but it would not be seeing the light of day anytime soon, and it would spend much of that dormancy alongside the force's other top-secret case files, including the one about the undergraduates, and the one about Landaverde. According to the Landaverde report, General Ramírez del Cid killed him, too.

– 2 –

KURT AND CARLOS USED FUNDING THEY DRUMMED UP FROM the Danish government's development arm to fly themselves and about a dozen Honduran luminaries, including Julieta and a prominent televangelist named Alberto Solórzano, to Guatemala on February 19, 2012. The explicit purpose of this trip was to study an anticorruption initiative there, but Kurt and Carlos also hoped that the group would bond.

Certain things about the two of them were fairly irresistible, such as their fearlessness, their cross-cultural bromance, and the fact that they *chose* to live in Nueva Suyapa. So it was no surprise that the travelers hit it off and decided to create an organization dedicated to the second leg of the Double Fight, to overhauling the institutions of criminal justice.

By the time the Alliance for Peace and Justice held its introductory press conference on March 8, at the Marriott in Tegucigalpa, it included not only ASJ, the national university, and Pastor Solórzano's gargantuan association of Protestant churches, but also a trade federation, an umbrella of NGOs, and a number of other entities.

This new alliance had gone ahead with the event even though, two days earlier, Kurt and Carlos had received what felt like a warning not to. The Cobra policemen who had been guarding them and their staff for about five years just hadn't shown up. According to the charity's records, when General Ramírez del Cid soon received its complaint about this, he remitted it to a subordinate who was not even in a position to resolve the issue.

After about a month, the Cobras did come back, but even so, Kurt and Carlos were in a precarious spot given that their lightly armed bodyguards were under the command of the brass their alliance was aiming to sack, prosecute, and jail. For the time being, it would primarily try to do that by prodding the Directorate for the Investigation and Evaluation of the Police Career, or the DIECP, a brand-new agency that was supposed to jettison crooked cops.

Though the alliance was technically separate from ASJ, in practice, it was something like an appendage to it. Its weekly meeting happened at the charity's office, and its executive director reported directly to Kurt and Carlos. Kurt's role was largely strategic and technocratic; he helped produce the well-researched reports the alliance would release, and his relentless email and WhatsApp nudging was the fuel that kept the whole operation churning along. Carlos, meanwhile, served as one of the alliance's statesmen; after a media coach taught him how to condense messages into sound bites, as well as which rhythms, expressions, and outfits worked on air, he became a regular fixture on the talk-show circuit. By the end of the year, the host of *Frente a Frente* would publicly anoint him as a sort of Landaverdean figure: "There are people who are willing to sacrifice their lives to combat corruption . . . men like Carlos Hernández, who expose themselves, who risk themselves, who might get themselves killed."

Because Julieta and Pastor Solórzano could arrange a meeting with pretty much anyone in the country, Kurt and Carlos suddenly found themselves operating in rarefied air. The man who was then the in-country rep for the United Nations Development Programme—

which, along with the US Department of State and the Open Society Foundations, would fund the alliance—later shared his impression of the two friends: "I think that in my entire career, which spans twenty years with the United Nations, they are among the most honest people I have ever met, among the best examples of integrity, commitment, and principled behavior I have ever encountered. And I'm not exaggerating about that."

One person Kurt and Carlos occasionally attended meetings with was Porfirio Lobo Sosa, or Pepe Lobo, the folksy, wishy-washy conservative who had been elected president after the coup. "I should say to you that I support all actions that are valid and will help us move forward" was the sort of hot air he was known to spew out to the press.

According to Carlos, the president once pulled him aside, placed his hand on his back, and said, "Don't get involved in all this stuff, man. This stuff is very dangerous. This stuff is not for you."

———

ONE OF THE MI–92 COPS HAD TURNED HIMSELF IN, BUT AS OF AUGUST 2012, the other three were still on the lam, despite the fact that Cholo had run a number of three-to-five-day search operations in the rural area where they were supposedly hiding out.

The Landaverde investigation had also been a dud. Cholo kept insisting that he and the official detail were on top of it—"for the umpteenth time I am asking you to be patient," he once wrote to Hilda—but Kurt, for one, was losing faith. "He had information, but none of it was panning out," the gringo later said. "Was he just taking our money? Did he *really* have that information? I was never quite sure."

But then, in accordance with a key tenet of the Cholo Experience, Cholo (or someone else) delivered. In early September, a twenty-one-year-old sicario was charged with murdering Landaverde. His name had first come onto the detail's radar through a tip, and since then, several witnesses had confirmed that he really was the triggerman.

Because he was already in prison for another crime, no capture had to be made.

Cholo, of course, took a lot of credit for this, and for what it's worth, Julieta, who could fact-check him through her many contacts in the criminal justice system, saw no reason to doubt the veracity of his claims. Kurt wasn't as convinced, but he kept running Cholo anyway, and on November 1, a second M1–92 cop turned himself in. According to Julieta, Cholo had a hand in that. "He used to send us photos from the places where he searched," she later said. "These were small rural communities, so it's likely the fugitives realized he was there. . . . I think this cop decided that surrendering was better than getting captured or killed."

Was Kurt trusting Cholo too little, too much, or just the right amount? That was a doozy of a question, but on the back of these two advances, he renewed the operative's contract for a few more months. Still at large were two M1–92 cops, the second Landaverde sicario, and whoever else had authorized, planned, or covered up the two killings.

WHAT THE DIECP HAD THE AUTHORITY TO DO, AND WHAT THE ALLI-ance had been pushing it to follow through with, was to subject every last cop to a confidence test that included a polygraph, a drug screen, and a financial audit. In the past, the force had gone to great lengths to avoid such inquisitions. For example, according to a well-informed political commentator, when the previous security minister announced a purge, the top brass mutinously occupied his office. "In Honduras," the minister said, after he had fled the country, "it is easier to depose a minister than to fire a single corrupt cop."

Clearly, the DIECP was in need of an incredibly valiant leader, but to Kurt's dismay, a gray-haired creature of the Honduran bureau-cracy named Eduardo Villanueva had been appointed at a meeting that the public was inappropriately barred from entering. On October 29, 2012, Villanueva informed the alliance that in the prior four months, his agency had put 145 cops through the confidence test and asked the Security Ministry to purge 70.

This was far from a thundering performance—the force was fourteen thousand officers strong—but at least it was a step in the right direction, and for the time being, the alliance wanted to be supportive. "We have agreed with the DIECP to put together a workshop ASAP on both the science and constitutionality of the polygraph," Kurt wrote to some contacts, on November 5.

Accurate lie detection is one of the white whales of criminal investigation. In the 1910s, a Harvard student hypothesized that when humans speak deceptively, their blood pressure spikes. He did some prototyping around that concept, and later on in life, while consulting for DC Comics, he created Wonder Woman, a superhero whose lasso could force those it enwrapped to tell the truth. By that time, 1941, the polygraph as we know it today was in use—a subject answered a series of yes-no questions while a cuff around his upper arm measured his blood pressure and heart rate, while a tube around his torso measured his breath rate, and while galvanometers clamped onto his fingertips measured his sweatiness.

This rudimentary gadget does not clairvoyantly spelunk through the depths of the human mind. What it does is detect stress, and while, yes, that stress could certainly be the byproduct of a guilty subject's nervous lying, it could also be the byproduct of an innocent subject's concern that this mid-century contraption was going to unfairly ruin his life. Because of that ambiguity, some see the polygraph as pseudoscientific hogwash, as a method little better than the trial-by-ordeal farces of the past. But the truth of the matter is not that extreme.

Research suggests that polygraph accuracy is materially better than a coin flip. That being said, it is still considered to be too error prone for certain applications. In the United States, for instance, polygraph results are generally not admissible in court, and nongovern-mental employers cannot use them as part of their hiring. American law enforcement agencies, however, can and do use the machine to screen potential candidates; this has undoubtedly weeded out many bad apples, but it has also undoubtedly screwed over a number of blameless applicants.

On November 27, in response to an appeal filed by a group of Honduran cops, four of the five justices on the Constitutional Chamber of the Supreme Court ruled that the DIECP's use of the poly-graph was unconstitutional. Since their decision was not unanimous, since that one justice held out, the officers' appeal was now going to have to go before the full slate of fifteen justices. But given how lop-sided the chamber-level vote was, it sure seemed like the polygraph was about to be outlawed.

An outraged Julieta told *La Tribuna* that the Constitutional Chamber was totally ignoring the fact that "the public security situation is a national emergency." There was no denying that the poly-graph would precipitate some number of unjust dismissals, but from the alliance's perspective, that collateral damage would be worth it, because there was no other feasible way to transform the force.

The power that the Supreme Court was about to strip away from the DIECP had been granted to it by the National Congress. Nevertheless, Juan Orlando Hernández, the president of the legislature, assured the press that he would respect the judiciary's decision.

But in reality, this was a man who didn't believe he had to kowtow to the checks and balances, and he was about to show that, at just forty-four years of age, he was the most powerful person in the entire country.

Throughout Juan Orlando's childhood in a rural western state, his father, a former army colonel, had forced him to wake up before daybreak and do chores with the farmhands—feed the cows, milk the cows, harvest the corn. Those were some serious man-of-the-people bona fides, but unlike some other Honduran politicians, he didn't maintain affectations that deliberately romanticized his rustic roots. He had gone on to get a law degree from the national university and a master's in public administration from the State University of New York at Albany, and in adulthood, he would act not like a campesino but like a globe-trotting executive. He was ambitious, hyperactive, transactional, pragmatic, decisive, well informed, well spoken, and well clothed, the type of guy who might pop up in the middle of a meeting to synthesize whatever was being discussed on a white board. And though he was a member of the conservative National Party, he could talk about clean energy and human rights as competently as he could talk about foreign direct investment and Jesus Christ.

On December 10, two days before the Supreme Court was scheduled to rule on the polygraph, once and for all, the National Congress, which, according to one politician, typically obeyed Juan Orlando with "a spectacular domesticity," created a commission to "investigate" the justices. Then, around 1:30 a.m. the following night, a time of day when Juan Orlando was known to do business, he addressed the legislature in its chamber, the Hemicycle. He kicked things off by unconvincingly alleging that a criminal conspiracy was behind the Constitutional Chamber's ruling.

The legislature had appointed all fifteen of the justices to their seven-year terms but didn't have an unambiguous right to terminate them—and it most certainly wasn't allowed to get rid of them just because it disapproved of their rulings. Nevertheless, at 3:58 a.m., a majority of the congresspeople in attendance voted to defenestrate the four justices who had gone against the polygraph.

The handful of people who theoretically could have resisted Juan Orlando's end run around the rules did not do that. President Pepe Lobo, who supported the defenestration, instead called for "harmony" among the various branches, and the chief justice didn't put up a meaningful fight, perhaps because his clerk was one of the replacement justices named.

Juan Orlando had rescued the purge, but he had also shown that beneath his shell of corporatized refinement, he was, in essence, an unapologetic political thug. For many Hondurans, that wasn't necessarily a turnoff. The country was only a few decades removed from autocratic rule, and one survey showed that just 41 percent of respondents agreed with the following: "Democracy has its problems but is still better than any other form of government." In other words, there was a fairly pervasive school of thought that said society's most intractable problems, like rampant crime and a contaminated police force, could be solved only by an agile strongman.

Perhaps there was an element of truth to that, but the next question had to be, Was Juan Orlando playing fast and loose with the constitution to altruistically solve intractable problems or to selfishly empower and enrich himself? With someone as slick and strategic as him, there would always be multiple angles to consider. In the case of the defenestration, here is just one of them: Juan Orlando had recently won the National Party's presidential primary, and the runner-up was planning to ask the Supreme Court to authorize a recount. So—well, well, well—had Juan Orlando replaced those four justices simply to safeguard his electoral victory?

Politics is a game of multiplayer, multidimensional chess, and Juan Orlando had made his gambit to dominate the board right when Kurt and Carlos had finally gained access to it. They could have retreated from the terrain he arrayed, but they instead kept playing, even though in this type of match, players could be turned into pawns.

———

"I'M MOVING A PIECE IN OPERATION RUBÍ."

The person who sent that thrilling sentence to Kurt and Carlos on February 14, 2013, was Omar Rivera. In 1994, at the impressively young age of twenty-three, he had been elected councilman of El Progreso, a city of over a hundred thousand people. He went on to work in Mel's government, and since the coup, he had been running a small charity that was now part of the alliance. But he was a political animal through and through. "I'm a warrior, I'm a tractor, I'm a bulldozer," he later said of himself. "My approach to politics is fearless."

Kurt and Carlos had come to accept that what came to them naturally—cooperativeness, studiousness, assuming the best—would earn them allies and access but not results. Therefore, according to Kurt, their new attitude toward government officials was, "If you're going to be brave, we'll support you; if you're going to be shitty, we'll try to get rid of you." That was why they had brought Omar, a feisty wheeler-dealer who never met a microphone he didn't like, into their inner circle.

He regularly sent them Homeric emails that were part primer on how politics works, part dramatis personae, and part step-by-step game plan. His "Operation Rubí" dispatch explained how to get rid of Attorney General Luis Rubí, the man in charge of the Public Ministry.

"I like this email a lot," Kurt replied.

He liked it a lot because, as one alliance member succinctly put it, "Rubí has been accused of negligence and corruption and is considered to be incompetent and a liar." Putting aside whatever he may or may not have done to contribute to the vanishing of the M1–92 policemen, he had seemingly engaged in some other misconduct. For example, according to the Administrative Office of Seized Assets, he apportioned thirty-one impounded vehicles for his and his family's use.

Yet he wasn't even necessarily the "shittiest" official then running an institution of criminal justice. Carlos had recently escorted four foreign experts on police reform to meet with the purge's key players, and in his mind, it was "very clearly a failure."

The DIECP, which had already cost taxpayers over a million dollars, had thus far recommended that just 230 cops be dismissed, and of those, only 31 had actually been purged. And most disturbingly,

Villanueva, the chief of the DIECP, had been letting the brass tell him which cops to evaluate, even though the whole point of his agency was that it was supposed to be independent of the force.

This pathetic excuse for a purge could be blamed not just on Villanueva but also on the two people who actually had the authority to fire officers, Security Minister Pompeyo Bonilla and the chief of police. Though General Ramírez del Cid was still on the force, he had been replaced as top cop by Juan Carlos Bonilla, aka El Tigre.

Whoever was in charge of casting villains in direct-to-video action movies would have had a field day with this warhorse of a man who towered over his subordinates, whose face was pockmarked and cartoonishly mean-featured, and whose noggin has been compared, quite aptly, to an Olmec head. The unusual way he shook hands seemed choreographed, like everything else he said and did, to unnerve and emasculate: With his fingers spread completely apart, he inserted his claw into yours such that the primary touchpoint was the webbing between his thumb and index finger; then, after making you wait for a second that felt like a minute, he coiled you—tightening his pinky, then his ring, then the others, one by one, until you beheld the power of his grasp. And throughout that entire nerve-racking experience, you were well aware that according to the many legends about this man, that hand you were touching did not play fair, in either love or war. He had fathered thirty children with fourteen different women, and when a Salvadoran journalist once asked him, point-blank, if he had ever murdered someone, his response was, "There are things that one takes to the grave."

Which perhaps explained why he had been so intent on dodging the polygraph. For all its faults, he did seem to respect its capabilities—a foreign journalist would soon discover that one of the only wall decorations in his spartan home was a caricature of himself chasing President Pepe Lobo, Juan Orlando, and Minister Bonilla with a polygraph machine in his hands.

There was undeniably a measure of black comedy in the way these superpowerful men conducted themselves, but all in all, the fact that Attorney General Rubí, Villanueva, Minister Bonilla, and El Tigre were in charge of safeguarding the most violent nation on earth was nothing short of tragic. When Kurt gave a speech about these issues on March 7, at the Church of the Servant in Grand Rapids, Michigan, he got choked up: "Honduras is hurting. My friends are hurting. My neighbors are hurting. I am hurting. . . . What's hard and sad and depressing is that it often feels like corruption and violence are growing faster than our efforts to stop them. We've done investigations. We've made proposals. We've held press conferences. But it feels like that's not doing anything. . . . Putting this presentation together has helped me be a little more hopeful, helped me feel like, even though we're not seeing results yet on the security issue, we're on the edge. Nah, maybe not even on the edge yet, but at least in the right place."

In mid-March, he, Julieta, and two other alliance members expressed their frustrations at a meeting with the country's heavyweights: President Pepe Lobo, Juan Orlando, Attorney General Rubí, Minister Bonilla, and El Tigre. Doing that took some serious gall given that some of the people the alliance wanted to axe were there in that room.

"I think that power is making me sick :-)" Kurt wrote to Carlos and two other contacts, the following Sunday. "I got home on Friday night and started vomiting and had diarrhea. . . . But now I'm getting better. I think that last meeting went really well."

"What's happening to us?" Carlos, who had been out of town, replied to just Kurt. "All Saturday and today I had an upset stomach, vomiting and diarrhea. . . . I'm never doing this travel craziness again."

"That's bizarre," Kurt wrote back. "We are connected in a strange way."

The political personage most aligned with the alliance's way of thinking had always been Juan Orlando, so on April 2, Kurt and a few others met up with him. Together they finalized an audacious plan that would begin with some public humiliation and hopefully end with new leadership atop the institutions of criminal justice.

A day later, Juan Orlando announced that an unprecedented spectacle was about to occur. His legislature and the alliance were going to jointly grill the country's criminal justice chieftains, one after the other, on live television, at primetime. In anticipation of the theatrical dressing-down those leaders were surely going to experience, the press decided to call this event the Catwalk.

Omar soon sent Kurt, Carlos, and the executive director of the alliance a one-thousand-word email with seventeen attachments to make sure his "brothers in arms" understood the stakes. While, yes, they might have been on the verge of canning those "shitty" officials, there was also a risk that the Catwalk would turn out to be a worthless dog and pony show or, even worse, one of Juan Orlando's self-serving machinations. If that was, in fact, how this played out, then the alliance's credibility—its political lifeblood— would vanish, because going forward, they would be seen as Juan Orlando's lackeys.

"We will now have to wait and see," Omar wrote in a follow-up message, "if what the legislators told us in private will become concrete in public, in the Hemicycle."

THERE WAS A TIME WHEN CARLOS SPENT HIS DAYS FRATERNIZING with schoolchildren in a marginalized barrio, but now he was in the Hemicycle, with a camera pointed at his face as he questioned Villaneuva, the chief of the DIECP, who was standing behind a rostrum with Juan Orlando and the rest of the congressional leadership at a dais to his rear.

In reference to the cops who held some type of rank—that is, the ones who mattered most—Carlos said, "You told us that we have

1,060 police officials. . . . Can you confirm that you have only applied 32 comprehensive confidence tests to those 1,060 officials?"

This question was designed to embarrass Villanueva, but Carlos was still mastering the art of political show business, so before he even let him respond, he shifted his microphone to the left and said, "My colleague here has another question."

Omar was wearing a sport coat but no tie, and as he pontificated, his expression alternated between irritation and disgust, and his right hand flitted around like a conductor's. "I would like Mr. Villanueva to listen very carefully to the question I am about to ask him. Sir, you have stated that the police chief is the one who sends you the lists of which officers to evaluate comprehensively. Is that correct?"

"Yes," Villanueva responded.

"It was the chief of police?" Omar repeated, rubbing it in.

This caused Juan Orlando to interject, "I'd like to avoid a dialogue here."

"Very well then," Omar continued. "The police chief sent you the list. My question is simple then. Have you comprehensively evaluated—I'm talking about the toxicological test, the psychometric test, the financial investigation, and the polygraph test—have you applied all of that to the last two police chiefs?" Who he was referring to was completely obvious, yet he still proceeded to name their names: "I'm talking about El Tigre and General Ramírez del Cid." And then, after playing with that forbidden fire, he decided to spell out his implication: "Because if you haven't, we run the risk that the two people who sent you those lists are drug addicts, or have illicitly enriched themselves, or have otherwise acted outside the law."

In fairness to Villanueva, there probably weren't too many people in the country who would have had the guts to hook those two menacing characters up to a polygraph machine, but that happened to be his job, and his excuse for shirking his duty was, to put it lightly, unconvincing. "If you are asking me why I haven't done a comprehensive evaluation of El Tigre," he said, "then I will respond nobly. That particular functionary was named by the president of the Republic of Honduras, and according to the members of the American Polygraph Association, a special protocol will be needed to polygraph him."

The next victim prodded out onto the Catwalk was Attorney General Rubí. After the executive director of the alliance asked him what appeared to be a simple question—How do you go about identifying and sanctioning underperforming prosecutors?—Rubí, an oafish man with a receding hairline, awkwardly stood in silence . . . for . . . sixteen . . . seconds . . . and then finally said, "I would like to tell you that—I suppose you're an NGO? Is that correct? If I'm not mistaken. Please answer me. You people are an NGO?"

"We are a coalition of large networks of civil society organizations," the executive director replied.

"To me, that indicates that you are a group of people, a group of institutions. But of those, none are NGOs? Huh?"

"What is your concrete question, Mr. Attorney General? Are there NGOs in our alliance? Yes, there are NGOs. There are also churches, labor syndicates, and other groups like youth organizations, women's organizations, and campesino organizations."

The seniormost attorney in the entire nation then started talking haltingly as he fidgeted, picked up his papers, put them back down, dropped his pen, rubbed his hands together, and then picked his pen up off the floor. Without clarifying why he had harped on the NGO matter, he employed an oratorical technique that seemed to fuse spoken-word poetry with a psychedelic trance: "I would like to tell you that running an institution like the Public Ministry, which knows a man from the time of his birth until the time of his death, which does an enormous quantity of activities, which knows about the air, which knows about the land, which knows about the trees, which knows the men, which knows the women, which knows the children, which knows the water, which knows the forests, which knows democracy, which knows narcotrafficking, which knows itself, all of it . . . " The recording the alliance preserved of this gets cuts off there, so it's theoretically possible that Rubí somehow landed his homily, but according to Kurt, his performance was "a crash and burn."

The following evening, Minister Bonilla explained that he had not axed many of the cops he intended to because before he had had a chance to make their removals official, they had gone on medical leave. Cops on medical leave cannot be fired, so what was being suggested here was that in the nick of time, a fortuitous wave of handicapping ailments had yanked a bunch of cops off the chopping block.

Next El Tigre, who was wearing a peaked military cap and a dark blue uniform adorned with decorations, declared, "I have just ordered the entire high command to take the confidence test. Me included."

At the conclusion of the Catwalk, on April 12, Juan Orlando did some chest thumping: "Now decisions must be made. . . . Anyone who doesn't have the courage to match the situation we are living through should not be in a position of power."

Not long after that, Kurt, Carlos, Omar, Julieta, and Pastor Solórzano went to discuss those decisions with Juan Orlando and Pepe Lobo at the president's mansion. The Catwalk was, any way you spun it, a Juan Orlando power play, so in front of everyone, Pepe Lobo made a show of scolding the younger politician. He reminded everyone that he, Pepe Lobo, had the authority to fire Minister Bonilla, and he insisted that, though he might ultimately do it, he didn't want any of them pressuring him to do it.

By the first of May, Minister Bonilla had been replaced; Villanueva had offered to resign; and Attorney General Rubí had been suspended. But the writing was on the wall.

Juan Orlando's legislature had recently given itself a clear right to impeach the attorney general, which had been possible only because the four constitutional justices who used to block that sort of thing had been defenestrated out of the picture. And as it turned out, the mere threat of impeachment was enough—Rubí resigned in June.

At the time, Kurt was in New York after having gone on a family vacation to the Grand Canyon. "I fell asleep very HAPPY!" he wrote to Carlos, Omar, and Julieta. "When I get back, we have to go out and celebrate. I feel like we did a good job and also that God is doing work."

– 3 –

I T WAS GENERALLY ASSUMED THAT CONGRESSIONAL APPOINT-
ments were made based on partisan finagling and backroom palm-
greasing, but the understanding the alliance had come to with Juan
Orlando was that it would get to help the legislature set up a virtuous
and depoliticized procedure for selecting the next attorney general.
As soon as it began negotiating the details of that procedure with the
congressional leadership, however, it became clear that the National
Party, which controlled the legislature, was scheming to appoint an
attorney general who would further its own interests.

On *Frente a Frente*, on July 9, 2013, Omar called this behavior
"absurd," a word which, in the decorous patois of the Honduran talk-
show circuit, was quite a strong insult. He blasted the National Party
for trying to rush through the appointment and reiterated the alliance's stance that it shouldn't happen until March 2014, when Rubí's
five-year term was supposed to have ended. This seemingly banal timing issue was actually engulfed in partisan passions, because there was
an election in November—Juan Orlando was running for president,
and every congressional seat was up for grabs. The point being, if
the attorney general were chosen next year, then the next legislature,

which was expected to be way less National Party dominated, would get to make the call.

Two days later, Carlos informed Kurt, who was still stateside, that Juan Orlando's chief adviser had called into that *Frente a Frente* episode and "publicly accused us of being traitors. It seems like Juan Orlando got very angry. Thank God I didn't go on the program, because I had to be the 'conciliator' afterward. . . . But I do think we proved ourselves to those who think we just follow Juan Orlando's instructions."

The next day, Kurt, who was clearly feeling guilty about his prolonged absence, related a dream he had had to Carlos and Julieta. "We were going into a meeting," he wrote, "and you guys were giving me a hard time about having left the country for so long :-) I'm back next Tuesday."

The alliance kept on lobbying for the type of appointment it wanted, and Omar felt they shouldn't accept anything short of that. But talented politicians know how to seduce their detractors, and once the legislators decided that the appointment was, most definitely, going to happen now, they offered the alliance a seat on the board that was going to nominate five candidates for congress to choose from.

Omar, the political whiz kid, thought they should stay away unless a series of stringent demands were met, but as Kurt put it in an email on August 11, he, Carlos, Julieta, and a few of the alliance's other key players felt that "ultimately, it is better to be inside the process than outside."

Five days later, Carlos and the six other members of the nominating board gathered in the Supreme Court of Justice building, around a shiny black table in a room with framed portraits, tan-and-gold drapery, and ornamental columns. Carlos felt like three of the nominators would go about this objectively—in addition to himself, there was Julieta, who had her own seat through the national university, and Dr. Custodio, who, six years removed from his spat with Dina, was still the national human rights commissioner. Then there were three nominators who had received congressional appointments themselves and therefore could have hidden loyalties and agendas: two Supreme Court justices and, in representation of the national association of attorneys, Rubí's former deputy. And finally, there was the seventh seat. Though it was held by a seemingly apolitical entity, the national association of private universities, Carlos was concerned, because the association had chosen to appoint Luis Eveline, whose wife was both a congressional candidate and a member of Juan Orlando's party.

Carlos had never been involved in this type of high-level sausage making before, but he still brought along a proposal for how the board should go about doing its vetting. According to him, much of that was adopted, which meant that, for the first time ever, the five nominees were going to have to survive a rigorous tournament with round-by-round eliminations.

Fifty-one contenders threw hats into the ring.

The nominators scrutinized their résumés from three p.m. on Friday, August 23, until three a.m. the following morning. Then, on little sleep, they spent all of Saturday interviewing the forty-six candidates who advanced, working until the early evening when, with the power out in the Supreme Court building, they had to illuminate their workspace with cellphones.

Thirty-eight contestants proceeded to the next round, a psychometric evaluation in a military building on Monday morning. "I'm walking out of this a bit exhausted," one of the aspirants told *La Tribuna*. "The psychometric test included more than eight hundred questions. . . . The examiners tried to get at the most intimate aspects of your personality and social life."

With the exception of Luis Eveline, who had been MIA since that first meeting, the board got together that night and used a pre-established scoring mechanism to determine which thirteen candidates advanced. Carlos thought that most of them were qualified to be the next attorney general, which was a testament to the tournament's impartiality, as was the fact that they had just eliminated Óscar Chinchilla. Chinchilla had been the only justice on the Constitutional Chamber not to oppose the polygraph and, relatedly, the only one not to get defenestrated. Ergo, he was presumed to be Juan Orlando's ally.

When the thirteen remaining contestants submitted themselves to a three-hour polygraph exam the following day, the questions asked of them included, Have you ever stolen from the government? And have you ever consumed marijuana, LSD, heroin, amphetamine, glue, cocaine, crack, methamphetamine, paint thinner, ecstasy, morphine, gasoline, or mushrooms?

Later that day, all the nominators, Luis Eveline included, met up to select the five nominees, and as they deliberated behind closed doors, the press anxiously waited.

When Carlos emerged, however, he revealed that the tournament had been hijacked: "Luis Eveline, who hadn't been here for this entire process, showed up today with the stance that we should reverse course and apply the polygraph to everyone that we interviewed. . . . This was clearly meant to benefit a particular someone."

The pre-polygraph winnowing down had been unanimously supported by all the nominators then in attendance, but at this meeting, the two justices and Rubí's ex-deputy had sided with Eveline. "This goes against our principles and our desire to do things correctly," Carlos continued, "so Dr. Custodio, the rector of the national university, and I all walked out."

The three of them soon resigned.

By invitation of the hollowed-out nominating board, some previously eliminated candidates took the polygraph, and on Friday, the five nominees were announced. One was—surprise, surprise—Chinchilla, and one was a replacement for the candidate who had gotten the highest marks on the tests but who withdrew in solidarity with the resigners.

The National Congress assembled the following morning, and at the conclusion of what *La Prensa* described as "a strenuous marathon session sullied by claims of multimillion-dollar vote purchasing, intense lobbying, internal scuffling, and street protests," Chinchilla was enthroned.

The alliance denounced this "contaminated and dubious" appointment, but according to Carlos, none of this had come as a shock. "Juan Orlando was not my friend," he later said. "This was purely about opportunism. We tried to take advantage of the opening he gave us to influence things, but with politicians, you always have to remember that they are not looking out for your well-being. They are looking out for their own interests."

This was not how he and Kurt wanted Honduran politics to work, but it *was* how it worked, and, ever pragmatic, they were willing to take this betrayal on the chin. That wasn't terribly hard to do, because taking a step back, they felt like Chinchilla, for all his faults, was a massive upgrade from Rubí. Their first meeting with the new attorney general, on September 12, was a bit uncomfortable, but ASJ wasn't going to stop collaborating with his prosecutors, and the alliance wasn't going to stop trying to revamp his institution.

"Politics is not for purists," Kurt later reflected. "No official was squeaky-clean. If you wanted to influence decision-making and change the country, you had a few choices. . . . One was to criticize, to throw stones from afar. That would have had no impact. Another was to get in bed with politicians and become a yes-man. If you did that, they would have just signed meaningless agreements with you and taken pictures of themselves doing it. We chose another option, where we tried to be close enough to the government to influence it, but far enough away to tell the truth about it, too. Where was that line? That's where we lived. It was often very stressful."

———

CARLOS WAS NOW A MOVER AND SHAKER WHO SOUGHT TO HELP THE poor by breakfasting with politicians and by hosting press conferences that were catered with hors d'oeuvres. Reporters could call him at any moment to ask for a comment on whatever happened to be churning through the news cycle, and it wasn't all that unusual for camera crews to just camp out in ASJ's foyer, waiting for the sagacious big shot to descend.

Being one of the media circus's mainstay acts was a burden, not a thrill. Carlos knew that if he declined to give on-the-record responses, journalists would stop hitting him up, and he would lose his invaluable stump. And he also knew that if his takes weren't thoughtful and well informed, he could damage ASJ and the alliance's reputations or promote bad policymaking. Getting ready for whatever might come at him meant late nights of reading after long days at the office, and even when he was well prepared, the commentating could still feel like walking a tightrope. "I have to be very careful about both what I say and how I say it," he later explained. ". . . That's hard, though, because I'm an emotional person. Sometimes I have to take a deep breath and calm my mind. It's always a difficult balance."

The range of topics he had to stay up to speed on was wide, because in parallel to its efforts to reform the criminal justice system, ASJ had been attempting to rehabilitate other parts of the government, too.

For example, a few years earlier, the charity released a series of damning studies about the country's public schools. Roughly a quarter of the teachers on the payroll never even showed up, and between 2001 and 2010, the average pupil received just 125 days of class per year, or 75 fewer than they were supposed to. These exposés contributed to the education minister's firing, and his replacement, who took over toward the start of 2012 and worked hand in hand with the charity, purged the ghost teachers and imposed some semblance of accountability across the entire system. This produced immediate results. In 2013, a nationwide army of volunteers ASJ conscripted to monitor the public schools confirmed that 200 days of class was achieved.

Healthcare was another ASJ theater of operations. Back in March

2013, the charity revealed that the federal storehouse that supplied the country's public health system had been purchasing overpriced medicines, expired medicines, diluted medicines, and counterfeit medicines. To illustrate how sinister these cons were, on national television, Carlos crumpled up a "blood-pressure pill" that contained no active ingredients. His mother had hypertension—was the medicine she had been taking a placebo? And how many other Hondurans had suffered or died because of these scams?

A week after ASJ released its report about this, the Public Ministry raided the storehouse, and soon thereafter, six of the swindlers were arrested. And once Juan Orlando was inaugurated as the president of the country in January 2014, he transferred responsibility for medicine purchasing to a trust that was overseen by the United Nations.

Speaking of the new president, Juan Orlando's first act on his first day in office was to sign a letter of intent with Carlos that, after about nine months of negotiations, became a historic accord, one that was supposed to supercharge ASJ's anticorruption efforts. The administration was going to be granting it an accountant's-eye view of five different branches—security, education, healthcare, taxes, and infrastructure. With this privileged access to information, the charity was undoubtedly going to discover a massive amount of fraud, embezzlement, and graft, because the Honduran bureaucracy was an absolute abomination. The Inter-American Development Bank had recently given civil services across Latin America a score between 0, being the worst, and 100; the average country got a 38, the second-worst country got a 21, and Honduras got a *12*.

On October 6, 2014, *Frente a Frente*'s venerable host, Renato Álvarez, got into position at the center of his metallic art-deco desk with two of the president's advisers to his right, and Carlos and the president of Transparency International, a Berlin-based anticorruption organization with chapters all across the world, to his left. The connection there was that ASJ had recently become its Honduras chapter.

As Carlos explained the new accord to the viewership, Renato listened with his neck craned and hands in a triangle. Once his guest finished, he asked for a clarification: "So Transparency International and the Honduran government are going to work together on creating transparency?"

"Exactly," Carlos replied.

"I'm going to tell you an anecdote," Renato continued, before turning toward the president's advisers, removing his eyeglasses, and throwing up a let's-cut-the-crap finger wag. "When I saw little Carlos Hernández, at the start of Juan Orlando's government, announcing that he was going to be working with the new administration, I said to myself, 'They are going to coopt the Honduran chapter of Transparency International!'"

This was the riddle of Juan Orlando. He would dangle a special opportunity in front of you that really did seem like a once-in-a-lifetime shot to improve Honduras, but if you bit on it, you risked getting a hook or pacifier lodged in your mouth. Kurt and Carlos were going to have to grapple with this dilemma over and over and over again, and so were the gringo diplomats who dealt with Honduras.

In the annals of American diplomacy, collaborating with flawed heads of state was nothing new, though within the Americas at least, the justification for doing so has evolved over time. For the nineteenth-century presidents—Monroe, most famously—it was about preventing European colonization near the United States' shores; for their turn-of-the-century successors, it was about helping American corporations doing business abroad; for FDR, it was about making sure nearby nations didn't ally with the Axis; for the Cold War presidents, it was about stymieing the spread of communism; and for Obama, it was about reducing the number of migrants showing up at the Rio Grande.

Because the forty-fourth president had a crisis on his hands. In 2014, US Border Patrol agents apprehended an unprecedented 68,631 unaccompanied minors, over a quarter of whom had come from Honduras. And that was just one facet of the migration problem; another was that the asylum system was completely overloaded.

According to American law, if a foreigner shows up at a port of entry and claims to be in danger, she has the right to try convincing an asylum officer that her fear is "credible." And if she manages to do that, she is then entitled to an asylum hearing at which a judge must determine whether she is likely to be "persecuted" back home. Just think about that—it's hard enough for American juries to determine whether or not a crime *has* happened in their own backyard; as part of the asylum process, officers and judges must more or less forecast whether or not a crime *will* occur in a distant land.

This system was shaky to begin with, and then the number of applicants skyrocketed to an unmanageable level. Back in 2009, just 5,369 adults made credible-fear claims at the southern border; by 2013, that number had septupled.

And the various challenges at the border showed no signs of abating. The population of Honduras was nine million, and according to a survey that asked if you intended to live or work in another country within the next three years, one-third of Honduran respondents said they did.

Republicans generally blamed the migration problem on "pull factors," like the president's sympathetic handling of the undocumented, while Democrats generally blamed it on "push factors," like the violence and poverty that plagued Central America.

When President Obama's new ambassador, James D. Nealon Jr., was sent to Tegucigalpa in 2014, his marching orders were to reduce migration by alleviating the push factors. He quickly befriended Kurt, who had essentially been trying to do just that for a very long time. "We shared the same goals," Nealon later explained. ". . . We began meeting often, sometimes a couple times per week."

Another person Nealon regularly interacted with was Juan Orlando, who was known to invest a lot of energy in glad-handing gringo officials. "While a member of congress," *The Washington Post* reported, "he lent his office to State Department officials, who used it to rally Honduran lawmakers to support the Iraq War." And according to what one senate aide would tell *The New Yorker*, "He calls you by your first name and tells people in Washington what they want to hear."

Which begs the question, Was Juan Orlando empowering ASJ through this unusually magnanimous accord because he thought that would be fantastic for Honduras, or because he knew it would placate the gringos? And to the extent he was wanting to placate the gringos, who possessed a seemingly limitless spigot of aid money, was his ultimate goal to help Honduras or himself?

In a January 2015 op-ed in *The New York Times*, Vice President Biden explained why the Obama administration had decided to ask Congress to triple what the American government typically provided to Central America. "Last summer," he wrote, "as our countries worked together to stem the dangerous surge in migration, the leaders of El Salvador, Guatemala, and Honduras asked for additional assistance. . . . I made it clear to these leaders that the United States was ready to support them—provided they took ownership of the problem. . . . And they responded. Honduras signed an agreement with Transparency International."

————

TWO MORE RED FLAGS SOON ROSE UP ABOVE JUAN ORLANDO.

On April 22, 2015, the Constitutional Chamber of the Supreme Court, which his legislature previously stacked, ruled that the presidential term limit was unconstitutional. That meant Juan Orlando could run in future elections and, in theory, be president for a long time.

Days later, when he returned from yet another one of his trips to Washington, he tried diverting the press corps' attention to a more flattering topic. "We are the only country in the world that has an accord with Transparency International," he reminded everyone.

The other flag was an even darker shade of red.

Between 2010 and 2013, the leadership of the Honduran Institute for Social Security had embezzled over $300 million from its coffers. The broad strokes of this monumental scandal had been in the public domain for a while, but then, in May 2015, a shocking new twist was introduced when a journalist alleged that some of the looted funds had found their way into Juan Orlando's presidential campaign.

In response, protesters known as the Indignant Ones rushed out into the streets. These demonstrations were a sincere expression of fury and disgust—after all, that money was supposed to have gone toward medical care for the poor—but they also ended up being the coming-of-age bash for a newish left-wing political party known as Libre. It was led by Mel, the couped-out ex-president, and one of its main propellants was a fervent hatred of Juan Orlando.

At a rally on May 13, Mel attacked not only his party's antichrist but also the institutions the antichrist loved to associate himself with. "Where is the American embassy on this?" he said. "Where is the ambassador, Transparency International, and the Organization of American States? Why are they all silent about these acts of corruption? They are the ones who certified this government as 'transparent.'"

That wasn't quite right. ASJ, Transparency International's local chapter, hadn't "certified" the government, but in fairness to Mel, he hadn't been the one who concocted that fiction. It was Juan Orlando who had taken care of that by assiduously presenting the transparency accord as a prize when, in reality, it was supposed to be more like a scarlet letter.

As for the charity's supposed silence, Carlos had, in fact, denounced the social security scandal on multiple occasions. And then, at a press conference on May 18, he unveiled a new slogan, "Whoever Falls . . . Falls," which meant that the Public Ministry should prosecute whoever participated in the pilfering and whoever violated campaign finance laws—without exception.

Mel obviously would have preferred a more explicit skewering of the president, but the allegation about his campaign was still preliminary, and ASJ's tagline did have a very specific implication—they had cribbed it from the Peruvian prosecutor who famously took down one of that country's ex-presidents.

Just as Carlos had hoped, media members started repeating his slogan. But then Juan Orlando did something brilliant: He made it *his thing*.

On June 3, after admitting that, unbeknownst to him, something like $135,000 of the embezzled money had been donated to his campaign, he said, "'Whoever Falls . . . Falls' is the message that the law and justice must be blind. No matter who someone is, if he made a mistake, and there is evidence of it, then he must pay." Going forward, the protesters who supported him would wave "Whoever Falls . . . Falls" signs at the Indignant Ones.

This put Kurt and Carlos in a very uncomfortable position. They were committed to political neutrality, and over the years, they had opposed a number of Juan Orlando's moves, but in light of the prominent roles their charity had played in some of his escapades—the Catwalk, the attorney general appointment, the transparency accord, and now this slogan thing—the Honduran Left, writ large, saw it as the president's lapdog.

At a press conference in early June, Kurt, who rarely appeared in the media, tried doing some damage control by clarifying that "the accord is not a prize for being transparent." But he knew that the real proof they weren't Juan Orlando's stooges was going to be publishing reports about the branches they now had access to, because those reports were inevitably going to expose a plethora of misdeeds within the president's government.

The problem with that was, Kurt and his team were absolutely drowning in the heaps and heaps of documentation that had been turned over to them. Racing to get these audits done, with ASJ's reputation on the line, was one of the most stressful experiences of his life.

Carlos's sons took to the streets to protest with the Indignant Ones, and for the most part, he agreed with the marchers. But one source of friction between ASJ and the movement was what to do about Attorney General Chinchilla.

The demonstrators wanted him to be impeached, because they believed he had sat on evidence about the social security scandal, and because they felt he would never go after his patron, Juan Orlando. But funny enough, Carlos had come around. "I am not defending him," he said on *Frente a Frente*, on June 27, "because I opposed how he got appointed. But I do think it's important to acknowledge that in the past twenty months, the Public Ministry has taken much stronger actions." For instance, the ministry had been seizing assets from cartels, which, according to Kurt, had turned Honduras into "a hostile environment for traffickers—they don't want to live in a country where the government takes your house, your four-wheelers, and your zoo." And as far as Carlos could tell, Chinchilla had been supporting, not obstructing, the social security investigation.

That conception probably wasn't pulled out of thin air, given that, across its various programs, ASJ had several windows into the Public Ministry. And two months after Carlos publicly complimented the attorney general, the charity was granted additional access. "We already work with ASJ on homicides and crimes against minors," Chinchilla explained, in a video produced by the alliance's PR machine, "and now we are going to expand on that." He was going to let the charity get involved in a wider range of cases, and to celebrate that, he and Carlos took some grip-and-grin photographs.

– 4 –

IT IS HARD TO PINPOINT EXACTLY WHEN KURT STOPPED RUNNING Cholo, but both the undergraduates' case and the Landaverde case had been dead for a while. There had been some achievements— the two M1–92 cops who turned themselves in were both convicted, and so was the sicario who shot Landaverde. But when Kurt, Carlos, Julieta, Hilda, and Cholo initiated the Double Fight, several years earlier, they had hoped to punish more of the culprits involved.

And as of December 2015, the most crucial component of the Double Fight, the police purge, had hardly advanced. That month, Omar, who had quit the charity he used to run to work at ASJ full-time, addressed this on *Frente a Frente*. "There are still rotten apples on the force," he declared. "And the reason why is the ineptitude of those who govern us—their trepidation, their cowardice, how afraid they are of the people they need to purge. . . . In the past three years, the DIECP has sent out at least 1,279 case files indicating that a police officer has failed a confidence test. . . . Yet only 260 have actually been removed from the force, and the majority of those were rank and file. . . . We have come here today to say this cannot go on."

Omar delivered that last line with a stirring intensity and a magisterial handwave. But so what? Who cared? He and Carlos had been saying stuff like that for years, repeatedly, like broken records, in every single forum they could.

But then, out of the blue, came what felt like a deus ex machina.

How and why it happened is still a mystery, but after years of dormancy within Casamata, the internal inspectorate's top-secret case files, the ones that described how General Ramírez del Cid and a cabal of crooked cops assassinated both the drug czar and Landaverde, leaked to *El Heraldo*. And soon thereafter, on April 4 and 5, 2016, that newspaper broke one of the stories of the century.

Apparently, the meeting where General Ramírez del Cid and his syndicate planned the hit on the drug czar had been *filmed*, because the boneheaded cop who was instructed to disable the room's video camera had instead unplugged the monitor showing its feed. Since the inspectorate had had access to that video, its report and the *El Heraldo* article based on it were filled with all sorts of cinematic details; this allowed the Honduran public to bear witness to a type of malfeasance that had previously been left to the imagination—cops deciding that the ideal time to murder the drug czar was right after he dropped his daughter off at school; cops cracking jokes and laughing up a storm during a discussion of that nature; and cops divvying up a bag of cash sent to them by their client, a narcotrafficker who wanted to make an honorable public official disappear.

Another astonishing aspect of these revelations was the prominence of the people implicated. General Ramírez del Cid had been the national police chief; his two immediate predecessors in that post had also allegedly been involved with the murder plots; and his two immediate successors, one of whom was El Tigre, had allegedly seen the inspectorate's bombshell case files but chosen not to forward them to the Public Ministry.

At a press conference on April 5, Kurt, Carlos, Julieta, and Hilda stood shoulder to shoulder with Omar as he demanded a purge, for what felt like the millionth time.

But things were different now.

Five days later, Juan Orlando called.

———

THE SPECIAL COMMISSION FOR THE PROCESS OF THE PURGE AND TRANS-
formation of the National Police first gathered on April 13, with Carlos,
Omar, and the other commissioners around a conference table in the
Security Ministry's headquarters. Carlos and two of the other attendees were technically "advisers," as opposed to "commissioners," but in
practice, that distinction mattered little. What did matter was that
this small group of civilians had been given a mandate, by both Juan
Orlando and the legislature, to disembowel and revitalize the force.

Before Carlos and Omar accepted the president's invitation to be
part of this, they and Kurt had discussed the risk that it would turn out
to be some type of sham, and in no time at all, things did go sideways.

The security minister, Julián Pacheco, who was Juan Orlando's
representative in the room, presented a list of the thirty-two cops he
planned to get rid of. This was a brazen violation of the autonomy that
Juan Orlando had promised the commission, and to make matters
worse, the minister was saying that he intended to let those officers
retire voluntarily, with generous severance packages *and* a promise not
to investigate their pasts. Furthermore, he had scheduled a ceremony
to celebrate their retirements.

Carlos had already learned his lesson about getting himself into
boardrooms where he was outnumbered, and one of the main reasons
he and Omar had agreed to step into this one was that it consisted
of Pastor Solórzano and the director of his Evangelical organization,
Pastor Jorge Machado, both of whom sat on ASJ's board of directors;
Vilma Morales, the former president of the Supreme Court who once
helped Kurt and Carlos with Dionisio's case; and finally, an ex–labor
minister who previously collaborated with the Labor Project. This six-
person block of like-minded individuals collectively had enough lever-

age to foil the security minister's plan and to ensure that the purge began in accordance with their specifications.

"We cannot continue allowing our streets to be bathed in blood as a consequence of the behavior of perverse police officers," Omar soon told the press. ". . . Now is the time for change, the precise moment for a transformation. It is now or never. All sectors of society are in tune. We cannot fail. We cannot fail Honduras."

Here was how the purge worked. The commission would ask the Public Ministry, the DIECP, the American embassy, the police force itself, and a variety of other institutions to send over whatever info they had on a particular batch of cops. Pastor Machado, the commission's secretary, and a team of ASJ lawyers would then condense that intelligence into slides for the commission's meetings. "We often had to take breaks to pray and quiet our minds," Carlos later said, "because we were given access to information that was very, very, very heavy."

Based on what was presented, the commissioners and their advisers would then adjudicate an officer's fate, while having no choice but to wonder, *Will this guy retaliate?* As they all would have known, the first serious effort to purge the force had ended when the civilian in charge of it died in a mysterious car accident.

On April 21, the commission purged three of the nine cops who held a generalship and announced that General Ramírez del Cid and another one were suspended pending a more thorough investigation. Their decision about General El Tigre was delayed, because his personnel file had somehow gone missing from the force's archive—according to what one source told *La Tribuna*, it had been devoured by rats.

The generals may have seemed like the scariest cops to terminate, but Omar worried more about those who had climbed up to the cusp of the hierarchy's summit but hadn't yet gotten to enjoy being a top dog. Nevertheless, in late April, the commission showed the door to thirty-one of the forty-seven officials who held the second-highest rank. One of the axed policemen soon told the press, in a very irate tone, "To hell with it. There's no reason to be afraid, man. You know what? They are the ones who are scared."

The purge was probably the most dangerous thing ASJ had ever been involved in, so it paid a British security consultancy to assess the situation. "The list of people who today potentially represent a true threat to ASJ is getting longer," the consultancy noted in its report.

That list presumably included the purged brass; General Ramírez del Cid, El Tigre, and the third general still in limbo; however many cops were now expecting the commission to fire them; and whoever else was sick and tired of seeing Carlos and Omar in the news, on an almost daily basis, opining about everything under the sun. "We rate the probability of a 'very serious' security incident as 'very high' to 'certain/imminent,'" the consultancy concluded.

On *Frente a Frente* on May 10, General Ramírez del Cid warned Omar not to get too "excited," a statement which, in Honduran-talk-show-speak, had a pretty ominous undertone.

El Tigre took a more conciliatory approach. He privately met up with the commission to proffer a deal: dirt on other cops in exchange for him getting to keep his standing. He wasn't doing policework anymore—he was the military attaché to the Honduran embassy in Colombia—so if the commission wanted to slyly avoid having to humiliate him, they could have just sent him back to his golden exile.

Around May 11, the country's intelligence services notified Carlos about a plot against him and his family. It is always hard to know what to make of such reports, but this concerned the global president of Transparency International so much that he took the time to mention it at an anticorruption summit in London, in a salon that contained British Prime Minister David Cameron and US Secretary of State John Kerry.

The Honduran government had already assigned cops and soldiers to serve as bodyguards for the commissioners, their advisers, and their families, and as an additional precaution, Omar had relocated to a secure residence. The British security consultancy urged Carlos to follow suit, because according to them, the terrain in Nueva Suyapa "is conducive to ambushes."

That was probably good advice, but Carlos had a profound, almost umbilical connection to the barrio—it was integral to his identity, his faith, and his love story with Bernarda—and throughout his tenure there, he had managed to survive a number of life-threatening quagmires.

So he decided to stay put.

On May 17, the commission purged 36 of the 108 officials who held the third-highest rank, though as Carlos soon explained on a radio show, "Those who got ratified have only passed through the first filter. . . . Nobody should be celebrating yet."

The main entrance to his and Kurt's compound was off the alley behind Genesis, and the only other access point was a garage on the bottom floor of his house. On the morning of May 31, he went down there with his son, Carlos Daniel, who went to college in New York and had just come home for his summer break. After the two of them got into the black armored SUV that the American embassy was lending to Carlos, his driver slid open the garage door.

At that point, the driver noticed something, grabbed it, and passed it back to Carlos. It was a piece of paper with letters cut out from a newspaper glued onto it, in the style of a ransom note. It read, "you are going to pay Hard," and beneath that was a photo of a black SUV riddled with bullets.

A handful of questions immediately entered Carlos's mind, including, *What's more important—the purge or my family?* He didn't have all the answers yet, but sitting there next to his son, feeling what it feels like to fear for his child's life, he knew one thing for sure: He had lost Nueva Suyapa forever.

The Hernández family stayed in a hotel that night and then shuffled among other domiciles for the next week or two. Carlos felt afraid, which, in his mind, was a sign that his faith was flickering, because the Bible clearly states, "Do not fear, for I am with you."

Kurt soon arranged for the four of them to fly to Michigan, which was where Omar's family was going to be hiding out, too. Carlos and Omar could have stayed with their wives and kids but decided not to. "This was him playing the Superman role," Carlos Daniel later said, "which, to this day, I think was dumb. . . . Why was it so important for him to go back?"

On June 21, the commission purged General Ramírez del Cid, that second suspended general, and El Tigre.

TO MAKE CULLING THE RANK AND FILE EASIER, THE COMMISSION established new standards for the force's personnel. "There were cops who were sixty-five or seventy years old," Omar later explained. "They shouldn't have been out on patrol. There were five hundred of those. We put them on a pension. . . . There were officers who couldn't read or write. . . . We created a process to evaluate abilities, faculties, education, and physique."

On December 15, 2016, the commission purged 405 cops, which was an especially large batch. Dealing with all the logistics involved must have been a lot for Pastor Machado, a bald man with a black goatee who, as the commission's secretary, handled the purge's nuts and bolts. His security detail dropped him off at home around seven and then left for the night, at which point the pastor joined his family for dinner. Soon thereafter, his wife's detail—two soldiers who felt like part of the family by now—walked outside.

There were supposed to have been two cops stationed out front as an additional layer of security, but for some reason, at that moment, they weren't there, and therefore, they didn't see what happened next: Masked gunmen jumped out of a black Nissan Pathfinder and opened fire.

Hearing this from inside his house, Pastor Machado took cover with his grandchildren for what felt like an eternity. Then, when the coast was finally clear, he walked outside.

One of his wife's bodyguards was already dead, and the other was wounded and wailing.

Soon thereafter—suspiciously soon, the pastor felt—a bunch of cops arrived at the scene, and he had no idea whether they had come to help or hurt them.

Telenoticias soon reported that that black Pathfinder was registered to a purged policeman, and on December 23, the Machados evacuated to Grand Rapids, Michigan.

Kurt addressed this incident in a speech he gave at the LaGrave Avenue Christian Reformed Church in Grand Rapids, on January 19, 2017. "This is what these people do," he said. "Makes you scared. Makes you full of fear. . . . But every time this type of stuff happens, the commission says the same thing: Nothing will stop us until we have the police force that the Honduran people and God want."

Throughout 2016, the commission had purged a total of 1,865 cops, and as of April 2018, the second anniversary of the purge, 4,627 cops, or about a third of the original force, would be gone.

Historically, the typical cadet was an uneducated young man who was put through a few months of military-style training. Between 2015 and mid-2018, however, most of the 8,273 cops hired graduated from a brand-new police academy, where the eleven months of coursework included police-community relations, where one of the entry requirements was a high school diploma, and where a quarter of the class was female. The alliance had lobbied for the educational reforms, and the commission had helped bring them to life. And during this period of institutional transformation, the force was also endowed with a new governing law, a new crime lab, a new 911 center, a new internal affairs unit, and hundreds of new patrol cars.

According to a Washington-based think tank called the Wilson

Center, the purge "rid the Honduran National Police of corrupt and criminal elements, opening the door to professionalization and a new relationship between the police and society. . . . As national-level police reforms go, this one does not appear to have any close parallel in Latin America in recent decades, making judgments about its sustainability unusually tentative."

———

JORGE BARRALAGA HAD BEEN IN COMMAND OF THE POLICE STATION that the four M1–92 cops slipped away from. Almost six years later, on July 30, 2017, federal agents stormed his house, not because of his role in that particular fiasco, but because over the course of a public-service career in one of the poorest countries in the Western Hemisphere, he, his family, and their associates had amassed a princely fortune by laundering money for narcos. According to some forensic accountants cited by *La Tribuna*, about $80 million had been shuffled among their bank accounts in the prior few months.

In an effort to facilitate these types of prosecutions, the purge commission forwarded information about over a thousand cops to the Public Ministry. The case against Barralaga was built predominantly with intel from other sources, but the commission likely played a role in making it happen, even if just by pressuring the ministry to go after dirty cops in general.

One person who believed the commission absolutely did have a hand in Barralaga's downfall was David Romero, a left-wing radio host who, according to Omar, had a personal relationship with the ultra-wealthy ex-cop. Romero told his listeners that Omar and Julieta had manufactured the case as vengeance for the M1–92 vanishing act and also insisted that they and Carlos were "Juan Orlando's pawns—they work for him; they are his spokespeople; they do whatever he says."

In Romero's mind, this was a grievous sin. "I believe in karma," he said, during an on-air discussion about Omar. "If you do evil and unjust things, either you or your kids will pay"—he audibly slammed his desk. "If your kid suddenly gets sick, dies in an accident, or gets murdered, don't cry so much. Instead, start reflecting on all the shit you did in your life."

One could be forgiven for suspecting that Romero was an easy-to-ignore shock jock operating on the fringes of the country's media landscape, not just because of his over-the-top style, but also because, back in 2004, he had pled guilty to raping his own daughter. But the truth is that, after he served out his sentence, he became something of a hero to the new Honduran Left, largely because, from his two pulpits, Radio Globo and Globo TV, he was an unrelenting thorn in Juan Orlando's side—it was he, Romero, who first linked the social security scandal to the president's campaign. In other words, in certain circles, Romero had a great deal of credibility, and though his broadsides against Carlos, Omar, and the purge could be a bit extreme, the criticisms they sensationalized were worth taking seriously.

Since prior purges had muddled along or flamed out, the commission chose to act very quickly, very aggressively, and very decisively, which, of course, led to there being false positives. "We lost very good people with lots of experience," one senior policeman lamented. "I don't understand why they were purged. . . . Those people now unfairly bear a mark." Even Agent Cruz, the detective who ably worked the Dionisio case, wasn't spared. "I gave everything I had to that job," she recently said. "I even sacrificed my health. . . . Getting fired like this made me feel defrauded."

Though purged cops had the right to appeal to the commission, according to the Wilson Center, only two of the one hundred officers who did so were actually reinstated. (Later on, significantly more cops would get reinstated via court order.)

False negatives did even more damage to the commission's credibility. A prominent Honduran NGO accused ten high-ranking cops ratified by the commission of human rights violations, and the Associated Press would later report that three of the seniormost figures on the rebooted force, including the chief of police, once helped facilitate a narcotics shipment. The commission would respond to that story by asserting that it was based on a forged document, one likely leaked by a group of purged cops who were trying to delegitimize the reform, but even so, it pledged to re-vet the three officials.

From the perspective of the Honduran Left, the mistakes the commission made were not honest—what determined whether or not a cop got canned was whether or not that cop served Juan Orlando's interests, and it was Minister Pacheco, a former spymaster, who puppeteered the fame-hungry, out-of-their-element commission.

While it is true that the minister had the final call on all purge decisions, according to the commissioners and their advisers, he usually abided by their recommendations, and they came to those without any type of outside interference. In many cases, however, all they had to rely on was information that came to them from the force's archive, and those types of files were generally thought to be vulnerable to manipulation.

Another issue came to light in mid-2017, when *El Heraldo* reviewed the force's payroll and noticed that thirty-nine supposedly purged cops were still on it. Relative to the thousand-plus officers who had been axed by then, this was a pretty minuscule discrepancy, but what made it such a bad look for the purge was that one of the officers who slipped through the cracks, supposedly by using the old medical-leave trick, was Juan Orlando's cousin. And a couple of years later, that cousin would be accused of some very, very serious crimes.

There are even more critiques of the purge floating around in the public discourse, including that the materials that sparked it, the internal inspectorate's reports about the assassinations of the drug czar and Landaverde, were fabrications. According to Kurt, however, "almost all the critiques of the purge are cheap. . . . The people who sold this alternative version of reality were the purged cops. They all say, 'I'm a good cop. I didn't do anything.'" While he will concede that, yes, there were certainly false positives and negatives, that, yes, the powers that be likely protected certain officers, and that, yes, the post-purge force was still far from exemplary, he felt like the purge's critics refused to accurately size up those flaws and compare them honestly against its benefits.

That might have been how Kurt wanted public opinion to work, but the problem was that he was now living in an extraordinarily polarized country—in a poll conducted in 2013, the year before Juan Orlando took office, on a scale from one to ten, with one being the most left-wing, and ten being the most right-wing, 6 percent of respondents self-identified as ones, and 18 percent as tens; when that poll was repeated in 2017, 15 percent were ones, and 30 percent were tens. In other words, nearly half the population was now a radical, and therefore, almost everything could be seen only through the lens of us-versus-them. The Left thought that Juan Orlando, who was running for reelection in November 2017, was a budding criminal autocrat—why would anyone with that mindset ever even consider compliment-ing the purge, one of the president's crown-jewel achievements?

Carlos had originally expected the purge to take six months, but it dragged on for years and permanently tore him away from the com-munity where he used to joyously walk around and mingle with neigh-bors. The Security Ministry got him and his family set up in a house surrounded by a wall in one of the ritziest neighborhoods in all of Tegucigalpa, and whenever he went anywhere, it had to be inside a bulletproof vehicle.

"What I resent about my job is the loss of freedom, not being able to do what I want," he recently said. "Take something as basic as going on vacation. I might want to go to Tela, but if I do, I am going to have to worry about getting noticed . . . because what we did impacted entire criminal structures. What if someone there knows that I con-tributed to purging a narco-policeman? And then take someone like

Joryina"—a Genesis grad who was purged from the force. "I used to have a good relationship with her mother, but now she steers clear of me, and so do her brothers and uncles. . . . My social life has become very constrained, and one reason for that is that people are scared to be friends with me. . . . Whenever I travel to another country, I rent a car. Why? To enjoy the sensation of freedom. I get in alone. I drive. I turn on the radio. I listen to music. And I sing."

What made this life-in-a-fishbowl situation all the more unpleasant was that the fancy house, fancy truck, and fancy bodyguards all fed the perception that he was a Juan Orlando flunky filching from the state, when, in his head, he was proud of the fact that he had refused to take a salary from the government.

Kurt and Jo Ann continued to live in Nueva Suyapa, but without their favorite neighbors, it wasn't the same. "It's sad," Kurt admitted. "We lived next door to each other for so long, and almost every day, we would sit around and talk, just processing our days. Since he had to leave for security reasons, that has become much less frequent. I think our friendship has suffered."

- 5 -

KURT AND CARLOS HAD STARTED THE ALLIANCE IN 2012 because the annual number of homicides in Honduras had almost tripled in a seven-year span. After that, however, this terrible trend reversed—while 7,172 people were murdered country-wide in 2012, in 2017, 3,866 were.

Juan Orlando probably deserves some credit for this given that, during his time in power, the police budget was ratcheted up, Criminal Investigation was revamped, an FBI-like entity was created, a military police force was deployed, two maximum-security prisons were constructed, and a number of narcotraffickers were extradited to the United States.

Kurt and Carlos also feel that ASJ, both acting alone and through the alliance, contributed to the reduction in violence. That's quite a grandiose claim, but it isn't entirely implausible in light of the fact that, as one well-traveled scholar from Rio de Janeiro State University put it, "Never in my life have I seen an NGO that has so much power over a country's criminal justice system." For instance, Peace and Justice had been solving murders in a handful of dangerous barrios, and on a news program in 2015, Carlos gave just one tiny example of how else the charity might have improved public safety: "As of last December, there were only eighteen investigators in all of San Pedro Sula, the city with the highest homicide rate in the world. . . . After we presented our study, the authorities sent out forty more."

The charity now occupied three additional houses within walking distance of the original. Carlos would zip in and out of this jerry-rigged campus with his armed entourage in tow, his internal restlessness visible in the way his fingers fidgeted with his smartphone. Kurt was usually upstairs, managing the day-to-day from his office, a pleasant space with a white board, a fish tank, a photo of Jo Ann, a painting of a Honduran child, a framed *New York Times* article about Peace and Justice, and a bowl of Hacky Sacks.

What most of their 130 or so employees did, once they passed by a retinue of guards, opened up a steel door with their fingerprints, and sat down in cubicles, was identify the government's shortcomings. For instance, they found that between 2014 and 2017, the Health Secretariat didn't do any of its hiring through a merit-based process, as was required by the law. The charity would then publicize its findings through written reports, press conferences, and media appearances, and whenever possible, it would help the government correct the issues, which could be as nitty-gritty as procurement-manual verbiage and software-installation plans.

One of its big success stories was the Property Institute. As part of the transparency accord, the charity had given the institute a failing grade for 2014, a 19 out of 100, because it discovered all sorts of corruption as well as irregularities on almost every land title it reviewed. Kurt and Carlos, who had been working on land titling for over a decade, knew that this sleaze and incompetence put devious entrepreneurs in a position to screw over poor homeowners. Fortunately, the institute's leadership had been willing to collaborate with ASJ, and for 2017, the charity gave it an 80 out of 100—pen-and-paper processes had been digitized; a number of the bureaucratic crooks had been indicted; and virtually all the audited titles were clean.

The charity had also slapped the Health Secretariat, the Education Secretariat, and the Security Ministry with atrocious baseline grades. They hadn't managed to transform those institutions yet, but they were hoping to do so soon, and they weren't the only ones who had some amount of faith in the current administration's commitment to rooting out corruption. According to a Transparency International survey, in Honduras, 55 percent of respondents felt that the government was doing a good job of fighting corruption, which was the third-highest result among 119 other nations (the global average was just 30 percent.)

The upcoming election, however, had the potential to throw a wrench in the charity's plans, because Juan Orlando, the man granting them access to the government's innards, was facing a challenger who, to put it lightly, was not an ASJ fan.

Salvador Nasralla was a flamboyant master of ceremonies who hosted game shows, emceed beauty pageants, and did color commentary for soccer matches. Though he was in his sixties, he had recently married Miss Honduras 2015, who was just twenty-six. The conservative establishment did its best to portray him as an egocentric clown, but he was not nearly as unserious as his condensed biography might suggest. Long ago, he had given lectures on business and engineering at the national university, and as he veered into politics during the Juan Orlando era, his one-note focus on high-level corruption, his untarnished outsider status, and his sardonic, off-the-cuff, know-it-all style were just what the Honduran Left was looking for. He didn't wear an ideology on his sleeve, and it was hard to predict how he would actually govern, but what was most important about him was that he was the anti–Juan Orlando candidate. The two parties backing him, the larger of which was Mel's Libre, were calling their unified front the Oppositional Alliance Against the Dictatorship.

Throughout the campaign, Nasralla maligned the purge, and Carlos worried that if he ended up winning, he would unwind it. He also worried about what a President Nasralla would mean for his personal safety. The candidate hadn't publicly opined on the government-provided security details that were then guarding the purge commissioners and advisers, nor did he mention the ones that had been guarding Kurt and ASJ ever since Dionisio's assassination, but there were definitely some people in his left-wing milieu who felt that these arrangements were an exorbitant waste of taxpayer resources.

And what would a President Nasralla do to the ASJ projects that relied on the commander in chief's cooperation? The answer remained to be seen, but most likely, he would cut them off, because he considered the charity to be subservient to his nemesis.

Yet ASJ remained officially committed to nonpartisanship. Pushed to reveal who they really wanted to win, however, Kurt later said, "I'll describe it this way. We guessed it would have been easier to work with Juan Orlando for another four years, because we already had relationships with him and his ministers. . . . But I still thought that if Nasralla won, we'd be able to influence him and work with him, too." And here is what Kurt says he thought about Juan Orlando at the time: "He always had a dark side, like all presidents in Honduras do, but he was also young and energetic and got shit done. . . . I can't think of anything where he ever explicitly said, 'Yes, we will do that,' or 'I will do that,' and then didn't." As for what motivated the president deep down: "He wanted them to do a *Narcos* series about him cleaning up the country."

Kurt and Carlos clearly didn't think of themselves as being pro–Juan Orlando, but some of their behavior was interpreted that way. For example, though Carlos publicly called the Constitutional Chamber's abolition of the presidential term limit "incorrect and questionable," ASJ didn't persistently condemn the ruling. According to Kurt, the reason why was that, in their view, reelection wasn't inherently bad—by then, almost every other country in Latin America had done away with the one-term cap.

That's a viable argument, but when he and Carlos talk about this, they do seem to skate over how Juan Orlando's legislature connivingly stacked the Constitutional Chamber, and also that, in almost every other country in the region, either the total number of terms was capped, or presidents were prohibited from serving consecutively— whereas the chamber had imposed no such restrictions.

Reflecting back on this years later, Kurt acknowledged, "If we could do it over, I might do it differently. . . . But now as I'm making my argument, I'm like, maybe we did make the right choice."

Then there was the charity's 226-page baseline report about the Infrastructure and Public Services Ministry, which was completed six months before the election. It revealed that many of the ministry's "employees" never showed up for work, and that on one site visit, the charity had found a room filled with National Party campaign materials.

Kurt and Carlos's main goal with these exposés wasn't to disgrace bureaucrats but to repair institutions, so before publishing them, they always gave the respective ministry and the president's team a chance to refute the allegations and to commit to a remediation plan, which, whenever possible, was presented at the same press conference where the charity unveiled its findings. In this case, the infrastructure ministry, after being slow to respond, vowed to create such a plan as long as the charity waited to publish until after the election.

There were some ASJ employees who thought the charity shouldn't consent to that, because delaying publication could be perceived as protecting Juan Orlando. But ultimately, Kurt and Carlos did decide to hold tight, basically for the exact same reason: They didn't want the baseline report to somehow influence the election.

At the time, this internal debate must have felt fairly academic, because it was hard to see how one report could have possibly swung things. A CID Gallup poll from September had 37 percent of respondents intending to vote for Juan Orlando, 22 percent for Nasralla, and 17 percent for the Liberal Party candidate, a coolheaded intellectual who Carlos, on a personal level, wanted to win. And given that 61 percent of respondents had a favorable impression of Juan Orlando, versus just 37 percent for Nasralla, it sure seemed like the incumbent had this in the bag.

———

TWO-THIRDS OF HONDURANS DID NOT HAVE CONFIDENCE IN THEIR country's elections. The most visible issue was electioneering. Party reps were known to dole out cash bribes as well as food and clothing, and come Election Day, you could expect to see a tractor with a National Party flag draped on it rolling around Nueva Suyapa, ostensibly to patch up the lanes.

Violence was also a factor. Last cycle, between the primary and the general, the body count had included ten mayoral candidates, four congressional candidates, six relatives of candidates, and twenty-one party reps. This time around, a journalist reported that in San Pedro Sula, MS-13 "was threatening to kill anyone found voting for President Juan Orlando Hernández."

In the lead-up to the big day, when 27,188 candidates would be vying for 3,016 positions, ranging from president to legislator to council member, 18,140,619 ballots were distributed to the 5,688 polling stations where citizens could find their assigned voting tables.

Each of the ten political parties was given enough credentials to staff all the voting tables nationwide, the idea being that they would police one another. But most of the parties were too small to even come close to doing that, and if one of the major parties gained control of a table—through intimidation, bribery, or purchasing credentials—then there were all sorts of ways to cheat. *The Economist* actually obtained a recording of a National Party training seminar at which the party reps there were literally taught some of those techniques, such as nullifying unfavorable ballots by adding superfluous markings.

The entity in charge of pulling off the election and ensuring its sanctity was the Supreme Electoral Tribunal. Traditionally, the two major legacy parties, the National Party and the Liberal Party, had each gotten one seat on the tribunal, and as a tiebreaker, the third seat had gone to the tiny Christian Democratic Party. That allocation had made sense in the past, but with the meteoric rise of Libre, it was no longer fair. Nevertheless, the last legislature—Juan Orlando's—had chosen to maintain it.

Two weeks before the election, David Matamoros, the National Party man who was the president of the tribunal, put its electronic transmission system through a dry run, because in the past, there had been some snafus with it. According to *La Tribuna*, "Matamoros insisted that, this time, there wouldn't be any incidents."

To minimize the potential for violence, starting four days before the election, the right to bear arms was suspended, and starting one day before it, the sale of alcohol was prohibited. On Election Day itself, Sunday, November 26, 2017, more than thirty thousand cops and soldiers were deployed to maintain order.

At seven a.m., Matamoros fired the proverbial starting gun at a ceremony in a high school gymnasium, at which point Juan Orlando, who had been queued up at a polling station, proudly did his civic duty. "Has everyone else already voted?" he then jokingly asked.

Over the course of the day, thousands of observers monitored the polling stations as millions of Hondurans cast ballots. ASJ and a consortium of foreign charities had organized their own small observer brigade, so Carlos was out and about in Tegucigalpa, wearing a gray vest and carrying a clipboard.

When the polls closed, and the Christmas lights strung up around the capital lit up kaleidoscopically, nothing seemed to be amiss. Now it was just a matter of waiting for the tribunal to start announcing results, which was expected to happen shortly.

Around 6:30 p.m., before the tribunal had given word, a well-known businessman told the press that according to his firm's exit polling, Juan Orlando had an "irreversible" lead. Everything that man said, however, had to be taken with a grain of salt, because he used to be Juan Orlando's security minister.

Nevertheless, a half hour later, in a ballroom packed with National Party activists, the first lady thanked the creator of the universe, and Juan Orlando proclaimed, "We won the election!"

He could say that all he wanted to, but the organ with the final call hadn't released any results yet, and as time ticked by, and continued to tick by, and continued to tick by, the tribunal's silence began to feel ominous.

Carlos, who had set up a sort of control room in a hotel salon, was nervous that there was chicanery going on behind the scenes, and that the mere suspicion of that would lead to civil unrest and its corollary, violent repression. "We were calling the country's political leaders," he later said, "trying to calm things down and get them to hold tight. Because both sides wanted to declare themselves victorious."

Nasralla partisans were chanting outside the nearby hotel where the tribunal was headquartered, and it wasn't until two a.m. that Matamoros finally showed his face. His press conference shocked the nation. With 57 percent of the vote counted, Nasralla held a sizeable lead—he was up by a full five points.

After the sun illuminated the streets the following morning, the long-shot candidate celebrated amid a jamboree of fist-pumping supporters as an accordionist in aviators played some tunes. The Liberal Party candidate soon conceded to him, and according to an ASJ employee, at the charity's devotional that morning, Kurt told his staff, "We have a new president. Everything is going to be OK. It could be better, but it's healthy for the country to experience a dramatic exchange of power."

WHEN MATAMOROS RELEASED THOSE INITIAL RESULTS, HE MADE sure to specify that 90 percent of the votes from Tegucigalpa and San Pedro Sula, the country's two major cities, had already been counted. That meant that the uncounted votes were going to be disproportionately rural, which suggested that Juan Orlando was still alive, because he was especially popular out in the countryside.

The previous day, the party reps at each voting table had examined the ballots and written down their final count on a tally sheet; those tally sheets were then sent electronically to the tribunal, unless they couldn't be—for whatever reason, no internet, say—in which case they were put into a box with the corresponding ballots and trucked to the capital with a military escort. Matamoros explained that they were going to be factoring those tally sheets into their count as they arrived at the tribunal's warehouse in Tegucigalpa, and that they would have them all by Thursday. A spokesman for the armed forces soon clarified why, in a country that can be traversed in a matter of hours, this was going to take several days: "Our deployment of the trucks was a bit slow, but that was only because we wanted to avoid causing vehicular congestion."

Observers floated around the tribunal's warehouse as electoral workers processed the tally sheets that came in. At ten p.m. on Tuesday, Matamoros announced that with 71 percent of the vote counted, Nasralla's lead had shrunk to two points.

Nasralla started going apeshit. The main thrust of his very loud allegation was that Juan Orlando was in the process of stealing the election through his docile pet, Matamoros. With accusations like that being hurled around, and with the streets teeming with riled-up partisans, the country was beginning to feel like a payload attached to a burning fuse. And what about all those soldiers now descending upon the capital? Were they just coming to deliver tally sheets, or were they also going to be bringing Nasralla's supporters to heel?

President Trump had been in office for nearly a year but had yet to appoint an ambassador to Honduras—he never would—so on Wednesday, between 11:13 a.m. and 12:18 p.m., Kurt sent a series of emails with the subject "Very worried in Honduras!" to a bunch of officials in Washington, whose contact info he had gotten from a friend:

1. They say that 100 percent of the counting will be done by tomorrow and we are all guessing Juan Orlando will be proclaimed winner.

2. This could easily result in violence, abuses. . . .

3. The U.S. does not have an ambassador here. . . . BUT the U.S. is VERY powerful here.

Our suggestion:

1. Wait for the results tomorrow—

- If Nasralla wins and Juan Orlando accepts, we are all set.
- If Juan Orlando is proclaimed winner (much more likely), next to no one will accept it and we will have violence, etc. . . .

2. That the U.S. send a high-level State Dept person here who can throw their weight around tomorrow

3. ASJ and lots of other people will ask for a recount—TALLY SHEET BY TALLY SHEET—with all parties present, with International supervisors, on Live TV. . . . And the US Rep can push for that to happen.

What do you think?

That evening, the tribunal announced that with 83 percent of the vote counted, Juan Orlando had taken the lead by a tenth of a point. Matamoros also disclosed that the tribunal's IT system had crashed—it had gone dark for almost nine hours. He presented this as an innocuous hiccup, but from Nasralla's perspective, it was nothing short of a smoking gun.

Things soon got out of hand. Around eleven p.m., Nasralla, Mel, and a throng of protesters broke through the metal gate in front of the tribunal's warehouse, and according to *La Tribuna*, they were "about to take away the ballots and electoral boxes" when the dispersion of tear gas stopped them.

Over the coming days, most of the Nasralla protesters who took to the streets did nothing more ferocious than bang on pots and pans, but in addition to that, roadways were blockaded, stoplights were smashed, tollbooths were torched, and a statue of a historic president was decapitated. "This is going to be permanent," Nasralla warned. "The people will be demanding what they want for one or two years, until this country is no longer a country."

The tribunal, meanwhile, worked through something called the special scrutiny process, which consisted of recounting the ballots associated with the 1,031 tally sheets that had some type of irregularity on them. At rows of folding tables in the warehouse's vast interior, yellow-gloved scrutinizers counted as observers peered over their shoulders. According to the brigade sent by the Organization of American States, which is basically the United Nations of the Western Hemisphere, at 5 percent of the special scrutiny tables that marked their tallies as valid, shady-looking ballots were included—for instance, ones that had no crease on them, even though the ballot-box openings were designed such that the ballots had to be folded to fit.

When the tribunal wrapped up this process, on Monday, December 4, it announced that with 100 percent of the vote counted, Juan Orlando had 42.98 percent of the total, and Nasralla had 41.39.

In Honduras, whoever gets the most votes wins—a majority is not needed—but this thing was still far from over, because Nasralla was demanding a recount.

Three days later, Matamoros agreed to recount about a third of the vote, which was almost exactly what Nasralla wanted. If done in a credible fashion, this recount had the potential to settle the election in a way that even the loser would have to respect. That was why, that night, Kurt, Carlos, and another ASJ executive rushed to the tribunal's warehouse, and that was also why they had encouraged the chargé d'affaires then running the American embassy, Heide Fulton, to come along with them.

Matamoros sat down with them in a conference room. The ASJ trio explained that they wanted to observe the recount but would do so only if the tribunal wrote down the rules of engagement beforehand, delineating protocol as specific as what happens when a scrutinizer has to go to the bathroom. According to Kurt, Matamoros initially agreed to this but then stepped away to speak to someone on the phone, and when he circled back to the conference room, he shot down their ultimatum. Kurt was under the impression that Juan Orlando had been on the other end of that line. "That was when we left," the ASJ executive later said. ". . . I could see that Juan Orlando had this guy in his pocket."

Matamoros denies speaking to anyone on the phone, and according to him, what he told ASJ was, "We're not going to sit down now and spend twelve or fifteen hours, maybe an entire day, writing everything down when no one else is asking for that."

When Matamoros held a press conference at the warehouse later that night, the chargé d'affaires was in attendance. Then, two days later, she returned to the warehouse for another one of his press conferences, except this time, she stood right beside him. The physical location of her person mattered a great deal, because in Honduras, the American government is seen as a sort of political referee. Therefore, when the recount ended on December 10—with the tally budging but not enough to matter—the chargé d'affaires's two appearances at the warehouse were interpreted to mean what *La Tribuna* slapped on its front page: FULTON CALLS FOR THE TRIBUNAL'S RESULTS TO BE ACCEPTED.

Soon, from a podium set up in front of the American embassy, Nasralla accused the gringos of aiding and abetting a highway robbery of an election. But he also knew that they were the only ones who could possibly keep Juan Orlando and Matamoros in check, so on December 13, he stooped to pandering, clarified that if he won, he wouldn't kick the American military out of its Central American home at the Soto Cano Air Base. And then, four days later, he headed north on a last-ditch mission to make his case in Washington.

On his layover in Miami, however, he got the news. The tribunal had called the election.

It was over. Officially.

WHO REALLY WON?

It's hard to say, given that some of the key controversies remain unresolved. Take that server crash. According to the Organization of American States' computer expert, the tribunal's server had been improperly configured, the crash was therefore entirely predictable, and the evidence of what happened during the blackout was not properly preserved. That sounds dodgy, and perhaps it was, but according to the European Union's brigade, its "technical experts, who were in the data center at the time, confirmed the purely technical nature of the incident. . . . They did not observe any indication of alterations to the database, which, had it occurred, would have been easily identified."

In any case, the type of cheating imagined here should have been detectable without having to parse all this computer talk, because the party reps at each voting table were supposed to have received a copy of the original tally sheet, and the tribunal published all the tally sheets it used in its count online—the idea being that if the tribunal, the military, or anyone else altered a tally sheet after it left a polling station, through either physical or digital means, the defrauded party could easily demonstrate the discrepancy.

Nasralla's team had copies of 14,363 of the 18,128 tally sheets. According to the European Union, "Following a cross-check between a large random sample of the tally sheets provided by the opposition and the originals published on the tribunal's website, our mission concluded that there was virtually no difference between the two sets." As for the tally sheets that Nasralla's side didn't have copies of, who the hell knows?

That is just a taste of the mind-numbing thicket of esoteric complexity that hovers over this election. At least one facet of its legacy, however, is easier to grasp.

A dusk-to-dawn curfew was imposed the Friday after the election, and in the five days after that, at least 1,351 people were arrested. The civil unrest was not harmless—hundreds of shops were damaged; seven police stations were destroyed; 253 security-force officers were, according to the government, injured; and one cop was killed with a Molotov cocktail. But the Office of the United Nations High Commissioner for Human Rights in Honduras determined that the government used excessive force, and that in the turbulent two months between Election Day and the inauguration, at least sixteen killings and sixty injuries could be confidently attributed to either cops or soldiers.

This time of year, Kurt and Carlos would normally be gearing up for their annual coast-to-coast bike ride, an eight-day jaunt across the country that was meant to raise awareness about educational issues, though really, they mainly did it to have fun. Kurt and Jo Ann would ride tandem, and last time around, over a hundred friends, colleagues, and bodyguards had joined. In light of what was going on in the country, however, they decided to cancel the ride.

"Over the past couple years," Kurt wrote, in a January 2018 post on his charity's website, "I can think of only two or three occasions that brought me to tears. However, in the days after Honduras's recent election, I found myself standing before the staff of ASJ, weeping. . . . We have celebrated so much progress in Honduras over the years—new laws, stronger systems, two hundred days of class, a declining homicide rate—but in the chaotic moments after the election, in the middle of so much uncertainty and polarization, I questioned if we had really moved forward."

"There was a lot of shade being thrown at ASJ," Kurt's sister-in-law remembers. "For Kurt, that was some of the hardest stuff. It just really hurt his feelings." The man who was once the executive director of the alliance was among those who felt the charity had dropped the ball. "Their silence made them accomplices," he explained. "They are Transparency International. They have a moral obligation to the Honduran people. But instead, they decided to not sacrifice their political positioning, the power they had gained through an unholy alliance with Juan Orlando."

"Silence" isn't quite right. According to the charity's records, in December 2017 alone, Carlos and Omar appeared in the media 34 and 149 times, respectively. That being said, there did seem to be a hint of hesitancy in the timing and verbiage of some of those statements. Their critics interpreted this as them subtly trying to promote a Juan Orlando win, but according to what Kurt wrote in an email at the time, there was another reason for it, which was that the American embassy and the Organization of American States "repeatedly said they prefer we not muddy the waters. So we have been saying we want a recount of all the tally sheets, but we have also been trying to give the US/OAS time-space."

Maybe he and Carlos erred in another way. They had pushed Fulton, the chargé d'affaires, to go to the tribunal's warehouse the night the recount was announced, because they thought she would be able to induce Matamoros to play fair. But what about the optics? "We didn't think of that," Carlos admits. "Her mere presence . . . led to the business community, the people, the armed forces, and the opposition all thinking that the United States was backing the tribunal."

That oversight seemed to be a consequence of their biggest blind spot. They had thought they could work with Juan Orlando as long as *they* said and did the right things, but when you are tangoing with a cunning strongman, when he is pushing and pulling you in all the right spots, making you feel like the belle of the ball, it is not always easy to determine what the "right thing" is. And furthermore, if you dance with him long enough, your reputations will bleed together, no matter how many times you insist that the two of you are not formally wed. For a while, ASJ had lent the president an air of moral legitimacy, but after this train wreck of an election, the emperor's clothes were off, and his stink had rubbed onto everyone around him.

Kurt and Carlos desperately wanted to show their haters that they would enthusiastically work with whoever held power, but for the next four years—at least—they weren't going to get that chance. And despite the continued reputational damage they would necessarily incur, they had no intention of getting off Juan Orlando's dance floor. "Whether or not we personally support Honduras's new elected leaders," Kurt wrote, in that post to his charity's site, "we consider it our job for the next four years to try to make their administration as effective as possible. *This is not a partisan position but a Christian one.* We know from experience that when governments fail, those who suffer are the poorest and most vulnerable."

On January 18, a government entity called Surprise Visit uploaded a video to YouTube titled *This Is How a New Story in Nueva Suyapa Begins.* At first, the mood is solemn—melodramatic piano music plays in the background as you see a series of scenes in slow motion and black-and-white. First there's B-roll of a run-down health clinic, then there's Juan Orlando earnestly holding court at a press conference, and then there's the president pulling a woman into a warm embrace. Once the second act of the video begins, everything is suddenly in color, and uplifting percussion enlivens the score. It seems as though something truly incredible is coming . . . and there it is! Men with shovels, wheelbarrows, saws, and ladders are constructing a new health clinic, and the doctor who will one day run it says, "Mr. President, we thank you for your determination, for your effort, and for the way you are transforming communities."

– 6 –

THE AMERICAN GOVERNMENT HAD BEEN DISBURSING AID TO its southerly neighbors for quite a long time, and the germ of this munificent tradition, believe it or not, was a three-month junket that John D. Rockefeller's grandson, Nelson, went on in order to familiarize himself with his family's Latin American holdings. The young heir came back from that trip with an altruistic mission, and in 1941, President Franklin D. Roosevelt made him the first ever coordinator of inter-American affairs.

From there, the aid machine expanded. "In this year of 1953," an American official wrote, "more than two thousand Americans from such towns as Keokuk, Elko, and Bennington are helping people to fight against suffering and want in places like Tegucigalpa."

The president who drastically amplified these efforts was Kennedy. In 1961, he assured an audience of Latin American diplomats that within a decade, the countries that accepted his administration's assistance would find themselves in a situation where "basic education will be available to all, hunger will be a forgotten experience, and the need for massive outside help will have passed." His flagship aid program sent a huge sum, $617 million, to Central America between 1962 and 1972, and, reflecting back on that period, a member of his administration would write, "Some university faculties were almost denuded as professors left their tranquil campuses to instruct the natives in the dank far reaches of the world."

This all-out attack on Central American poverty did not bring about the desired results, yet still, pretty much every single president since Kennedy has put his own particular spin on the fixing-Central-America challenge. What led President Obama to do his own turbo-charging of the aid machinery was the US Border Patrol reporting that in 2014, 237,860 people from Honduras, El Salvador, and Guatemala were apprehended at the southern border. At the time, that was considered to be an alarmingly high number.

For a few years thereafter, the number of apprehensions was lower, but then in 2019, a couple of years into Trump's presidency, 607,774 Hondurans, Salvadorans, and Guatemalans were apprehended. In other words, the migration spike had spiked.

Determining the degree to which Obama's aid programming impacted migration would be a very complicated task indeed, but his successor, for one, felt that the path forward was clear. "Honduras, Guatemala and El Salvador are doing nothing for the United States but taking our money," President Trump tweeted, in December 2018. "Word is that a new Caravan is forming in Honduras and they are doing nothing about it. We will be cutting off all aid to these 3 countries—taking advantage of U.S. for years!"

It was an awkward time for the United States to be retrenching from Honduras, because in March 2019, the American embassy in Tegucigalpa broke ground on what was projected to be a $529 million new headquarters. Because of the way appropriations worked, it was going to take some time for the flow of aid money to actually dry up, but soon enough, the 1.5 million Hondurans who were benefiting from USAID-backed charities and programs were going to be left in the lurch. In June 2019, one such program laid off 140 agricultural technicians who had been helping 125,000 poor Hondurans get through a drought. And on the twentieth of that month, the leadership of ASJ began reckoning with this new paradigm on the top floor of its office in Tegucigalpa.

The charity's Honduran and American boards were both there, sitting at desks arranged into a U shape—Carlos was in the middle, with his elbows on the table; Kurt was at the end, next to the snack buffet, which he frequently visited; and a translator in the corner of the room was whispering into a microphone, in either English or Spanish, so whoever was wearing headphones could understand what was being said. About half the charity's funding had been coming from the American government, and as of New Year's Day 2020, that stream of money was going to have all but disappeared.

Kurt presented eight different budget scenarios for the upcoming year, in each case detailing how many of the charity's 150 employees would have to be let go—worst case: 111.

Which scenario they hit would depend on how much money they raised between now and November, which was when the unlucky staff members would have to get their two-month notices. Unfortunately, it was a bad time to be fundraising, because the charity had just tapped its donor base harder than ever before to fund the ongoing construction of its new headquarters, which, including the land, would end up costing $5.2 million.

Kurt and Carlos, who are quite proud of the fact that ASJ's first office was in a garage, had begrudgingly decided to move forward with this project in order to accommodate the charity's large and growing staff and large and growing ambitions. But in an ironic twist, this building-cum-symbol-of-hope was going to be completed in January 2020, right when the charity was bound to shrivel.

Kurt is an almost pathologically optimistic person, and he told his fellow board members that he wasn't trying to scare them or suggest that this was their problem to fix. Then his wife, Jo Ann, who is somehow even more impervious to worry than he is, argued that it was too soon to even discuss the funding shortfall.

No real solutions to this seemingly urgent crisis were proposed until one of the gringos, a six-foot-nine orthopedist, suggested that they pray with intention. The group had already taken several twenty-minute prayer breaks, but everyone seemed to think that this was a superb idea. They all closed their eyes as the giant doctor declared that God is great, powerful, and wonderful.

———

ASJ'S OFFICE WAS CHRISTENED ON SCHEDULE. THE TWO-STORY, GLASS-and-concrete edifice sits on top of a four-level parking structure that punctures the top of a hill. The workspace is open-plan, except for Kurt's and Carlos's offices, which, of course, share a wall. The facility's most notable quality is that it is exceptionally secure—a thick fence runs along its street-facing perimeter, and there are guard shacks, metal detectors, and barracks for the guards.

As over 150 donors, most of whom had flown down from the United States, took their seats in the building's sizeable ballroom in order to begin celebrating its ribbon cutting, Kurt, who was wearing a red shirt and a gray sport coat and holding his "Keep Calm and Carry On" mug, was standing near the doorway. A reporter in attendance found a moment to ask him if he was at all embarrassed about the charity's new palace. "Yes," he replied. "This is a country where people don't have homes."

He soon stepped up to the podium. "It's kind of crazy to think about all the stuff that's happened in the last twenty years," he began, before spending about thirty minutes revisiting some of that "stuff": he and Jo Ann following Carlos and Bernarda to Nueva Suyapa; he and Carlos failing to help Fidelia get her husband's killers arrested; and the step that arguably made them who they are today, the founding of Peace and Justice. "We had no idea if it would work, or if we would get ourselves killed," Kurt said. "We also had no money, so we were willing to be creative and brave—or, as some would say, a little bit crazy."

He next talked about the murder of the two undergraduates, and how since then, the country's homicide rate had more than halved. "ASJ didn't do that by ourselves," he said, "but we were an important part of making it happen. . . . If the homicide rate had stayed the same, some seven thousand more people would have been killed."

What Kurt's donors, who are primarily middle-class Dutch Mid-westerners, usually get from him is a sort of PG version. For instance, he described Cholo as nothing more complex than an "ex-cop" who "made sure our cases went to the right people." He doesn't ever seem to deliberately lie, but when speaking as a fundraising memoirist, he can get a little loose, sometimes insinuating that ASJ deserves more credit for something than it does, and sometimes relating stories he remembers vaguely with a confidence they don't quite deserve. He is not an outwardly vain or boastful man; in fact, he almost always presents what he has done as a "we" thing and has disavowed the chance to become famous in Honduras. But whether intentional or not, some mythmaking has clearly gone on with him. One donor would soon privately remark, while tearing up, "Kurt's heart is tender. God decided to use him this way. He's like a Moses."

To be clear, Kurt's PG versions don't gloss over everything. He told his donors all about the black cloud hanging over the char-ity: "The president was reelected. I would say most people think he shouldn't have been allowed to even run for a second term. . . . And there was also seemingly a fair bit of fraud. He probably didn't even win. . . . So the president, who is in charge of all this stuff—police, education, health—is super unpopular. . . . It's very tempting to join those throwing stones. If we just said, 'We hate this president, too! Let's get rid of him!'" Kurt pumped his fist. "Lots of people would applaud. They would say, 'Yeah! ASJ finally joined the light side, the white side, finally came over from the dark side.' But not only would a lot of the public applaud; a lot of the bad guys would, too—the cops who've been purged, the drug traffickers, the people in education and health doing bad stuff. . . . We can't just hang up our gloves for two years and let things get worse."

The charity had raised more money than it expected to, so though fifty-five employees did have to be let go, no programs were shuttered, and Kurt was able to assure his donors that his people still had their eye on the prize: "There are three million school-age kids in Honduras, and 1.1 million of them don't go to school. . . . That is a tragedy . . . and the government has no plan. . . . We held our first press conference about this last Wednesday. Fifty media members were here in this room. Yesterday, one of the main Honduran newspapers ran an editorial titled '1.1 Million.' . . . We are trying to thread the needle, trying to be close enough to power to influence it, but far enough away to still speak the truth."

This was, of course, not the first time Kurt and Carlos had replanted their flag on this we'll-work-with-Juan-Orlando-warts-and-all stance. But unfortunately for them and everyone else still associated with the president, a certain rumor was in the process of blowing up into a truly jaw-dropping revelation.

———

THE US STATE DEPARTMENT HAS ESTIMATED THAT THE YEAR BEFORE Juan Orlando took office, 87 percent of the cocaine that entered the United States traveled through Honduras first. Fast-forward to 2019, however, and that estimate had plummeted to just 4 percent. Juan Orlando, the guy who had supposedly pulled off that miracle, was therefore celebrated as a global poster boy for the War on Drugs.

The notion that he himself was in on the trade was first seriously introduced toward the beginning of the police purge, when Ramón Sabillón, one of the generals who was about to get axed, hinted, on television, that the president's brother was a narco. At the time, this message didn't pack that much punch because there were several reasons to doubt the messenger—the press had been accusing General Sabillón of suppressing the internal inspectorate's report about the drug czar's murder, and Juan Orlando had previously demoted him, so there was a chance he was just trying to exact revenge.

But then, eight months before the election, a narco who used to run a cartel called the Cachiros took the stand in New York City and claimed that Tony Hernández, the president's brother, once solicited a bribe from him.

And as it turned out, there was really something there. In November 2018, a year after Juan Orlando won his second term, Tony was arrested in Miami and indicted in a Manhattan federal court. According to the DOJ, he was a narco who offered other traffickers a special type of deal: In exchange for them kicking up to him, his brother's government would let them be. One of the prosecution's witnesses was a narco who claimed to have been present when El Chapo handed Tony a million bucks.

Juan Orlando had sixteen siblings, so it was hard to imagine he was close with all of them, but the narcos singing in New York were sure making it sound like the president was involved in Tony's dirty dealings. This indicated that, at some point in the future, the DOJ might use these same witnesses to go after the commander in chief.

When Tony was found guilty, three months before ASJ's building inauguration, Juan Orlando tweeted, "What is there to say about a conviction based on the testimonies of confessed murderers?" He had a point. The Cachiro and that other narco who testified had cumulatively fessed up to 134 murders and were both obviously trying to earn themselves reduced sentences by cooperating with the DOJ. And furthermore, both seemed to have originally surrendered themselves in anticipation of Juan Orlando extraditing them, so it was possible that they held a grudge. These were the sorts of thought-provoking arguments that Juan Orlando's lawyers might one day use in his defense in court, but there was another potential witness who was going to be much harder to discredit.

When Honduran cops arrested a narcotrafficker named Nery López, back in June 2018, they discovered secret compartments in his vehicles that contained grenades, about $193,000, and a number of spiral notebooks that documented López's business dealings. Juan Orlando's initials, JOH, appeared within those ledgers, and according to what one of López's lawyers would later tell Univision, the notations about "*Bersache*," as in Versace, were also references to the president.

At the time of Tony's conviction, López was being held in a Honduran prison known as the Pit, and his lawyers were in the process of negotiating a cooperation agreement with the DOJ. If the gringos were, in fact, planning to pursue Juan Orlando, then López would likely be the centerpiece of their case, because unlike the Cachiro and that other narco, he actually had something physical to substantiate what he said.

Juan Orlando seemed to be well aware that this inmate posed an existential threat. According to one of López's attorneys, his client received unauthorized visits from the president's older brother, a wheelchair-bound military vet, and also from a Miami-based private eye employed by their family.

Eight days after Tony's conviction, the warden of the Pit arranged for López and another prisoner to be brought out into a hallway so he could tell them that visitations were prohibited for the rest of the day. There was nothing terribly odd about that, given that López had a leadership role in his cellblock. But what was curious was that about twenty-five minutes later, the warden summoned the two of them out to the hallway again, this time to reverse course, to inform them that visitations were back on. And at that point, a masked individual opened an adjacent door, and six inmates burst through it.

It seemed meaningful that this well-choreographed ambush happened in clear view of a security camera, and also that the footage ended up on the internet—for about thirty seconds after López already appears to be dead, the assailants wildly stab, hack, and shoot his corpse. This made the video feel like a warning, a warning about what happens when you talk to the DOJ about Juan Orlando Hernández.

The day after the attack, a government official preposterously suggested that López had been killed because he was going "to prove that the drug ledgers were falsified."

Six weeks later, one of López's lawyers was murdered.

Three days after that, sicarios silenced the warden forever.

———

THAT IS WHERE THINGS STOOD AS OF THE BUILDING KICKOFF.

It may be hard to fathom how Kurt and Carlos could have justified interacting with the president and his underlings in any way, shape, or form, but it is important to note that he wasn't an outlier within the uppermost echelons of Honduran politics. The narcos in New York were claiming to have also bribed his two predecessors, Pepe Lobo and Mel; Pepe Lobo's son had been convicted of narcotrafficking; Mel's brother had long been the subject of the same type of rumor; the perennial power atop the Liberal Party, Jaime Rosenthal, had been charged with laundering money for narcos; and his son and nephew had both pled guilty to similar charges. The point being, if Kurt and Carlos resolved to sit on the sidelines until the presidential sash was draped over an unimpeachable politician, they might be sitting out for a very long time, and meanwhile, what was going to happen to those 1.1 million kids?

The counterargument was that it wasn't possible to help the country's pupils when the president the education minister reported to was *this* evil, and that even attempting to improve the Education Secretariat was inadvisable, because whatever small and ultimately irrelevant enhancements you managed to achieve would end up becoming shiny feathers in the cretin's cap.

"Carlos and I are very sensitive to those criticisms," Kurt admits. "They're often being made by people we care about, people whose opinions we value. We're always struggling within ourselves about what is the right thing to do."

Some good came from their decision to stay the course. Juan Orlando let ASJ audit the agency that made the country's pandemic-related procurements, and when the charity released its report, in June 2020, the headline was that at a cost of $47 million, which was at least $12 million more than the going rate, the agency had purchased seven mobile hospitals from a shell company in Miami that subcontracted the work to a Turkish firm with no prior experience in the field. Enough said. The head of the agency wound up in prison.

Though that tale was disturbing, during the lockdown, it was overshadowed by even juicier news. For instance, American prosecutors indicted El Tigre, the purged police general, because according to them, he had served as Juan Orlando and Tony's muscle, the bruiser who guarded their cocaine shipments and assassinated their adversaries. Implicit in that was the following: Not only had Juan Orlando received dirty campaign contributions through his brother, but also, he was a full-fledged narco himself. The president of a country!

The DOJ generally doesn't indict sitting heads of state, but there was an election scheduled for November 2021, and Juan Orlando was too unpopular to even bother running.

The contest pitted the National Party's candidate against Mel's wife, Xiomara Castro, and Jaime Rosenthal's son, who had served out his sentence in an American prison. Nasralla dropped out of the race and threw his support behind Xiomara, and as soon as she was sworn in on January 27, 2022, the first female president in the country's history, her predecessor became fair game.

A few weeks later, a contingent of Honduran cops led Juan Orlando out of his home. His face was obscured by sunglasses, a cap, and a disposable mask; his wrists and ankles were shackled; and to bring his fall from grace full circle, he was being escorted by General Sabillón, Xiomara's new security minister.

About two months later, on April 21, the ex-president was loaded onto a DEA aircraft, and his wife posted a previously recorded video online. "I am innocent," Juan Orlando declared. ". . . And I will leave you with this phrase: 'You will know the truth, and the truth will set you free.'" A jury in New York would later conclude that he was, in fact, a drug trafficking conspirator, even though they were informed—by him—that he once signed an agreement with Transparency International.

Soon after Juan Orlando's extradition, Carlos addressed it on an update call with the charity's supporters. "We worked with Juan Orlando," he said, "who the United States is now calling one of the biggest narcotraffickers in the world. . . . This wasn't a surprise, because his name had come up more than a hundred times in trial testimonies in New York. What was a surprise was learning that the United States had been investigating him since 2004. . . . They didn't say anything about that to us. On the contrary, they celebrated him, praised him, and recognized him as the president leading the fight against narcotrafficking. . . . Honestly, sometimes when I reflect on this, I feel used. Used, on the one side, by Juan Orlando, who wanted to legitimize himself by cozying up with civil society. . . . And also used by the United States, because we did the thing they had been wanting to do for many years but never accomplished: We purged the police."

"I think this is sometimes what happens when you stand up for justice instead of hiding," Jo Ann added. "Sometimes you get caught in the middle and attacked. That doesn't necessarily mean you did something wrong, but it does mean you need to do a lot of reflecting on how to move forward."

ACCORDING TO KURT, "PRETTY MUCH EVERYONE AT ASJ WAS HOPING the National Party would lose the election, but we also knew that would be a challenge, because whoever came in, at least part of them would be wanting payback for anything we helped the previous administration do, like the purge. During the two-month transition period, we actually had tons of meetings and lots of contact with the new administration. . . . So we were like, *Oh, maybe this isn't going to be like we expected; maybe they are going to want our help*. . . . But around the end of January, I think they decided that it wasn't politically convenient to be meeting with ASJ."

The charity still releases reports, puts on press conferences, and speaks to the media about the government's failings, but because Xiomara's team has largely boxed them out, their opportunities to work directly with bureaucrats are few and far between. And anytime they do publicly float a critique, they can expect a bombardment of responses like this, which came from a congresswoman: "That guy is with ASJ. That's really all you need to know. They were complicit with the narco-government. Their opinions have no credibility."

"I used to believe ASJ was half good," Salvador Zúñiga, the Lenca leader who Kurt wrote about in his dissertation, recently said. "But as they became publicly aligned with the government of Juan Orlando, who did so much harm, I realized, no, they are useless. *Useless*. They should disappear. They should leave this country."

The heartiest animosity tends to be reserved for Omar, an emphatic man who really did seem to relish the limelight. As Kurt himself will admit, "Maybe like 20 to 30 percent of the time, I felt he hit the wrong note, sounded too pro-government, too Juan Orlandoish."

The most damaging thing Omar ever did to ASJ's reputation, however, wasn't something he said but something he did, namely, quitting to become director of a government watchdog that, oddly enough, was funded by the government. He made that transition toward the end of Juan Orlando's tenure, and since the president was presumed to have influence over the watchdog's board of directors, many interpreted Omar's move as: Juan Orlando rewards lackey with bright shiny job.

Carlos, whose public appearances tended to be more understated, isn't quite as despised as Omar, but anytime he commentates, he gets it on social media.

"That clown is one of the people who licked Juan Orlando's butt."

"This asshole should have been taken away with Juan Orlando."

"These animals shouldn't even open their mouths."

"They should just put him to sleep."

Once upon a time, Carlos was a man who led an exceptionally communal and openhearted life, but in order to protect himself, he now shuts himself off. "I never just casually listen to the news or browse social media anymore," he explained. ". . . We pay a monitoring company to show me what I need to see. . . . And I know this is a little extreme, but if a friend or someone at church starts saying this or that, I immediately cancel them, delete their contact from my WhatsApp."

The fog of hatred he lives under isn't just hurtful; it's frightening, too, partly because Xiomara's administration removed ASJ's government-provided security details. The charity now employs a smaller team of guards, but according to Carlos Daniel, Carlos's son, who lives abroad, "I think of Honduras as being a place where anyone in my family could be killed. . . . I think about that all the time. . . . I've had deep, deep conversations with my brother about this. Not just about our dad's job being dangerous, but also about how far away we are from him, and that we had this weird-ass childhood and life. One thing my brother is still pissed off about is that there were always people in our house"—in Nueva Suyapa, it was the neighbors; post–Nueva Suyapa, it was the guards. "Maybe that means we didn't get to have enough personal conversations as a family."

THE NATIONAL ANTICORRUPTION COUNCIL, OR CNA, IS ANOTHER watchdog partly funded by the government. Like ASJ, it exposes corruption, but unlike ASJ, it doesn't then try to buddy up with bureaucrats to fix their problems for them. This philosophical difference is reflected in attitudinal and aesthetic ones—while ASJ's events and multimedia tend to feel academic, family friendly, and conciliatory, CNA's tend to feel dramatic, swaggering, and acerbic. Its typically black-and-red graphic design looks like it could be promotional material for a low-budget horror movie, and its executive director, Gabriela Castellanos, is known for her cutting wit. To many of the Hondurans who felt that the Juan Orlando era *was* a horror movie, CNA's approach felt spot-on. Therefore, as ASJ became more and more tainted, Gabriela's star rose.

And she went on to prove that she wasn't just some partisan Juan Orlando basher, simply by continuing to do her job once the new administration took over. At a CNA press conference on May 24, 2023, she declared that Xiomara had turned "the presidency into a family dining table with room for her spouse, children, siblings, aunts and uncles, nephews and nieces, brothers-in-law and sisters-in-law. . . . Her council of ministers looks like an image of a genealogical tree." In one especially illuminating episode, three senior government officials who were all named José Manuel Zelaya—one of them being Mel—attended a meeting with the army's top brass.

Gabriela did not ultimately find this amusing. She argued that nepotism at this scale was a serious form of corruption and warned that a single family holding this much power put the country at risk of a totalitarian future.

Xiomara's administration has proved to be very sensitive to criticism, so, predictably, Gabriela was berated. "Our more than twelve years of resistance out in the streets," the finance minister tweeted, "is what proves who we really are in the face of this defamation by CNA, which looked the other way to cover up the corrupt narco-tyranny. . . . CNA's cynicism and perversity are unacceptable." Another official accused Gabriela of representing "a reactionary faction of the US government that wants to destabilize the country in order to promote a coup."

Over the years, Kurt and Carlos had tried to coordinate with Gabriela, but their sense was always that she wanted to keep a distance. Soon after her nepotism press conference, however, she asked them to come to her office, because, as she would explain to them there, she was afraid for her life.

What exactly she perceived to be a death threat is best left unwritten, but she was worried enough to flee the country, on June 18. Kurt and Carlos, who had dealt with this type of situation before, became her unofficial caretakers—their security people and a consultant they helped her find hardened her home and office in Honduras, and Kurt found her a free place to stay in the United States, which his third child, Andrea, a Honduran woman he and Jo Ann adopted as an adult, got set up with internet.

On July 20, when Gabriela held a press conference to announce that she had returned to Honduras, Kurt and Carlos were sitting alongside her. "Thousands of Hondurans abandon this country every single day because of all the barbaric things going on here," she said. ". . . But I am one of the stubborn Hondurans who wants to rescue this country from dark forces. . . . I don't want to become a martyr, but fighting back is our way of life, and we are not going to cede a single centimeter in this fight." While she spoke, Kurt looked down with a funereal expression, and after she finished, Carlos added, "We will not tolerate this. We cannot be shut up."

Later asked to reflect on this episode, Kurt said, "The Libre party is saying the same thing about Gabriela that they do about us, that she was part of the narco-state, and that she didn't say anything for the twelve years the National Party held power. . . . It's disturbing, because the accusations against CNA are even more unfounded than they are against us. . . . There's also a little piece of this that feels like—I'm trying to think of the right adjective. It's like, well shit, you know, if they can make this stick to her, then I feel less bad that maybe we did do something wrong. . . . You know what I'm saying? I'm not describing it well, but I think you get the idea."

On the whole, Kurt and Carlos feel like they made Nueva Suyapa and Honduras better, but the truth is that their two-plus decades of all-in altruism, all-in courage, and all-in faith have not gotten them anywhere close to a satisfying conclusion. The country they have risked their hides for over and over again is still light years away from being Switzerland, or South Korea, or even Costa Rica, and it's possible, if not likely, that the two friends will not live to see the national transformation they seek.

Their dalliance with Juan Orlando saw them soar up to incredible heights and then get cut back down to size, and perhaps this was God's ultimate test—perhaps he wanted to see what they would do once he showered them in some of their countrymen's vitriolic animus and rubbed a harsh reality in their faces, showed them that, on this idiosyncratic quest of theirs, there probably wasn't ultimately going to be glory, adoration, or even a list of unqualified wins.

Maybe all Kurt and Carlos can ever expect is more toil, a lifelong climb that, instead of bringing them higher up a ladder, keeps them pinned to the side of a spinning wheel. Most people would not be able to tolerate such a frustrating endeavor, but Kurt and Carlos have, and Kurt and Carlos do, and what sets them apart, it seems, is their bond—its permanence, its wholeheartedness, its alchemy, its fit.

"If I could find a woman that complements me that well," one former employee said, "I would be the happiest man alive. . . . I saw them fight a couple times. It was very intense. . . . But afterward, they always hugged and said, 'I love you.' Because they really do. . . . That's their secret ingredient: love."

Nothing encapsulates this more than a sequence of events that happens with surprising regularity. Someone will say something during a meeting, and then, at the exact same moment, Kurt and Carlos will look up, not at the speaker, but at each other. What happens next is that their eyes widen, and they grin, because they just know, through some type of telepathy, that they're thinking the exact same thing. Sometimes, they don't even bother to share it.

ACKNOWLEDGMENTS

I had a great team: Farley Chase (agent), Gina Iaquinta (editor), Maria Connors (editorial assistant), Bill Vourvoulias (fact checker), Sarah Johnson (copy editor), Becky Homiski (project editor), Rebecca Munro (project editor), Louise Mattarelliano (production manager), Steve Attardo (creative director), Peter Miller (publicist), Nick Curley (marketing), and Kadiatou Keita (marketing). And I'm extremely grateful to all those who spoke to me or provided materials, introductions, or advice. There are way too many of you to list, but I do feel the need to shout out my Honduran family, Abram Huyser-Honig, David M. Kennedy, Garrett Schabb, and the three women who I absolutely could not have done this without: Jill Leovy, my mom, and my wife.

A NOTE ON SOURCES

I went on five reporting trips to Honduras, with the longest one lasting about three months, and while there, I almost always stayed in Nueva Suyapa.

The source material for this book ended up including interviews with over 150 people, some of whom spoke to me multiple times, as well as a gargantuan trove of Kurt's emails and ASJ's documents, well over two thousand articles, many hours of archival news footage, a home library's worth of reports, studies, court filings, and books, a portfolio of photographs, and my own observations. For one not-particularly-long chapter I selected at random, I used, in one way or another—sometimes for specific facts, sometimes just for background—interviews with 31 people, 35 articles, 16 books, 6 court records, 135 ASJ documents, 1 folder of photographs, 2 reports, 3 videos, and a bunch of emails. And to give some sense of how many emails ASJ turned over to me, for the month of August 2013 alone, the archive ran to 232 pages and included 22 attachments.

To ensure this text was clear and digestible, I sometimes made some very minor tweaks to quotations. For example, Hondurans have a hard time pronouncing "Kurt," so they typically call him Alan, his middle name, and more often than not, the people I interviewed referred to Cholo as Roberto, which, as previously mentioned, is one of his aliases. Nevertheless, once I decided that I was going be calling Kurt "Kurt" and Cholo "Cholo," or, say, that I was going to be referring to Carlos del Cid as "del Cid," I virtually always called them that, even in quotations where the original speaker did not. That being said, all the names and nicknames in this book are real, with the exception of the one pseudonym I invented: Macario Pavón.

Another sacrifice I made to the altar of readability was not discussing, at length or at all, a number of topics, anecdotes, people, and nuances related to Kurt and Carlos, ASJ, Nueva Suyapa, and Honduras.

Below are some of the sources I utilized, organized by chapter, though the books are listed separately at the end, since I typically turned to them for multiple parts of the story. Note that this presentation is far from exhaustive because (a) I ought to be coy about who exactly I interviewed, (b) the emails and internal documents are not publicly accessible, and (c) I have no ill will toward trees, so, for example, while I might have pulled many articles about, say, Holy Week in Honduras or the 2017 election, I just provided a sampling.

And to just, for a moment, elaborate on that first point, I had the opportunity to interview Niño's sister, the one who accompanied Carlos when he drove her brother to the hospital. I am only willing to reveal that because she has since passed away. The point being, were she still alive and residing in Nueva Suyapa, there could theoretically be consequences to conclusively revealing that she spoke to me about a murder. And arguably, the same could be said of those who told me about, say, Delta Security Services or Juan Orlando Hernández.

Finally, I would like to offer a special hat tip to Jeffrey T. Jackson, whose book, *The Globalizers*, served as the basis for my lengthy description of the Cajón Dam.

Book One

CHAPTER ONE

"A sus 12 años acorralaba en colonia Nueva Suyapa." *La Tribuna*. March 20, 2005.

"Cómo ganado." *La Tribuna*. June 21, 2006.

"Cristianos evocan sufrimiento de Cristo en la Semana Santa." *La Tribuna*. March 22, 2005.

"Desde las entrañas de la capital." *La Tribuna*. September 29, 2003.

Gómez, Luis Alonso. "Disfrute en tranquilidad sus vacaciones de verano en el oriente de Honduras." *La Tribuna*. March 20, 2005.

"Hasta el 'tope.'" *La Tribuna*. January 24, 2006.

"Historia de Tegucigalpa." *La Tribuna*. September 29, 2003.

"Juan Orlando Hernández, Former President of Honduras, Indicted on Drug-Trafficking and Firearms Charges, Extradited to the United States from Honduras." US Department of Justice. April 21, 2022.

Lanza Valeriano, Raúl. "Ritos de Semana Santa en el pasado inmediato." *La Tribuna*. March 20, 2005.

"Latinoamérica en Semana Santa." *La Tribuna*. March 20, 2005.

"Miles de feligreses reviven la pasión de Jesucristo." *La Tribuna*. March 21, 2005.

"Most Extreme Airports." The History Channel.

"Nunca repararon calle." *La Tribuna*. April 18, 2005.

Palin, Megan. "Why This Airport Is One of the Most Dangerous in the World." News.com.au. May 24, 2018.

"Plane Crashes in Honduras, Killing at Least 131." *New York Times*. October 22, 1989.

"Playas del Atlántico y Pacifico a extranjeros y nacionales." *La Tribuna*. March 21, 2005.

"Programa de celebraciones de los 425 años de San Miguel de Tegucigalpa." *La Tribuna*. September 29, 2003.

"¡Qué bárbaros, ya es demasiado!" *La Tribuna*. July 6, 2005.

Schauer, Norita. "Sobrevivientes de accidente aeroterrestres reviven aquella terrible tragedia." *La Tribuna*. July 24, 1993.

"Sopa de pescado, el platillo más exquisito de Semana Santa." *La Tribuna*. March 22, 2005.

"Tegucigalpa la ciudad más importante de Honduras." *La Tribuna*. September 29, 2003.

"Terrible tráfico en El Prado." *La Tribuna*. March 26, 2007.

"Toncontín Airport." Alluring World.

"Toncontín International Airport." Airport Technology. August 1, 2011.

"Viajeros abarrotan empresas del transporte interurbano." *La Tribuna*. March 20, 2005.

CHAPTER TWO

"Niños de primer grado egresan de 'El Verbo.'" *Tiempo*. December 22, 1995.

Panchamé, Mario. "El uso de la oralidad para la construcción de una historia de identidad comunitaria en 10 colonias del Distrito Central de 1955 a 2010." Master's thesis, National Autonomous University of Honduras.

"Una misma comunidad, una misma historia: Tegucigalpa." ATD Cuarto Mundo. October 24, 2016.

Vásquez, Juan Carlos. "Solitaria deja chiquitos a niños en Nueva Suyapa." *El Heraldo*. October 2, 1995.

CHAPTER THREE

"'A mí nadie me lavó el celebro.'" *La Tribuna*. July 18, 1994.

Andino, Leonarda. "Comisionado de Derechos Humanos visita a representantes de etnias." *El Heraldo*. July 13, 1994.

Andino, Leonarda. "Con paso firme y exigiendo justicia llegaron indígenas." *El Heraldo*. July 12, 1994.

"Antidemocracticos quieren anarquizar el pais." *La Tribuna*. July 13, 1994.

Bárcenas, Xiomara. "En lamentable hecho de sangre termina peregrinación de etnias." *El Heraldo*. July 18, 1994.

Bárcenas, Xiomara. "Reina pidió a indígenas no magnificar hecho de sangre." *El Heraldo*. July 18, 1994.

de Foletti, Alessandra. "Los Lencas: Pasado y presente." *La Tribuna*. August 20, 2006.

"Diputados investigarán situación de indígenas de nuevo municipio." *La Tribuna*. July 15, 1994.

"Ejecutivo declara solventado el problema de los indígenas." *La Tribuna*. July 15, 1994.

"FF.AA. listas para garantizar libre circulación de personas." *La Tribuna*. July 12, 1994.

"FF.AA. no permitirá la toma de carreteras: Discua Elvir." *El Heraldo*. July 12, 1994.

"Gobierno crea dos comisiones para satisfacer demandas de indígenas." *El Heraldo*. July 13, 1994.

"Grupos étnicos satisfechos por la solidaridad de capitalinos." *El Heraldo*. July 15, 1994.

"Indígenas autorizan sólo a sus voceros para dar declaraciones." *La Tribuna*. July 14, 1994.

"Indígenas de todo el país llegan hoy a protestar frente a Casa Presidencial." *La Tribuna*. July 11, 1994.

"Indígenas llenar su 'morral.'" *La Tribuna*. July 16, 1994.

"Indígenas oficializan entrega de Planteamiento Único al Congreso." *El Heraldo*. July 13, 1994.

"Indígenas regresan satisfechos a sus tribus." *La Tribuna*. July 16, 1994.

"Indígenas sometidos a rigores del hambre." *El Heraldo.* July 14, 1994.

"Indígenas vuelven con nuevo 'look' y bien fortalecidos con Neurobión." *La Tribuna.* July 16, 1994.

"JNBS asiste hijos de los indígenas." *La Tribuna.* July 14, 1994.

Kinzer, Stephen. "Our Man in Honduras." *New York Review.* September 20, 2001.

Martínez Moure, Luis. "Manipulación de los indígenas." *La Tribuna.* July 13, 1994.

"Nuestra 'peregrinación' fue campanazo, dicen indígenas." *La Tribuna.* July 16, 1994.

Nulia Coto, Ramón Wilberto. "Intibucá y la esperanza: Lagunas, bosques enanos y choros." *La Tribuna.* June 17, 2006.

"Peregrinación indígena." *La Tribuna.* July 15, 1994.

"Proponen creación de municipio." *La Tribuna.* July 13, 1994.

"Reina ordena a FF.AA. impedir toma de carreteras." *La Tribuna.* July 12, 1994.

Río de sangre. Podcast. Bloomberg Green. September 14, 2020–October 19, 2020.

"Sacerdotes apoyan peregrinación por la vida, justicia, y libertad." *La Tribuna.* July 12, 1994.

"Sangre de indígenas en basílica de Suyapa empaña celebración de su retorno victorioso." *La Tribuna.* July 18, 1994.

"Se reportan 500 indígenas enfermos por larga marcha." *El Heraldo.* July 13, 1994.

"Soluciones, exigen al gobierno más de 4,000 indígenas al llegar a la capital." *La Tribuna.* July 12, 1994.

Turcios, Julio César. "Justicia, libertad y paz reclama marcha indígena." *El Heraldo.* July 11, 1994.

Van Engen, Jo Ann. "Short Term Missions: Are They Worth the Cost?" *Other Side* (January and February 2000).

Van Engen, Jo Ann, and Kurt Ver Beek. *Developing World Citizens: Learning to Listen to the Voices of the Poor.* White paper prepared for the Teagle Foundation. September 2007.

Ver Beek, Kurt Alan. "The Impact of Short Term Missions: A Case Study of House Construction in Honduras After Hurricane Mitch." *Missiology: An International Review* (October 2006).

Ver Beek, Kurt Alan. "International Service-Learning: A Call to Caution." *Commitment and Connection* 34, no. 4 (2002).

Ver Beek, Kurt Alan. "The Pilgrimage for Life, Justice and Liberty: Insights for Development." PhD diss., 1996.

Ver Beek, Kurt Alan. "Spirituality: A Development Taboo." *Development in Practice* (February 2000).

"Viene movilización indígena sobre la capital de Honduras." *El Heraldo.* July 11, 1994.

Villanueva, Armando. "Ejecutivo firma compromiso del gobierno con las etnias." *El Heraldo.* July 16, 1994.

Villanueva, Armando. "Reina: Insensatos quieren crear el caos en Honduras." *El Heraldo.* July 13, 1994.

CHAPTER FOUR

"Acribillan a leñador para robarle pistola." *La Tribuna*. December 19, 2003.

"Alarmante número de caídos en lucha contra delincuencia." *La Tribuna*. November 18, 2003.

Cáceres, Lorenzo. "Ley antimaras es irreversible." *El Heraldo*. September 30, 2003.

"Cada media hora llegaron los heridos al hospital." *La Tribuna*. December 26, 2003.

"Cerca del cielo está el infiernito." ElHerlado.hn. January 1, 2006.

"Colegios son 'canteras' para reclutan nuevos pandilleros." *La Tribuna*. April 11, 2005.

"Ejecutado hallan joven en colonia marginal." *La Tribuna*. November 24, 2003.

"Ejecutados a balazos hallan dos peligrosos asaltantes." *La Tribuna*. November 18, 2003.

"'El Chelito' juega 'burro' con la policía." *La Tribuna*. November 19, 2005.

"En auto llegan a asaltar a fieles de Virgen de Suyapa." *La Tribuna*. January 14, 2004.

"Era alumno de 'El Siniestro.'" *La Tribuna*. June 4, 2005.

"¿Es Herlan Fabricio el verdadero nombre de 'El Chelito?'" Revistazo.com. August 4, 2005.

Escoto, Orlando. "Descuartizadas, violadas y sin corazón hallaron a mujeres." *La Tribuna*. December 22, 2003.

Funes, Wendy Carolina. "'El siniestro' y compinches matan candidato a diputado." *El Heraldo*. December 6, 2004.

Gutiérrez Rivera, Lirio, Iselin Åsedotter Strønen, and Margit Ystanes. "Coming of Age in the Penal System: Neoliberalism, 'Mano Dura' and the Reproduction of 'Racialised' Inequality in Honduras." In *The Social Life of Economic Inequalities in Contemporary Latin America*, edited by Margit Ystanes and Iselin Åsedotter Strønen. London: Palgrave Macmillan, 2018.

"Hallan cadáver en la Montañita." *La Tribuna*. November 2, 2003.

Hernández, Wilfredo. "Capturan temibles mareros armados hasta los 'dientes.'" *La Tribuna*. October 17, 2003.

Hernández, Wilfredo. "Policía y pandillero mueren en enfrentamiento a balazos." *La Tribuna*. January 24, 2004.

Honduras: Zero Tolerance . . . for Impunity. Extrajudicial Executions of Children and Youths Since 1998. Amnesty International. 2003.

Horne Carter, Jon. "Gothic Sovereignty: Gangs and Criminal Community in a Honduran Prison." *South Atlantic Quarterly* 113, no. 3 (Summer 2014).

"La balean 'mareros' al oponerse a ser violada." *La Tribuna*. October 7, 2003.

La cara de la violencia urbana en América Central. Fundación Arias para la Paz y el Progreso Humano. 2006.

"Lo matan a triso en colonia Nueva Suyapa." *La Tribuna*. December 7, 2004.

"Lo matan por no dar anillo de oro." *La Tribuna*. November 1, 2003.

"'Los Puchos' se le revelaron a 'La 18.'" *La Tribuna*. August 1, 2005.

"Lucharé por 'Ley Antimaras,' reitera titular del Congreso." *La Tribuna*. January 19, 2004.

"Madrugadores y trasnochadores." *El Heraldo*. September 29, 2003.

"Maras in Honduras." YouTube video. Posted January 6, 2015, by Alexandra Rangel.

"Mareros ultiman a muchacho en Suyapa." *La Tribuna*. December 27, 2003.

"Más de 1,400 'órdenes de captura' no ejecuta policía, denuncia CSJ." *La Tribuna*. November 19, 2003.

"'Me refugié en las maras' y encontré el 'amor de madre.'" *La Tribuna*.

"Mejor me muero antes que derogar la Ley Antimaras." *La Tribuna*. November 16, 2003.

Miller, Christian T. "Dying Young in Honduras." *Los Angeles Times*. November 25, 2002.

"Misterioso deceso de taxista al enfrentarse a un 'celador.'" *La Tribuna*. September 28, 2003.

"MP culpable de tanta impunidad: CODEH." *La Tribuna*. November 5, 2003.

"Mutilado y con 'tiro de gracia' hallan ejecutado a 'El Siniestro.'" *La Tribuna*. December 26, 2004.

"Por violación caen jóvenes." *La Tribuna*. January 12, 2004.

"Reaparece 'El Siniestro' y elimina aspirante a diputado." *La Tribuna*. December 5, 2004.

"Resurgen 'Los Chacales,' otro grupo de exterminio." *La Tribuna*. April 21, 2005.

Rodgers, Dennis. "Slum Wars of the 21st Century: Gangs, *Mano Dura* and the New Urban Geography of Conflict in Central America." *Development and Change* 40, no. 5 (2009).

Ver Beek, Kurt Alan. "A More Perfect Love: Casting Out Fear to Become Courageous Christians." *Prism* (2010).

CHAPTER FIVE

"Le pisan los talones a banda de 'ruleteros.'" *La Tribuna*. April 15, 2005.

"Mareros matan otro cobrador de buses." *La Tribuna*. March 22, 2005.

"Pandilleros ultiman muchacha en Suyapa." *La Tribuna*. May 1, 2005.

"Tres muertos en ataques de maras en zonas capitalinas." *La Tribuna*. April 5, 2005.

CHAPTER SIX

"A 'regañadientes' entregan armas comités de seguridad ciudadana." *La Tribuna*. October 11, 2003.

"Capturan mareros que ultimaron universitarios." *La Tribuna*. May 20, 2005.

Honduras: Zero Tolerance.
La cara de la violencia urbana.
"Policía hiere uno de los menores más buscados." *La Tribuna.* June 4, 2005.
Johnson, Scott. "Vigilante Justice." *Newsweek.* December 16, 2004.

CHAPTER SEVEN

"Por venganza mata a hija de vecina." *La Tribuna.* June 4, 2005.

CHAPTER EIGHT

Anderson, Jon Lee. "Is the President of Honduras a Narco-Trafficker?" *New Yorker.* November 8, 2021.
Banegas, Efraín. "A pagar promesas y pedir milagros llegan miles de feligreses al Santuario de Suyapa." *La Tribuna.* February 2, 2008.
"Cacería sin límites en barrios de miedo." *La Tribuna.* July 30, 2005.
"Cae el resto de la banda 'Los Puchos.'" *La Tribuna.* August 4, 2005.
"Capturan a chico de 13 años acusado de matar a agente de DEA en Honduras." Agence France-Presse.
"Cerca del cielo está el infiernito."
"Drug Figure Loses Appeal Against U.S." Associated Press. December 3, 1995.
"EEUU califica riesgoso vivir en Honduras." Associated Press. August 13, 2005.
"'El Chelito' juega 'burro' con la policía."
"El gobierno tiene que poner más seguridad." *La Prensa.* August 12, 2005.
"Embajada agradece ayuda de taxista y hospital." *La Tribuna.* August 1, 2005.
"¿Es Herlan Fabricio el verdadero nombre de 'El Chelito?'"
"Evidencias hunden a jefe de 'Los Puchos.'" *La Tribuna.* July 31, 2005.
Fiallos, Carmen. "La aldea de Suyapa." *La Tribuna.*
Gómez, Luis Ernesto. "Slain Son's Resolve Lives On with Mom." *Santa Maria Times.* December 6, 2006.
"Honduras: Niño de 13 años era el asesino de agente de la DEA." Agence France-Presse. July 31, 2005.
"Liquidan agente de la DEA en Suyapa." *La Tribuna.* July 30, 2005.
Malkin, Elisabeth. "Amid a Crisis, Hondurans Heap Large Hopes on a Tiny Religious Icon." *New York Times.* October 18, 2009.
"'Mareros' son monstruos y máquinas de matar." *La Tribuna.* April 6, 2005.
"Máxima seguridad para 'El Chelito.'" *La Tribuna.* August 2, 2005.
"Medicina forense determinará edad de menor infractor." Revistazo.com. August 4, 2005.
"Policía no encuentra a 'El Junior' y 'El Pato.'" *La Tribuna.* August 2, 2005.
"Policía se mete a 'El Infiernito' para capturar al 'El Siniestro II.'" *La Tribuna.* July 31, 2005.
Ramírez, Mario Hernán. "Suyapa." *La Tribuna.* April 24, 2016.

"Redoblan seguridad en aldea de Suyapa." *La Tribuna*. August 8, 2005.

Rohter, Larry. "Seized Honduran: Drug Baron or a Robin Hood?" *New York Times*. April 16, 1988.

Seper, Herry. "Brutal DEA Agent Murder Reminder of Agency Priority." *Washington Times*. March 5, 2010.

"Temen atentados en renacer con la llegada de 'El Siniestro II.'" *La Tribuna*. August 1, 2005.

"Una captura por diligencia o por presión." Revistazo.com. August 4, 2005.

CHAPTER NINE

"Agentes de la D.G.I.C. capturan a 'El Junior.'" Revistazo.com. November 22, 2005.

"Cazan temidos cobradores de 'impuesto de guerra.'" *La Tribuna*. November 18, 2005.

"Compinche de 'El Chelito' responderá por muerte del agente de la DEA." *La Tribuna*. November 24, 2005.

"'El Chelito' intenta escaparse mientras se le practicaba examen físico." Revistazo.com. November 18, 2005.

Horne Carter, "Gothic Sovereignty," *South Atlantic Quarterly*.

"Lanzaron cadáver de joven en 'abismo.'" *La Tribuna*. August 8, 2005.

"No tenemos recursos para perseguir gente." *La Tribuna*. April 23, 2005.

"Porque lo 'quemaron' hermano de 'El Chelito' mata dos personas en Suyapa." *La Tribuna*. August 8, 2005.

"Se reproducen 'Los Puchos.'" *La Tribuna*. August 8, 2005.

CHAPTER TEN

"Arrestan a marero por muerte de un psicólogo del IHNFA." *Tiempo*. August 15, 2003.

"Atrapan a 'El Chelito' en el Divino Paraíso." *La Tribuna*. November 27, 2005.

"Atrapan ladrón en Nueva Suyapa." *La Tribuna*. November 23, 2005.

"Auto de prisión a exdirector de 'Renaciendo.'" *La Tribuna*. February 9, 2006.

"Busca Honduras a peligroso 'mara.'" El Porvenir.mx. November 22, 2005.

"Cansados de sus fechorías pobladores matan 'mareros.'" *La Tribuna*. April 21, 2006.

"50 mil pagaron por la fuga de 'El Chelito." *La Tribuna*. November 20, 2005.

"Cuatro muertes le atribuyen a sospechoso de matar psicólogo." *La Tribuna*. August 15, 2003.

"Custodios son responsables por la fuga de 'El Chelito.'" *La Tribuna*. November 23, 2005.

"Defensa también ayudará a centro 'Renaciendo.'" *La Tribuna*. February 9, 2006.

"'El Chelito' condenado a 4 años de internamiento." *La Prensa*. January 21, 2006.

"'El Chelito' habría pagado a policías para fugarse de Renaciendo." Revistazo.com. January 12, 2006.

"'El Chelito' juega 'burro' con la policía."

"'El Chelito' se escapa una vez más de Renaciendo." Revistazo.com. November 22, 2005.

"En manos de policía quedan tres 'puchos.'" *La Tribuna*. June 17, 2006.

Enríquez, Octavio. "'El Siniestro' vuelve a escapar de la cárcel." *La Prensa*. November 20, 2005.

"Fiscalía Contra la Corrupción debe investigar la fuga de 'El Chelito.'" *La Tribuna*. November 22, 2005.

"Frustran sexto intento de fuga de pandillero en Honduras." Associated Press. January 14, 2007.

"Fuga de 'El Chelito' le duró poco tiempo." *La Tribuna*. August 8, 2005.

Gutiérrez Rivera, Åsedotter Strønen, and Ystanes, "Coming of Age in the Penal System."

Honduras: Zero Tolerance.

Horne Carter, "Gothic Sovereignty," *South Atlantic Quarterly*.

Human Rights Violations in Honduras. World Organization Against Torture. December 2006.

"Informe revela inaudita situación de Renaciendo." *La Tribuna*. February 8, 2006.

"Jon Horne Carter: Gothic Sovereignty (March 9, 2022)." YouTube video. Posted March 14, 2022, by IU CLACS.

"Libre 'compinche' de 'El Chelito.'" *El Heraldo*. August 31, 2007.

"'Los Puchos' enfrenan a la policía en temible balacera." *La Tribuna*. February 5, 2006.

"Marero sería el asesino de psicólogo." *El Heraldo*. August 15, 2003.

"Mareros dan muerte a compañero porque quería dejar agrupación." *La Tribuna*. November 23, 2003.

"Máxima seguridad para 'El Chelito.'" *La Tribuna*. August 2, 2005.

"Otro crimen en 'El Infiernito.'" *La Tribuna*. February 7, 2006.

"Pistolero liquida a psicólogo del IHNFA." *La Tribuna*. August 14, 2003.

"Recapturan a 'El Siniestro' en Honduras." *El Diario de Hoy*. August 9, 2005.

"3 custodios acusados de torturadores de niños." *La Tribuna*. November 25, 2005.

"Viene demanda al país por abusos en Renaciendo." *La Tribuna*. February 9, 2006.

"Violaciones en Renaciendo denuncia la Primera Dama." *La Tribuna*. February 7, 2006.

"'Volaron tres angelitos' de cárcel de menores." *La Tribuna*. April 30, 2005.

CHAPTER ELEVEN

"Agentes policiales capturan exterminadores de 'El Infiernito.'" *La Tribuna*. June 3, 2006.

"Denuncian policías matones que aterrorizaban en colonia." *La Tribuna*. April 29, 2006.

Honduras: Zero Tolerance.

"'Los Puchos' ejecutan a un niño en 'El Infiernito.'" *La Tribuna*. April 23, 2006.

Miller, "Dying Young in Honduras."

"Prófugo está nuevo jefe de 'Los Puchos.'" *La Tribuna*. April 29, 2006.

"Resurgen 'Los Chacales' otro grupo de exterminio." *La Tribuna*. April 21, 2005.

Rodgers, "Slum Wars of the 21st Century."

"Unos 1,586 jóvenes han sido ejecutados." *La Tribuna*. April 2, 2005.

CHAPTER TWELVE

"Agentes policiales capturan exterminadores de 'El Infiernito.'" CONADEH. August 15, 2006.

"Apresan exterminador de cipotes pandilleros." *La Tribuna*. August 12, 2006.

"Asesinan testigos." *El Heraldo*. August 12, 2006.

"Balacera interrumpe evento de Mel Zelaya." LaPrensahn.com. August 12, 2006.

"Capturan supuesto asesino en serie." *El Heraldo*. August 12, 2006.

"Mel presidente." *La Tribuna*.

"Pobladores piden liberación del exterminador de 'Los Puchos.'" *La Tribuna*. August 14, 2006.

"Pondré agencia para seguridad del pueblo y 'Pepe' funeraria." *La Tribuna*. August 5, 2005.

Reyes, German H. "La historia no miente: A las autoridades les importa un pepino que se fuguen los asesinos." Revistazo.com. August 7, 2014.

CHAPTER THIRTEEN

Bumpus, John Paul, John Speed Meyers, and Pierina Ana Sanchez. "Reducing Homicide in Honduras: How the US Government Can Help." *Journal of Public and International Affairs* (2014).

Bumpus, John Paul, John Speed Meyers, and Pierina Ana Sanchez. "Case One: Honduras." In *Best Practices in Reducing Violent Homicide Rates*. Report produced by Woodrow Wilson School of Public & International Affairs.

Nazario, Sonia. "How the Most Dangerous Place on Earth Got Safer." *New York Times*. August 11, 2016.

Rojido, Emiliano, and Ignacio Cano. "Impact Evaluation of the 'Paz y Justicia' Programme to Reduce Homicides in Honduras." *International Journal of Comparative and Applied Criminal Justice* 46, no. 1 (October 2021).

Ver Beek, "A More Perfect Love."

CHAPTER FOURTEEN

"A cinco años del incendio de Comayagua, CIDH reitera a Honduras su deber de investigar los hechos y adoptar medidas de no repetición." Comisión Interamericana de Derechos Humanos. February 15, 2017.

"Comayagua Prison Fire Killed 355—Honduras Officials." *BBC News*. February 16, 2012.

"Descartan mano criminal en incendio de granja penal de Comayagua." *El Heraldo*.

Díaz, Juan César. "Honduras: Inician juicio por muerte de 361 reos en incendio en cárcel de Comayagua." *El Heraldo*. January 16, 2017.

Grillo, Ioan, and Mike McDonald. "Survivors Accuse Guards After Honduras Prison Blaze." Reuters. February 16, 2012.

Hernández, Javier C., and Randal C. Archibold. "Blaze at Prison Underscores Broad Security Problems in Honduras." *New York Times*. February 15, 2021.

"Honduras' Comayagua Jail Fire 'Caused by Cigarette.'" *BBC News*. February 21, 2012.

"Listado oficial reporta 376 reos muertos." *La Tribuna*. February 16, 2012.

Peralta, Eyder. "Honduras Prison Fire: Most in Comayagua Jail Had Not Been Convicted." *NPR*. February 16, 2012.

Zabludovsky, Karla. "Report Paints Dire Picture in Honduran Prison Fire." *New York Times*. August 2, 2013.

Book Two

CHAPTER ONE

"A pescar Blue Marlins." *La Prensa*. October 12, 2006.

"Acribillan guardia para robarla arma." *La Tribuna*. March 22, 2005.

"Asaltantes mata a otro guardia." *La Tribuna*. November 9, 2003.

Cayetano, Juan. "Pescador con fortuna." *La Prensa*. September 21, 2004.

"Colonias declaran la guerra a delincuencia." *La Tribuna*. April 18, 2005.

"Empleados del ministerio no hacen nada por el trabajador." Revistazo.com. December 6, 2004.

"Falta de controles permite que guardias de seguridad estén mal pagados." Revistazo.com. November 26, 2004.

"Forajidos matan guardia para robarle escopeta." *La Tribuna*. November 15, 2003.

Honduras: Zero Tolerance.

"The Influence of Central American Dynasties Is Ebbing." *Economist*. May 31, 2021.

"Justice Seminar: Dr. Kurt VerBeek." YouTube video. Posted June 2, 2011, by Association for a More Just Society.

"La seguridad privada en Centro América." Fundación Arias para la Paz y el Progreso Humano. May 2003.

"Lo renovamos a contrato a Delta Security por un año más." Revistazo.com. December 9, 2004.

"Matan guardia que vigilaba farmacia." *La Tribuna*. July 6, 2005.

Moreno, Jenalia. "Gangs Make Security Big Business in Honduras." *Houston Chronicle*. September 1, 2006.

"Policía apadrina algunas compañías de seguridad." *La Tribuna*. May 27, 2006.

"Por robarla la pistola matan a guardia de clíper." ElHeraldo.hn. June 5, 2006.

"Ser vigilante es tener un pie en la tumba." *La Tribuna*. April 19, 2005.

"Ultiman guardia de seguridad." *La Tribuna*. September 19, 2005.

Ver Beek, "A More Perfect Love."

CHAPTER TWO

"¡Allá está un Dios arriba que se va a encargar de juzgarlo!" Revistazo.com. December 6, 2004.

"Aún le quedan 35 días de vida a 'El Cajón.'" *El Heraldo*. July 8, 1994.

"El pago del bono educativo." Revistazo.com. April 6, 2005.

"El reclamo de sus derechos laborales le costó su empleo." Revistazo.com. December 6, 2004.

"El sol de las noticias: Dina Meza." YouTube video. Posted July 28, 2017, by Voces de un Diálogo.

"Empleados de Delta llegan masivamente a ASJ." Revistazo.com. December 16, 2004.

"¡Esta con la empresa o contra la empresa!" Revistazo.com. November 26, 2004.

"Funcionario niega que se vaya por presiones." *La Tribuna*. July 15, 1994.

"Hemos llegado a la conclusión que lo mejor es cumplir con la ley." Revistazo.com. December 9, 2004.

"He pedido un día libre y no me lo dan." Revistazo.com. November 26, 2004.

"Interview with Honduran Journalist and HRD Dina Meza." YouTube video. Posted March 11, 2013, by Front Line Defenders.

"Justice for Betanco." YouTube video. Posted July 16, 2009, by Association for a More Just Society, ASJ-US.

"La generalidad de las empresas de seguridad que operan en el Litoral Atlántico violan los derechos laborales." Revistazo.com. December 6, 2004.

"¡Los pagos no son estables y a uno no le dicen por qué le quitan el dinero!" Revistazo.com. December 7, 2004.

"Me despidieron por no pagar un uniforme nuevo." Revistazo.com. March 29, 2005.

"Mi renuncia no obedece a presiones políticas, sostiene Mauricio Mosse." *El Heraldo*. July 15, 1994.

"Miles de guardias de seguridad en desamparo." Revistazo.com. December 10, 2004.

"Nosotros no podemos perder nuestros derechos." Revistazo.com. November 26, 2004.

"Principal incumplimiento de las empresas principal de seguridad." Revistazo.com. December 6, 2004.

"Principal obstáculo para defender derechos laborales." Revistazo.com. December 3, 2004.

"Project Performance Audit Report. Honduras. El Cajon Power Project." The World Bank. June 30, 1989.

"Sin una ley efectiva, empresas de seguridad tienen luz verde para violentar derechos laborales en Honduras." Revistazo.com. December 9, 2004.

CHAPTER THREE

Baldemar Alvarado, Joaquín. "El significado de la Gran Huelga de 1954." *La Tribuna*. April 23, 2006.

"Delta de acuerdo en continuar con jornada de 24 horas." Revistazo.com. December 16, 2004.

"Dionisio Díaz García, más de una década del asesinato del 'abogado de los pobres.'" YouTube video. Posted December 8, 2016, by asj honduras.

"Documental 'La Ceiba, Honduras.'" YouTube video. Posted June 29, 2020, by Cucalambeana Online.

"En un mes haremos una reinspección para revisar si hay cumplimiento del acta de compromiso." Revistazo.com. December 9, 2004.

"Estado solo se fija en precios bajos de licitaciones." Revistazo.com. November 26, 2004.

"Justice for Dionisio Díaz García, Martyred Lawyer of the Poor." YouTube video. Posted July 16, 2009, by Association for a More Just Society, ASJ-US.

"No ha sido fácil pero vamos a seguir mejorando." Revistazo.com. April 8, 2005.

"Nosotros nos limitamos a conciliar entre las partes." Revistazo.com. December 6, 2004.

"Preocupada IJM por condiciones laborales de guardias." Revistazo.com. December 6, 2004.

"Reclamos de guardias de seguridad ahora son atendidos por empresa." Revistazo.com. April 7, 2005.

"Reunión de evaluación de cumplimiento de compromisos." Revistazo.com. April 6, 2005.

"Supervisor denuncia despido mientras empresa señala que fue traslado." Revistazo.com. April 6, 2005.

CHAPTER FOUR

"Exempleados demandan a SETECH exigiendo derechos laborales." Revistazo.com. October 23, 2006.

Marin, Robert. "Mano de la justicia cae sobre empresa Delta." Revistazo.com. August 18, 2006.

Meza, Dina. "Me siento como terminada la vida de tanto desvelo en Delta." Revistazo.com. September 5, 2006.

CHAPTER SIX

"Asesinan a otro abogado." ElHerlado.hn. December 5, 2006.

Bracken, Ali. "Living on the Frontline: Honduras." www.tribune.ie. September 7, 2008.

"CIDH pide protección para personal de la ASJ." ElHeraldo.hn. December 21, 2006.

"Denuncian más amenazas." ElHeraldo.hn. December 8, 2006.

"Exigen investigación." ElHeraldo.hn. December 7, 2006.

"Honduras no puede seguir llorando a sus mejores hijos." Revistazo.com. December 6, 2004.

"Justicia . . . Justicia . . . por la muerte del 'abogado de los pobres.'" Revistazo.com. December 11, 2006.

Mendoza, Claudia. "Condenan asesinato de abogado; piden protección para cuatro periodistas." Revistazo.com. December 5, 2006.

Mendoza, Claudia. "El pueblo hondureño da último adiós al abogado de los pobres." Revistazo.com. December 5, 2006.

Morazán, Rosa. "Ciudadanía exige castigo para asesinos de abogado de la ASJ." Revistazo.com. December 5, 2006.

"Periodistas amenazados protestan en los bajos del Congreso Nacional." *La Tribuna*. December 16, 2006.

"Piden seguridad para frenar ola delictiva." ElHeraldo.hn. December 6, 2006.

"Servicio memorial en honor al 'abogado de los pobres.'" Revistazo.com. December 15, 2006.

"Sicarios ultiman a defensor de los pobres." Revistazo.com. December 4, 2006.

"Sicarios ultiman otro abogado." *La Tribuna*. December 5, 2006.

"Suspender la licencia de operaciones a empresas de seguridad solicita la ciudadanía al gobierno de Honduras." Revistazo.com. December 13, 2006.

CHAPTER SEVEN

"Asesinan testigos." *El Heraldo*. August 12, 2006.

"Avanzan pesquisas en caso de abogados." ElHeraldo.hn. December 16, 2006.

"Embajada norteamericana interesada en esclarecer crímenes de abogados." Revistazo.com. February 27, 2007.

"Enfermera escapa de ser violada en pasillos del Hospital Escuela." *La Tribuna*. June 20, 2006.

"Exigen investigar la verdad." *La Prensa*. July 4, 2007.

"Imparables fechorías en Hospital Escuela." *La Tribuna*. November 24, 2005.

"Intentan violar mujer que acababa de parir." *La Tribuna*. February 6, 2006.

"Mareros invaden hospital para matar a joven quemado." *La Tribuna*. February 4, 2006.

Mendoza, Claudia. "Dos meses de espera . . . dos meses sin respuesta." Revistazo.com. February 6, 2007.

"Narcotráfico está metido en la campaña: Custodio." *La Tribuna*. September 15, 2005.

"Nuevamente burlada la seguridad del Escuela." ElHeraldo.hn. May 14, 2005.

"Pervertidos se infiltran en salas de niños del Materno Infantil." *La Tribuna*. June 19, 2006.

Schwartz, Mattathias. "A Mission Gone Wrong." *New Yorker*. December 29, 2013.

CHAPTER EIGHT

"A un año, impune crimen de abogado." ElHerlado.hn. December 5, 2007.

"Amenazan un testigo clave del crimen de Blanca Jeaneth Kawas." *La Tribuna*. December 11, 2003.

"Amnistía Internacional preocupada por Honduras." ElHeraldo.hn. August 8, 2007.

"Asesinan al quinto abogado." ElHeraldo.hn. December 23, 2006.

Bow, Juan Carlos. "Crímenes sin castigo en Honduras." *La Prensa de Nicaragua*. April 2, 2016.

"53 abogados perdieron la vida en forma violenta." *La Tribuna*. March 16, 2013.

"Crímenes de abogados siguen en la impunidad." ElHerlado.hn. January 4, 2007.

"Criminalista se va al exilio por amenazas de muerte." *La Tribuna*. December 16, 2006.

"Documental 'Blanca Jeannette Kawas.'" YouTube video. Posted November 27, 2018, by utvunah.

"Germán Antonio Rivas." Committee to Protect Journalists.

"Hallan ultimada a testigo de desaparición de fiscal." *La Prensa*. November 13, 2008.

"Hear No Evil, See No Evil." *Baltimore Sun*. June 19, 1995.

Hernández, Wilfredo. "Sicarios ejecutan a líder campesino." *La Tribuna*. September 12, 2005.

Honduras: Zero Tolerance.

"Investigan misterioso desaparecimiento de fiscal." *La Prensa*. October 28, 2008.

Kinzer, Stephen. "Our Man in Honduras." *New York Review*. September 20, 2001.

"Magistrados y jueces amenazados a muerte." *La Tribuna*. December 6, 2006.

"Parque Nacional Blanca Jeannette Kawas Fernández." *La Tribuna*. October 5, 2014.

"Report Nº 13/94." Inter-American Commission on Human Rights. February 2, 1994.

Santos, Benjamín. "La muerte de German Rivas." *La Tribuna*. November 29, 2003.

"Sicarios atacaron a periodista." ElHeraldo.hn. September 12, 2007.

CHAPTER NINE

Ahern, Patrick. "'Lawyer of the Poor' Killers Brought to Justice—but What About the Intellectual Authors?" *Honduras This Week*. March 23, 2009.

Bracken, Ali. "Living on the Frontline Honduras." www.tribune.ie. September 7, 2008.

"Culpables asesinos de abogado Dionisio Díaz." ElHeraldo.hn. February 27, 2009.

"Culpables los 2 implicados en la muerte de abogado." Tiempo.hn. March 1, 2009.

"Desmantelan enjambres de abejas en la Corte Suprema." Tiempo.hn. February 25, 2009.

"Justice for Dionisio Díaz García, Martyred Lawyer of the Poor."

"Reconstruyen crimen del abogado Dionisio Díaz." Tiempo.hn. February 20, 2009.

"Recuperado el juez picado por avispas." *El País*. February 26, 2009.

"30 años de cárcel para homicidas de abogado Dionisio García." *La Tribuna*. February 25, 2009.

"2008 Country Reports on Human Rights Practices—Honduras." United States Department of State. February 25, 2009.

"Viernes dictan fallo por crimen contra abogado." ElHeraldo.hn. February 24, 2009.

CHAPTER TEN

"Allanan casa de empresario tras asesinato de exdirector de centros penales." *La Prensa*. December 9, 2016.

"Bala perdida mata a mujer en el barrio Villa Adela de la capital." *El Heraldo*. October 6, 2018.

"Bala perdida mata a una mujer en Comayagüela." *La Prensa*. October 6, 2018.

Huyser Honig, Abram. "A Victory for Justice in Honduras." *Sojourners*. March 1, 2010.

"Justice for Betanco." YouTube video. Posted July 16, 2009, by Association for a More Just Society, ASJ-US.

"Justice for Dionisio Díaz García, Martyred Lawyer of the Poor."

"ONG pide despido de viceministro de Trabajo." ElHeraldo.hn. March 4, 2010.

"Universidades presentan precandidatos a magistrados." *La Tribuna*. August 26, 2008.

Book Three

CHAPTER ONE

"A policías 'sicarios' acusan de matar a hijo de la rectora." *La Tribuna*. October 26, 2011.

A NOTE ON SOURCES

"Alfredo Landaverde Frente a Frente [01/11/2011] [17/11/2011]." YouTube video. Posted December 7, 2011, by H Cortez.

Arce, Alberto. "Tres generales y un cartel: Violencia policial e impunidad en Honduras." *New York Times*. April 15, 2016.

Archibold, Randal C. "Peace Corps to Scale Back in Central America." *New York Times*. December 21, 2011.

"Asesinato de Landaverde es una exhibición más de un . . ." *La Tribuna*. December 8, 2011.

"Callan la voz cantante a favor de la depuración policial." *La Tribuna*. December 8, 2011.

"Condenable atentado contra *La Tribuna*." *La Tribuna*. December 6, 2011.

"Con permiso huyen policías ligado a la muerte de universitarios." *La Tribuna*. October 31, 2011.

"Da más miedo encontrarse a cinco policías que a los mareros." *La Tribuna*. November 4, 2011.

"Encontramos a la policía sin supervisión ni control; no hay disciplina, ni jerarquía." *La Tribuna*. November 4, 2011.

"Entre el dolor y conmoción sepultan hoy a hijo de rectora." *La Tribuna*. October 24, 2011.

"Faltan 'huevos' para combatir el narcotráfico en Honduras." *La Tribuna*. December 8, 2011.

Farah, Douglas, and Kathryn Babineau. "The Evolution of MS 13 in El Salvador and Honduras." *Prism 7*, no 1 (September 14, 2017).

Ferri, Pablo. "The Struggle to Survive in the Most Violent Country in the World." InSight Crime. December 14, 2012.

Finnegan, William. "An Old-Fashioned Coup." *New Yorker*. November 22, 2009.

Fox, Edward. "Dynamics of Honduran Police Corruption Narrow Chance for Reform." InSight Crime. January 31, 2012.

"Hay más de 10,000 denuncias contra policías desde el 2009." *La Tribuna*. November 4, 2011.

Hernández, Javier C. "An Academic Turns Grief into a Crime-Fighting Tool." *New York Times*. February 24, 2012.

"Intervienen posta en busca de policías sicarios." *La Tribuna*. October 27, 2011.

"Julieta Castellanos, electa rectora de la UNAH." *Proceso Digital*. April 24, 2009.

"La policía nunca informó al MP que sospechosos se irían de 'día libre.'" *La Tribuna*. November 1, 2011.

"Mi amigo está herido, llévenlo al hospital . . . él es hijo de la rectora . . ." *La Tribuna*. November 3, 2011.

"Mi hijo murió primero, a Carlos . . . mataron con disparo en la cara." *La Tribuna*. November 1, 2011.

Miroff, Nick. "Grim Toll as Cocaine Trade Expands in Honduras." *Washington Post*. December 26, 2011.

"MP duplica hermetismo en caso de universitarios." *La Tribuna*. November 10, 2011.

"No es política de la Policía Nacional matar personas." *La Tribuna*. November 15, 2011.

"Pedimos la reestructuración completa de la policía." *La Tribuna*. November 4, 2011.

"Policía requiere intervención inmediata con apoyo internacional: Castellanos." *La Tribuna*. November 8, 2011.

"Policía retrasa entrega de informe sobre la muerte de universitarios." *La Tribuna*. October 30, 2011.

"Policías le avisaron a Barralaga que huirían." *La Tribuna*. November 10, 2011.

"Presentan requerimiento contra Barralaga y Marco Tulio Palma." *La Prensa*. April 19, 2012.

"Rectora pide la pronta intervención internacional en el estado hondureño." *La Tribuna*. November 12, 2011.

Robles, Frances. "Honduras Becomes Murder Capital of the World." *Miami Herald*. January 23, 2012.

Schwartz, Mattathias. "A Mission Gone Wrong." *New Yorker*. December 29, 2013.

"'Si la intervención es la solución hay que hacerla': Lobo Sosa." *La Tribuna*. November 8, 2011.

"Solo escuchamos cuatro disparos como a las 2:10 de la mañana." *La Tribuna*. October 28, 2011.

"Subinspector fue el que disparo al vehículo en plena persecución." *La Tribuna*. November 8, 2011.

"Testigos revelan más detalles en fuga de policías." *La Tribuna*. April 16, 2013.

"Universitarios alzan la voz contra la violencia y claman por la paz." *La Tribuna*. October 28, 2011.

"Urge intervención en la policía." *La Tribuna*. November 2, 2011.

"100 Days of Resistance—Part 2: Fault Lines." YouTube video. Posted October 15, 2009, by Al Jazeera English.

CHAPTER TWO

Adams, David C. "El ascenso de Juan Orlando Hernández: Autócrata de origen humilde, presidente de Honduras por segunda vez." *Univision Noticias*. January 27, 2018.

Adams, David C., and Jeff Ernst. "From Humble Roots to President of Honduras: Juan Orlando Hernández—in Photos." *Univision News*. January 26, 2018.

"Alianza—Avances en los trabajos que realiza la DIECP." YouTube video. Posted January 15, 2013, by Alianza por la Paz y la Justicia.

"Alianza—Informe de violencia." YouTube video. Posted February 28, 2013, by Alianza por la Paz y la Justicia.

"Alianza—Llamado de la Alianza por la Paz y la Justicia es escuchado." YouTube video. Posted April 10, 2013, by Alianza por la Paz y la Justicia.

"Alianza—Mensaje a los que luchamos por una Honduras con paz y con justicia." YouTube video. Posted December 10, 2012, by Alianza por la Paz y la Justicia.

"Alianza—Participación de APJ en rendición de ctas en el congreso (DIECP)." YouTube video. Posted April 11, 2013, by Alianza por la Paz y la Justicia.

"Alianza—Participación de la APJ en la rendición de cuentas del Fiscal General Luis Rubí." YouTube video. Posted April 15, 2013, by Alianza por la Paz y la Justicia.

"Alianza—Supervisión de trabajos de depuración de la Policía." YouTube video. Posted January 15, 2013, by Alianza por la Paz y la Justicia.

Anderson, Jon Lee. "Is the President of Honduras a Narco-Trafficker?" *New Yorker.* November 8, 2021.

Arias, Ninfa. "'Corte' a cuatro magistrados de la Sala Constitucional." *La Tribuna.* December 13, 2012.

Arias, Ninfa. "Fiscal Rubí expone alarmante impunidad." *La Tribuna.* April 11, 2013.

"Arita y Villanueva ratificado Dirección de Investigación y Evaluación de la Carrera Policial." *La Tribuna.* December 1, 2011.

Carducci, Giuliana, Catalina Iglesias, Charlotte Gossett, Danilo Moura, and Dariela Sosa. "Advocating for Peace, Justice and Security in Honduras: An Evaluation of Alianza por la Paz y la Justicia." Transparency International UK Defence and Security Programme.

"CN ordena revisa la conducta de los magistrados de la CSJ." *La Tribuna.* December 11, 2012.

"'CN tomará decisiones porque el pueblo ya no aguanta más.'" *La Tribuna.* April 15, 2013.

"'Corte desconoce emergencia nacional en materia de seguridad.'" *La Tribuna.* December 5, 2012.

"CSJ provoca que policías comiencen batalla contra el estado: Rectora." *La Tribuna.* December 6, 2012.

"Cúpula policial a pruebas de confianza en 30 días." *La Tribuna.* April 13, 2013.

"Declaradas inconstitucionales pruebas de confianza a policías." *La Tribuna.* November 28, 2012.

"Depuración sería el primer tema: JOH." *La Tribuna.* December 11, 2012.

"Destitución es ilegítima, ilegal e injusta." *La Tribuna.* December 13, 2012.

"DIECP en el ojo del huracán." *La Tribuna.* April 5, 2013.

"DIECP perdió control de la depuración policial." *El Heraldo.*

"Dr. Kurt Ver Beek @ Church of the Servant." YouTube video. Posted March 7, 2013, by Association for a More Just Society, ASJ-US.

Ernst, Jeff. "Honduran President's Fall from Grace Poised to End in US Indictment." *Guardian.* January 26, 2022.

"Escalofriante: Fiscal admite que el 80 por ciento de los delitos queda impune." *Proceso Digital.* April 10, 2013.

"Esperábamos que depuración fuera de arriba hacia abajo: ASJ." *La Tribuna.* April 8, 2013.

"Fallo de la corte conspiraba contra Ley Orgánica de la Policía." *La Tribuna.* December 18, 2012.

Gabel Cino, Jessica. "Is a Polygraph a Reliable Lie Detector?" *Conversation*. September 28, 2018.

Harris, Mark. "The Lie Generator: Inside the Black Mirror World of Polygraph Job Screenings." *Wired*. October 1, 2018.

"Histórica 'pasarela.'" *La Tribuna*. April 9, 2013.

"Investigación está colapsada: Juan Carlos Bonilla." *La Tribuna*. April 11, 2013.

"JOH propone someter pruebas de confianza a plebiscito o referéndum." *La Tribuna*. November 29, 2012.

"Juan Orlando Hernández: Un líder valiente, reformador y . . . " *La Tribuna*. January 27, 2014.

"La Alianza por la Paz y la Justicia en Frente a Frente." YouTube video. Posted October 30, 2012, by Alianza por la Paz y la Justicia.

"Magistrados condenan la destitución de sus compañeros." *La Tribuna*. December 14, 2012.

"No aguantamos más." *La Tribuna*. April 4, 2013.

"Pasarela en el Congreso." *La Tribuna*. April 5, 2013.

"'Pepe' llama a la armonía entre poderes." *La Tribuna*. December 14, 2012.

"Polémicas empañaron proceso de elegir a las autoridades del DNIECP." *La Tribuna*. December 1, 2011.

"Policía a las puertas de una intervención internacional." *La Tribuna*. April 3, 2013.

"Polígrafo ya no será causa de despido." *La Tribuna*. December 19, 2012.

"Pompeyo Bonilla promete dejar sentadas bases de la depuración." *La Tribuna*. April 4, 2013.

"Resultados negativos a un año del proceso de depuración policial." *La Tribuna*. March 13, 2013.

"Sala Constitucional dejó muy debilitada la depuración policial." *La Tribuna*. December 19, 2012.

Sieff, Kevin. "Honduran President, a Trump Ally Implicated in Drug Trafficking, Tries to Win Over Biden." *Washington Post*. February 12, 2021.

Talbot, Margaret. "Duped." *New Yorker*. June 25, 2007.

"Transarán expediente a la CSJ sobre caso de Landaverde." *La Tribuna*. April 2, 2013.

"Villanueva le 'pasa la pelota' a Seguridad." *La Tribuna*. April 10, 2013

CHAPTER THREE

Aguilar, Leonardo. "El investigador que denunció los favores al narcoestado del fiscal que se va." *ContraCorriente*. August 29, 2023.

"Alianza—Posición de la APJ sobre la problemática de la elección del fiscal general." YouTube video. Posted August 30, 2013, by Alianza por la Paz y la Justicia.

"ALIANZA—Rechazo a elección del fiscal y nueva ley de MP." YouTube video. Posted July 10, 2013, by Alianza por la Paz y la Justicia.

"APJ /ASJ proponen herramientas tecnológicas #APP para elección CJS." You-Tube video. Posted July 15, 2015, by Alianza por la Paz y la Justicia.

Basu, Moni. "Daniel's Journey: How Thousands of Children Are Creating a Crisis in America." *CNN.* June 19, 2014.

Biden, Joseph R., Jr. "Joe Biden: A Plan for Central America." *New York Times.* January 29, 2015.

Carducci et al., "Advocating for Peace, Justice and Security in Honduras."

"Carlos Hernández opina sobre informe de la Junta Interventora del IHSS." You-Tube video. Posted March 6, 2014, by Alianza por la Paz y la Justicia.

"Carlos Hernández y Julieta Castellanos, en Treinta / Treinta (30/30) Edgardo Melgar." YouTube video. Posted June 8, 2015, by Alianza por la Paz y la Justicia.

"CICIH seria proceso muy lento; hay que buscar otro mecanismo." *La Tribuna.* June 8, 2015.

"51 abogados candidatos a fiscalía general y adjunto." *La Tribuna.* August 24, 2013.

"Cisma en la Junta Proponente." *La Tribuna.* August 29, 2013.

Clemens, Michael A. "Violence, Development, and Migration Waves: Evidence from Central American Child Migrant Apprehensions." Center for Global Development. July 2017.

"Con 12 casos sonados comienza Comisión del CN." *La Tribuna.* May 22, 2015.

"Congreso Nacional elige hoy al fiscal general y al adjunto." *La Tribuna.* August 31, 2013.

"Conviene o no que este gobierno nombre al fiscal general y adjunto." YouTube video. Posted August 1, 2013, by Alianza por la Paz y la Justicia.

"Corrupción y financiamiento de partidos políticos." YouTube video. Posted May 19, 2015, by Alianza por la Paz y la Justicia.

Cortázar Velarde, Juan Carlos, Mariano Lafuente, and Mario Sanginés. *Serving Citizens: A Decade of Civil Service Reforms in Latin America (2004–13).* Inter-American Development Bank. 2014.

"Cuentas y combate a corrupción." *La Tribuna.* October 7, 2014.

"Debe de continuar la coordinación entre FUSINA y operadores de justicia." You-Tube video. Posted March 18, 2015, by Alianza por la Paz y la Justicia.

"Déjenme trabajar, no tengo tiempo de pensar en nada más." *La Tribuna.* April 27, 2015.

"Denuncia de cheques del IHSS movió olla de corrupción." *La Prensa.* May 27, 2015.

"Estado comprará medicamentos sin intermediación de funcionarios." *La Tribuna.* March 26, 2014.

"Firma de convenio ASJ y MP." YouTube video. Posted August 25, 2015, by Alianza por la Paz y la Justicia.

"Frente a frente." YouTube video. Posted June 17, 2015, by Alianza por la Paz y la Justicia.

Gagne, David. "Honduras' Search for Corruption Antidote Might Be Fatally Flawed." InSight Crime. December 1, 2015.

"Hay que aprovechar este momento para fortalecer las instituciones." *La Tribuna*. June 5, 2015.

"Hay que fortalecer la Fiscalía Anticorrupción." *La Tribuna*. June 6, 2015.

Hernández, Carlos, Roland Hoksbergen, Katerina Parsons, and Kurt Ver Beek. "For a Government That Works: ASJ's Theory of Change, with a Case Study of Their Efforts in Education." *Christian Relief, Development, and Advocacy: The Journal of the Accord Network* 1, no. 1 (2019).

"Honduras firma acuerdo para combatir corrupción." *La Prensa*. October 6, 2014.

"Honduras se pasa al bando mayoritario de los países reeleccionistas." *La Tribuna*. April 25, 2015.

"Inteligencia del Estado indagará fuga de medicinas." *El Heraldo*. March 26, 2014.

"Intervienen almacén de medicamentos de Salud." *La Tribuna*. April 3, 2012.

"Intervienen entrega de medicinas en hospitales." *La Tribuna*. June 11, 2015.

"Junta Proponente deberá enviar lista de candidatos a fiscal general el 20 de agosto." *La Tribuna*. August 12, 2013.

"La reelección es un derecho del pueblo." *La Tribuna*. April 24, 2015.

"No más impunidad, piden en 'marchas de antorchas.'" *La Tribuna*. June 8, 2015.

"Noticias APJ—APJ propone cción anticorrupción de inmediata implementación." YouTube video. Posted June 19, 2015, by Alianza por la Paz y la Justicia.

"Omar Rivera, entrevista a profundidad, Canal 11." YouTube video. Posted June 4, 2015, by Alianza por la Paz y la Justicia.

"Otra entrega de medicamentos a 27 hospitales a nivel nacional." *La Tribuna*. March 25, 2014.

Palencia, Gustavo. "Honduras President: Graft-Linked Companies Helped Fund My Campaign." Reuters. June 3, 2015.

"Partido Nacional se moviliza en la capital: 'Caiga quien caiga.'" *La Tribuna*. June 8, 2015.

"'Porque no tenemos nada que ver con eso, moralmente estamos aptos para investigar.'" *La Tribuna*. June 4, 2015.

Preston, Julia. "New U.S. Effort to Aid Unaccompanied Child Migrants." *New York Times*. June 2, 2014.

"Proceso de selección de candidatos a Fiscalía divide a la Junta Proponente." *La Tribuna*. August 28, 2013.

"15 días más pide Junta Proponente." *La Tribuna*. August 17, 2013.

"Reactivan la Junta Proponente." *La Tribuna*. August 1, 2013.

Robbins, Seth, and Héctor Silva Ávalos. "No Time to Wait: Biden's Security Challenges in Central America." InSight Crime. January 20, 2021.

Rodríguez, Dagoberto. "Ministerio público ya tiene nuevos titulares." *La Prensa*. September 2, 2013.

Sabet, Daniel. "When Corruption Funds the Political System: A Case Study of Honduras." Wilson Center. August 2020.

"Sala Constitucional oficializa fallo sobre reelección presidencial." *La Tribuna.* April 24, 2015.

"Sociedad civil pide castigar a corruptos 'caiga quien caiga.'" *La Tribuna.* May 19, 2015.

"TVC Frente a Frente—Honduras es el primer país que firmará un acuerdo contra la corrupción." YouTube video. Posted October 6, 2014, by Tvcplay.

"Unos 2,500 maestros quedarán fuera de planilla de pago este mes." *La Tribuna.* March 19, 2013.

CHAPTER FOUR

"Adiós al festín de incapacidades médicas que tenían los policías." *La Tribuna.* June 5, 2016.

"Aprueban decreto que acelera depuración y transformación." *La Tribuna.* April 12, 2016.

Arce, Alberto. "Honduran Ex-Police Chief Says Government Faked Documents in Assassination Case." *New York Times.* April 22, 2016.

"Así ejecutaron al zar antidrogas Julián Arístides González." *El Heraldo.* April 3, 2016.

"Atentan contra Jorge Machado y la Comisión Depuración Policial." *La Tribuna.* December 16, 2016.

"Bloquean 42 bienes de lavado de clan Barralaga." *La Tribuna.* August 1, 2017.

"Comisión de depuración cancela a 405 policías por diversas razones." *El Heraldo.* December 15, 2016.

"Comisión Depuradora investigará informe divulgado por la Agencia AP que vincula a director de Policía con narcotráfico." *El Heraldo.* January 26, 2018.

"Decreto faculta al Ejecutivo a sacar cualquier policía." *La Tribuna.* April 8, 2016.

Dye, David R. "Police Reform in Honduras: The Role of the Special Purge and Transformation Commission." Wilson Center.

"Extrañas ratas devoraron hojas de servicio de policías." *La Tribuna.* April 27, 2016.

"'Hay dos carteles: Uno cachureco y otro liberal.'" *La Tribuna.* April 20, 2016.

"The Honduran National Police: Is progress Being Made in Cleaning Up and Reforming the Force?" YouTube video. Posted June 21, 2016, by WoodrowWilsonCenter.

"Honduras: Comisión para la depuración policial se compromete a brindar resultados." *El Heraldo.* April 13, 2016.

"Honduras: L 1.5 millones iba recibir cada oficial retirado." *El Heraldo.* April 15, 2016.

"Inicia evaluación de generales activos de la Policía Nacional." *La Tribuna.* April 15, 2016.

"Intervenidas las instalaciones antiguo cuartel de Casamata." *La Tribuna.* April 5, 2016.

"JOH juramenta Comisión de Reestructuración." *La Tribuna*. April 13, 2016.

"José Ugaz presidente de TI." YouTube video. Posted May 12, 2016, by Alianza por la Paz y la Justicia.

"Justice Lecture with Dr. Kurt Ver Beek—Jan 19, 2017." YouTube video. Posted January 23, 2017, by Association for a More Just Society, ASJ-US.

"Las empresas que más usó Barralaga de 'Lavadero.'" *La Tribuna*. August 2, 2017.

"Los crímenes que dieron origen a la cuestionada depuración policial en Honduras." CESPAD. January 13, 2020.

"Más de siete mil nuevos policías contra el crimen." *La Tribuna*. November 23, 2017.

"Miembros de la comisión depuradora denuncia amenazas a muerte." YouTube video. Posted June 1, 2016, by Alianza por la Paz y la Justicia.

"No posterguen la depuración policial: Omar Rivera." *La Tribuna*. April 8, 2016.

"'No voy a distraerme a limpiar la Policía Nacional.'" *La Tribuna*. November 2, 2017.

"Oficiales y agentes depurados siguen activos en la Policía Nacional." *El Heraldo*. June 25, 2017.

"Omar y Julieta Castellanos hablan de Depuración Policial Honduras." YouTube video. Posted December 9, 2015, by Alianza por la Paz y la Justicia.

"Policías también mataron a Alfredo Landaverde." *El Heraldo*. April 5, 2016.

"Pronunciamiento de APJ." YouTube video. Posted April 5, 2016, by Alianza por la Paz y la Justicia.

Puerta, Felipe. "Arrests of Honduras Police Reveal Setbacks in Purge." InSight Crime. October 16, 2018.

"Reestructuración comienza con 35 oficiales que se van." *La Tribuna*. April 14, 2016.

Risquez, Ronna. "Accusations Land Honduras Police Reform Commission in Hot Water." InSight Crime. February 5, 2018.

"Sociedad Civil aplaude la intervención en Casamata." *La Tribuna*. April 6, 2016.

"23 comisionados cancelados y 23 suspendidos." *La Tribuna*. April 30, 2016.

CHAPTER FIVE

"'Acepté documento con OEA sin pensar era trampa.'" *La Tribuna*. November 30, 2017.

"Alianza celebra triunfo y pide a TSE que oficialice el mismo." *La Tribuna*. November 28, 2017.

"Alianza: Unas 1,504 actas fueron clonadas." *La Tribuna*. December 12, 2017.

Cálix, Héctor. "Nasralla salta del deporte y la farándula a la política." *El Heraldo*. April 7, 2014.

Dada, Carlos, and Fred Ramos. "Honduras niega la reelección a su presidente." *El Faro*. November 27, 2017.

D'Amours, Julia. "Explainer: The 2017 Honduran Presidential Election." AS/

COA. November 21, 2017. https://www.as-coa.org/articles/explainer-2017
-honduran-presidential-election

"David Matamoros: 'Hasta que esté 100% se declarará a un ganador.'" *La Tribuna*.
December 1, 2017.

"Depuración se hizo en forma científica no se puede retroceder." *La Tribuna*.
November 17, 2017.

"Desfalco en el IP suma seis millones." *La Tribuna*. June 11, 2015.

"Destruyen estatua de Manuel Bonilla." *La Tribuna*. December 2, 2017.

"Election Update: Four Days Since Polling Ended." *Honduras Culture and Politics*.
November 30, 2017.

"'El voto es secreto pero el escrutinio es público.'" *La Tribuna*. November 24,
2017.

"Empresarios y sociedad civil piden a candidatos espera resultados del TSE." *La
Tribuna*. November 29, 2017.

Farah, Douglas, and Kathryn Babineau. "The Evolution of MS 13 in El Salvador
and Honduras." *Prism* 7, no 1 (September 14, 2017).

Final Report: General Elections 2017. European Union Election Observation
Mission.

"Human Rights Violations in the Context of the 2017 Elections in Honduras."
Report of the United Nations High Commissioner for Human Rights.

*Informe final de la Misión de Observación Electoral de la Organización de los Estados
Americanos*. Organization of American States. November 24, 2013.

"Is Honduras's Ruling Party Planning to Rig an Election?" *Economist*. November
25, 2017.

López Zúñiga, Eduardo Jair. "El director de TI de Honduras y su posición sobre
la reelección." *El Heraldo*.

Malkin, Elisabeth. "Honduran President Declared Winner, but O.A.S. Calls for
New Election." *New York Times*. December 17, 2017.

"'Mantenemos la posición de apoyar una construcción a este proceso creíble y
transparente.'" *La Tribuna*. December 10, 2017.

"Marcha pacífica de la Alianza en la capital." *La Tribuna*. December 4, 2017.

"Más de 30 mil aspirantes corren por 3 mil cargos." *La Tribuna*. November 25, 2017.

"Medios internacionales acusan a Zelaya y Nasralla de provocar caos y violencia."
La Tribuna. December 3, 2017.

"Militares retornan con el material electoral." *La Tribuna*. November 29, 2017.

"MOE-UE: Coincide con resultados de declaratoria del TSE." *La Tribuna*.
December 18, 2017.

"Nasralla dice que policías depurados podrían ser reintegrados." *La Tribuna*.

"Nasralla vuelve a pedir repetición de elecciones." *La Tribuna*. December 3, 2017.

"Ningún tipo de violencia se justifica: Sociedad Civil." *La Tribuna*. December 4,
2017.

"'No hubo adición, sustracción o modificación de los datos,' concluye el informe
del TSE." *El Heraldo*. December 9, 2017.

"Organismos electorales de América se unen a observación de elecciones 2017." *La Tribuna.* November 9, 2017.

"Países inician reconocimiento del Presidente Hernández." *La Tribuna.* December 21, 2017.

"Partidos pequeños brillaron por su ausencia en las mesas." *La Tribuna.* November 27, 2017.

"People and Corruption: Latin America and the Caribbean." Transparency International. 2017.

"'Posible conexión entre policías depurados y campaña de intimidación.'" *La Tribuna.* November 21, 2017.

"Processing an Acta: Rules and Procedures." *Honduras Culture and Politics.* December 16, 2017.

"Repetir las elecciones no es legal." *La Tribuna.* December 23, 2017.

Sabet, Daniel et. al. "Honduras Threshold Program: Endline Evaluation Report." Millennium Challenge Corporation. October 2020.

Salazar, Miguel. "The Honduran Government Is Trying to Steal an Election." *Nation.* December 6, 2017.

"Salvador dice haber entregado pruebas del frauda a Almagro." *La Tribuna.* December 19, 2017.

Segundo informe preliminar de la Misión de Observación Electoral en Honduras. Organization of American States. December 17, 2017.

"Simpatizantes de Alianza protestan." *La Tribuna.* December 1, 2017.

"Sistema de divulgación del TSE se paralizó." *La Tribuna.* November 30, 2017.

"Sitio InSight Crimen reconoce drástica reducción de homicidios." *La Tribuna.* November 17, 2017.

"Sobre la encuesta de CID Gallup." *El Pulso.* September 25, 2017.

"Statement from the Tribunal Supremo Electoral." *Honduras Culture and Politics.* November 24, 2017.

"Statistics and Fraud." *Honduras Culture and Politics.* December 17, 2017.

"Transcripción será anónimo y aleatoria: Theodore Dale." *La Tribuna.* November 13, 2017.

"The Transparency Agreement: A Documentary from ASJ." YouTube video. Posted July 17, 2019, by Association for a More Just Society—ASJ-US.

"TSE dio el banderillazo para el inicio de las votaciones." *La Tribuna.* November 27, 2017.

"TSE entrega a la OEA informe de las seis recomendaciones." *La Tribuna.* December 12, 2017.

"TSE: Hasta el jueves se conocerán resultados." *La Tribuna.* November 28, 2017.

"Velocidad y transparencia en el simulacro de nueva transmisión." *La Tribuna.* November 1, 2017.

"VOTO POR VOTO DE 4,752 MESAS." *La Tribuna.* December 8, 2017.

"What May Be Coming in the Honduran Election." *Honduras Culture and Politics.* November 27, 2017.

CHAPTER SIX

Adams, David C., and Jeff Ernst. "What Did Nery Know? A Prison Murder in Honduras Deepens Suspicions of Government Involvement in Drug Trafficking." *Univision News.* December 6, 2019.

Aguilar, Leonardo, and Jennifer Avila. "The Zelaya Clan Returns to Power in Honduras." *ContraCorriente.* May 27, 2022.

Anderson, Jon Lee. "Is the President of Honduras a Narco-Trafficker?" *New Yorker.* November 8, 2021.

"Anti-Corruption Advocate Flees Honduras After Receiving Threats." *Al Jazeera.* June 19, 2023.

Asmann, Parker. "Honduras President Selective When Targeting Criminal Crackdowns." InSight Crime. February 27, 2019.

Asmann, Parker. "Will Tony Hernández Conviction Upend Narco-Politics in Honduras?" InSight Crime. October 18, 2019.

Asmann, Parker. "Yet More Accusations Against Honduras President, But Will They Matter?" InSight Crime. May 5, 2020.

Ávalos, Héctor Silva. "Wild West of Honduras: Home to Narcos and Their Politicians." InSight Crime. September 10, 2019.

Clavel, Tristan. "Former Honduras Investment Minister Admits to Laundering Drug Money." InSight Crime. August 30, 2017.

Clavel, Tristan. "Honduran President Decries Drug Traffickers' Bribery Allegations." InSight Crime. October 9, 2017.

"Concentración de poder (2022–2026)." YouTube video. Posted May 24, 2023, by CNA Honduras.

Ernst, Jeff. "Hernández Conviction in Manhattan Spatters National Party and Ruling Party Libre in Honduras." *El Faro.* March 11, 2024.

Ernst, Jeff. "Prosecutors Present 'Drug Ledger' with Notes of Drug Shipments That Allegedly Mention the President of Honduras and His Brother." *Univision News.* October 3, 2019.

Ernst, Jeff. "Witness Directly Involves the President of Honduras in the Use of Drug Money for His Campaigns." *Univision News.* October 8, 2019.

Ernst, Jeff, and David C. Adams. "A Top Cop Feared by Drug Traffickers to Be Honduras' New Security Minister." *Univision News.* January 27, 2022.

"Fake Accounts, Coordinated Messages and Digital Troops: The Smear Campaign Against Gabriela Castellanos." *ContraCorriente.* January 19, 2024.

"Gabriela Castellanos regresa a Honduras y brinda conferencia con miembros de sociedad civil." YouTube video. Posted July 20, 2023, by Televicentro Noticias.

Goodwin, Zachary. "Massively Overpriced Contracts Hamper Honduras' Pandemic Response." InSight Crime. July 17, 2020.

"Honduras Anti-Corruption Activist Says She Left Country After Threats." Reuters. June 19, 2023.

Kinosian, Sarah. "Drug Clan Leader Testifies He Bribed Honduran President with $250,000." Reuters. March 11, 2021.

Mendez, M. "Diputada Ramos acusa a ASJ de ser cómplice de 'narco gobierno.'" Radioamerica.hn. July 19, 2022.

Papadovassilakis, Alex, and Parker Asmann. "From Ally to Extradited: Former Honduras President Sent to US on Drug Charges." InSight Crime. April 21, 2022.

Robbins, Seth. "How His Own Extradition Policy Exposed the Honduras President." InSight Crime. September 17, 2019.

Robbins, Seth, and Alex Papadovassilakis. "Former Honduras President Accused of Drug Conspiracy That Moved 500 Tons of Cocaine." InSight Crime. February 15, 2022.

Books

Acosta, Óscar, and Adriana Yu Shan. *Tegucigalpa ayer, Tegucigalpa hoy*. San Pedro Sula: Centro Editorial, 2011.

Alvarado, Elvia. *Don't Be Afraid, Gringo*. New York: HarperCollins, 1989.

Aquilina, Mike. *Villains of the Early Church*. Steubenville: Emmaus Road, 2018.

Arce, Alberto. *Blood Barrios*. London: Zed Books, 2017.

Bahr, Sergio Fernando. *Violencia y seguridad en las comunidades de Nueva Suyapa y Villanueva*. Tegucigalpa: Centro para la Prevención, Tratamiento y Rehabilitación de las Victimas de la Tortura, 2011.

Barahona, Marvin. *Pueblos indígenas, estado y memoria colectiva en Honduras*. Tegucigalpa: Guaymuras, 2009.

Barahona, Marvin, and Ramón Rivas. *Rompiendo el espejo*. Tegucigalpa: Guaymuras, 1998.

Bingham, Tom. *The Rule of Law*. New York: Penguin, 2011.

Blitzer, Jonathan. *Everyone Who Is Gone Is Here*. New York: Penguin, 2024.

Booth, John A., Christine J. Wade, and Thomas W. Walker. *Understanding Central America*. New York: Routledge, 2020.

Bunck, Julie Marie, and Michael Ross Fowler. *Bribes, Bullets, and Intimidation*. University Park: Penn State University Press, 2012.

Carlsen, William. *Jungle of Stone*. New York: William Morrow, 2016.

Carroll, Rory. *Comandante*. New York: Penguin, 2013.

Carter, Jon Horne. *Gothic Sovereignty*. Austin: University of Texas Press, 2022.

Cohen, Rich. *The Fish That Ate the Whale*. New York: Picador, 2012.

Coleman, Kevin. *La huelga de 1954 en las fotos de Rafael Platero Paz*. Tegucigalpa: Editorial Guaymuras, 2019.

Consejo Nacional Anticorrupción. *100 años de corrupción e impunidad en Honduras*. Tegucigalpa: Publigráficas, 2017.

Cruz, José Miguel. *Maras y pandillas en Centroamérica*. San Salvador: UCA Editores, 2006.

Danner, Mark. *The Massacre at El Mozote*. New York: Vintage, 1994.

Dudley, Steven. *MS-13*. Toronto: Hanover Square Press, 2020.

Easterly, William. *The White Man's Burden*. New York: Penguin, 2006.

Estrada, Oscar. *Honduras: Crónicas de un pueblo golpeado*. Brimfield: Casasola Editores, 2012.

Estrada, Oscar. *Tierra de narcos*. Brimfield: Casasola Editores, 2021.

Foxe, John. *Foxe's Book of Martyrs*. Newberry: Bridge Logos. 2001.

Frank, Dana. *Bananeras*. Chicago: Haymarket Books, 2016.

Frank, Dana. *The Long Honduran Night*. Chicago: Haymarket, 2018.

Galeano, Eduardo. *Open Veins of Latin America*. New York: Monthly Review Press, 1997.

Goldman, Francisco. *The Art of Political Murder*. New York: Grove Press, 2007.

Grandin, Greg. *Empire's Workshop*. New York: Holt Paperbacks, 2006.

Grillo, Ioan. *Gangster Warlords*. London: Bloomsbury, 2016.

Gutiérrez Rivera, Lirio. *Territories of Violence*. Hampshire: Palgrave Macmillan, 2013.

Haugen, Gary A. *Good News About Injustice*. Lisle: InterVarsity Press, 2009.

Indiano, César, Hilda Caldera, and Esther Hernández. *Alfredo Landaverde*. Tegucigalpa: ZAFRA editores, 2018.

Instituto Universitario en Democracia, Paz y Seguridad. *Democracia, elecciones, y violencia en América Latina*. Tegucigalpa: Publigráficas, 2017.

Instituto Universitario en Democracia, Paz y Seguridad. *Encrucijadas de la democracia en Honduras y América Central*. Tegucigalpa: Comunica, 2019.

Jackson, Jeffrey T. *The Globalizers*. Baltimore: Johns Hopkins University Press, 2005.

Kleiman, Mark A. *Against Excess*. New York: Basic Books, 1992.

Lakhani, Nina. *Who Killed Berta Caceres?* London: Verso, 2020.

Leiken, Robert S., and Barry M. Rubin. *The Central American Crisis Reader*. New York: Summit Books, 1987.

MacCulloch, Diarmaid. *Christianity*. New York: Penguin, 2009.

MacFarquhar, Larissa. *Strangers Drowning*. New York: Penguin, 2015.

Malone, Mary Fran T. *The Rule of Law in Central America*. New York: Bloomsbury, 2014.

Martinez, Óscar. *A History of Violence*. London: Verso, 2016.

Martínez D'Aubuisson, Juan José. *A Year Inside MS-13*. New York: OR Books, 2019.

Meza, Víctor. *Diario de la conflictividad en Honduras: 2009–2015*. Tegucigalpa: Centro de Documentación de Honduras, 2015.

Motley Hallum, Anne. *Beyond Missionaries*. Lanham, MD: Rowman & Littlefield, 1996.

Mouw, Richard J. *Calvinism in the Las Vegas Airport*. Grand Rapids: Zondervan, 2004.

Muse, Toby. *Kilo*. New York: William Morrow, 2020.

Nazario, Sonia. *Enrique's Journey*. New York: Random House, 2006.

Phillips, James J. *Honduras in Dangerous Times*. Lanham, MD: Lexington Books, 2015.

Pine, Adrienne. *Working Hard, Drinking Hard*. Berkeley: University of California Press, 2008.

Preston, Douglas. *The Lost City of the Monkey God*. New York: Grand Central, 2017.

Rivas, Ramón D. *Pueblos indígenas y garífuna de Honduras*. Tegucigalpa: Guaymuras, 2000.

Robicsek, Francis. *Copan*. New York: Heye Foundation, 1972.

Rushdie, Salman. *The Jaguar Smile*. New York: Viking, 1987.

Russell Lee, Matthew. *Narco Drama*. New York: Inner City Press, 2024.

Sachs, Jeffrey. *The End of Poverty*. New York: Penguin, 2006.

Saviano, Roberto. *ZeroZeroZero*. New York: Penguin, 2015.

Schoultz, Lars. *In Their Own Best Interest*. Cambridge: Harvard University Press, 2018.

Searcy, Teresa Andrews. *Falsely Accused*. Lincoln, NE: R. H. Publishing, 2010.

Ungar, Mark. *Policing Democracy*. Baltimore: Johns Hopkins University Press, 2011.

Vargas Llosa, Mario. *Sabers and Utopias*. New York: Farrar, Straus and Giroux, 2009.

Ver Beek, Kurt, and Nicholas P. Wolterstorff. *Call for Justice*. Eugene, OR: Cascade Books, 2019.

Wainwright, Tom. *Narconomics*. New York: PublicAffairs, 2017.

Washington, John. *The Dispossessed*. London: Verso, 2020.

Wheeler, William. *State of War*. New York: Columbia Global Reports, 2020.

Zamora, Javier. *Solito*. London: Hogarth, 2023.